The Politics of Reproduction

D1607813

The Politics of Reproduction

Beyond the Slogans

Rebecca M. Albury

Allen & Unwin

First published in 1999 by
Allen & Unwin
9 Atchison Street,
St Leonards NSW 1590 Australia
Phone: (61 2) 8425 0100
Fax: (61 2) 9906 2218
E-mail: frontdesk@allen-unwin.com.au
Web: http://www.allen-unwin.com.au

National Library of Australia
Cataloguing-in-Publication entry:

Albury, Rebecca.
   The politics of reproduction: beyond the slogans.

   Bibliography.
   Includes index.
   ISBN 186448 906 5.

   1. Human reproduction—Political aspects. 2. Human
   reproduction—Moral and ethical aspects. 3. Abortion—
   Political aspects—Australia. 4. Feminism. 5. Women's
   rights. I. Title

176

Set in 10/11.5pt Plantin Light by DOCUPRO, Sydney
Printed by South Wind Production Ltd, Singapore

10 9 8 7 6 5 4 3 2 1

In memory of
George Jerome McClure, Jr
and
Emily Winifred Roberts

Contents

Preface and Acknowledgments

Every book has a story behind it. In this case, it is a story about politics and scholarship. Few adults in English-speaking countries have been able to ignore the feminist campaigns for reproductive choices including access to abortion. Slogans like 'Abortion Is a Woman's Right to Choose' and 'Free Abortion On Demand' have helped to shape the public politics of abortion in many liberal democratic countries. Increased access to birth control and abortion services and the development of the technologies to assist conception have called attention to the complexities of the politics of human reproduction.

As an activist I have participated in the politics and some of the attempts at policy development and implementation. As a scholar I have tried to analyse the complexities of the shifting politics. This book is an exploration of my current understandings of the combination of the two. I have organised the argument around the familiar slogans of feminist reproductive politics for two reasons. The first is obvious: the slogans are well known and continue to form the basis of debate, even when the wording of the slogan is rejected as incomplete or misleading. The second reason is related to the first: the very familiarity of the slogans means that people use them without thinking about the assumptions that shape them, or the consequences of implementing them in specific ways.

I will explore some of the ways that new uses of old slogans reveal the complexity of the original demand by illuminating issues that were previously hidden. For example, the demand for choice about using technology to terminate an unwanted pregnancy sounds odd when converted into a demand for choice about the use of technologies of assisted reproduction to achieve pregnancies for women past menopause. Moving the political debate beyond the slogans of choice and rights requires the opening up of the meanings of reproductive decision making and the place of procreation in the lives of women. It also requires an exploration of the contexts in which women make decisions about fertility and raise children. The contexts range from the interpersonal considerations between a woman and her partner, through cultural meanings of motherhood whether religious or secular, to the relationships created in particular social institutions like health care services or workplaces, and include state regulation of aspects of reproduction.

The first chapter tells the story of Australian feminist campaigns about reproduction. It is a story in which I have been a political activist, but it is a social commentary, not a memoir. I will introduce some of the elements of the feminist interventions in the politics of reproduction that I will discuss further in later chapters. Chapter 2 is about the social constitution of women, using both cultural studies interpretations of the meanings of the bodily practices of feminine attractiveness—ranging from weight control through to cosmetic surgery—and social science analyses of the power relations implicit in reproductive medicine. Some of the public debates about women's health are contradictory because liberal democratic notions of self-ownership and bodily integrity fit awkwardly with assumptions that women's political agency is limited by widely accepted, apparently common-sense meanings of their bodies as weak or reproductive. In chapter 3, I consider the role of feminist campaigns in challenging the interpretation of the duty of state to regulate morality by regulating fertility control practices. Debates from feminist scholarship about ethics have contributed to new articulations of moral issues. Political activism has helped to shape a changing political agenda about sexuality, reproduction and physical safety for women and children. Women have become recognised as experts about their own lives who must therefore be consulted in the policy process. The changes have not gone uncontested. Those whose views have been challenged have reframed their arguments to include the findings of scientific medicine to support their moral positions, bringing together expert claims of doctors and religious leaders to counter women's claims to knowledge.

Chapter 4 takes up the demand for safe and accessible contraception in the context of feminist discussions of sexuality. An analysis of popular birth control advice books demonstrates that while the advice reflects the feminist demand that women be able to make choices about contraception it does not challenge the common-sense notions that heterosexual expression necessarily involves penis-in-vagina intercourse. In chapter 5 I discuss some of the politics that have led to the current contradictory policies about abortion in Australia. The abortion debate has strands that comprise all of the social groups with a major interest in fertility. Feminists and civil libertarian law reformers have contended with conservative moralists over government policy. Medical professionals have both participated in the debates and provided abortion services whether they were formally legal or not. Both the debates about and the practice of abortion continue even as some of the arguments are extended to concerns about the disposal of surplus frozen embryos in *in vitro* fertilisation (IVF) programs.

An exploration of feminist analyses of the meanings of motherhood in the lives of women is at the centre of chapter 6. Both critical and common-sense understandings of motherhood are a part of feminist interventions in policy debates about adoption and assisted reproductive technologies. A critical understanding of the cultural meanings of motherhood is particularly important at a time when both technology and rhetoric are rendering women invisible and allowing the enlarged image of a foetus to become a symbol of life itself. Finally in chapter 7, I return to storytelling to demonstrate the value of applying some of the insights developed in cultural studies to political arguments and political campaigns. This time I'll retell the stories that women and doctors have used to represent themselves and each other in their attempts to shape public policy. Too often these representations are adversarial and cast the other party as dangerous, selfish or thoughtless. I am searching, not for an elusive 'middle ground' hoped for by politicians and policy makers, but for a different grounding for the politics of reproduction.

My current understandings of the complexities inherent in the politics of reproduction are the result of years of research and teaching women's studies in Australian universities. I have also been an activist at a number of levels including social movement politics, the board of directors of a non-government organisation and membership of a Commonwealth government advisory committee. Each of these aspects of my life has provided an opportunity to reflect on the problems and pleasures of the others. I am middle aged, white and middle class. Life is, of course, more complex than this standard statement of relative privilege implies. In addition to lessons learned in my political life, a particular encounter with the medical profession in my personal biography is a shadow presence in my analysis of reproductive politics.

In 1984 one of my daughters, then fourteen, was diagnosed with Hodgkin's disease, a cancer of the lymphatic system. The rigorous treatment regime successfully eliminated the cancer, though it also produced some long-term effects. She was lucky; we all were. Years before, I had observed and supported a friend whose son had a cleft palate and decided the mediation of a course of difficult medical treatment for a child was a significant test for a parent. My own experience of supporting a child with cancer confirmed that opinion, but also raised questions for me about many of the assumptions that have shaped feminist health activism. For those with cancer, treatment choices are not completely open, nor are all outcomes equally good. The assumption that if the 'right' decisions are made or the 'proper' processes followed, things will turn out well, cannot be the basis of oncology treatment. Yet I saw medical staff respecting the wishes of children and parents in an attempt to make the disease and treatment a part of ordinary life: explaining each step of treatment carefully, finding ways to fit treatment regimes around the lives of the children, knowing when to advise against further treatment, continuing supportive relationships after treatment ended whether because of death or remission. Women's health activists demand that each of these practices should be a part of all service delivery. The demands are too frequently unmet in the treatment of adults.

Women's health activists have tended to argue that women's control of decision making or reproductive health services would lead to successful outcomes. Yet, even the best decisions about birth control, childbirth or infertility treatments may not lead to the desired outcomes: contraception fails sometimes, babies assume awkward positions during labour, infertility treatments fail to enable conception. The question for me has become, how can feminists support women in the decisions they make next, since the consequences of previous decisions and unpredictable biology continue to throw up new problems and opportunities? This has meant exploring the contexts in which reproductive health services are delivered, in which policies that regulate reproduction are made and in which the reproductive lives of women and men are lived. That exploration has revealed a terrain of considerable ambiguity and complexity which I discuss in this book.

+ + +

The contribution of friends, colleagues and students is a part of the story of this book. My friends in reproductive politics have discussed aspects of this argument with me for years. Thanks especially to Jeanne Rudd, Margaret Kirkby, Lynne Hutton-Williams, Marie Tulip, Vicki Marquis, Ceslily Murphy and Rosa Needham for conversation, politics and encouragement. Thanks too to the many activists in other states and to conference participants who have shared valuable insights and sources of information; it is impossible to personally thank you all. Colleagues in university teaching have read chapters, invited me to give papers and discussed ambiguities with enthusiasm. Barbara Baird, Dorothy Broom, Barbara Buttfield, Terri Jackson, Dorothy Jones, Lenore Lyons-Lee, Mary Medley, Helen Meekosha, Rose-lyn Melville, Margie Ripper, Lyndall Ryan, Toni Schofield and Trish Vezgoff will recognise the results of conversations over many years. They also know what is left out. The book would have a different shape without the constant engagement of students with these issues. Thanks to all of you, especially the women at Macquarie University who argued in 1982 that I should think about abortion and infertility treatment within the same framework, and the members of Women in Society and the Sociology of Gender Relations classes at Wollongong University who kept on pushing me to relate theoretical issues to social and political practice. Thanks to Elaine Buckman, Nicole Rankin and Naomi Watson who wrote BA (Honours) theses on related material, and to Erika Haubold who is completing a PhD about masculinity and abortion debates; the supervision relationship takes on an extra dimension when both parties are working on complementary projects. A significant proportion of chapter 1 appears in a different form as an essay in *Australian Feminism: A Companion* (1998).

Research is time consuming even when well supported. Nicole Rankin was also a research assistant without compare on a part of the project funded by an Australian Research Council small grant in 1991 and 1992. I also received small useful grants from Wollongong University over many years. Thanks, too, to John

Bern and James Wieland for help in organising teaching time and study leave in a way that enabled me to finish the book. I must express my special appreciation of Ann Aungles and Susan Dodds, good friends, colleagues and intellectual companions. Librarians in many university and state libraries have generously offered help. The inclusion of very recent news events has been made easier by the clipping service that Diane Proctor oversees for the Australian Reproductive Health Alliance and the existence of Ausfem Polnet, an electronic discussion group founded and managed by Elizabeth Shannon. Jeanne Rudd compiled the index. Kerry Lawrence massaged away many of the stresses of long hours of word processing and read part of the manuscript. Jane McClure, Katherine Albury, Alicia Albury and Graham Barwell each offered unique blends of support and distraction.

The story would not be complete without Allen & Unwin; thanks to the publisher's thoughtful readers, to Elizabeth Weiss with her carefully crafted array of carrots and sticks and to Karen Ward and Emma Cotter for efficiently supervising the process that turned the manuscript into a book. Even with all this help, there are deficiencies; they are my own. I invite readers to join with my friends and students who have heard me out and then said, 'But, Rebecca . . . '. Without their reservations the arguments here would have been weaker.

Rebecca M. Albury
April, 1998

1 An Introduction to the Politics of Reproduction

Women tell each other fertility stories. Each new stage of women's reproductive life is marked by a new set of stories—menstruation, early sexual encounters, pregnancy, birth and menopause. Having a story to share often seems like a passport into particular communities of women. Women's magazines tell fertility stories: stories about innovative treatments for infertility and the resulting multiple births; accounts of mothers coping with injured or disabled children; searches by adopted people for the knowledge that will fill gaps in their identity; longings by relinquishing mothers to know what happened after they said goodbye to their babies; advice from doctors and psychologists about managing pregnancy, birth and early mothering. Here or in self-help groups women with extraordinary experiences can discover that they are not alone. All of this storytelling provides a shared language for speaking about reproduction. Using the shared language, each woman can interpret the meanings of physical changes or social demands whether apparently ordinary or extraordinary.

There are other stories about fertility and reproduction that contribute to the shared language. In these stories the voices of women are relatively quiet. Some of those stories are in the language of medicine, where the doctor explains and interprets the meanings of the changes in a woman's body. Some stories are legal, using the language of legislation and judicial practice to regulate women's experiences of fertility. There are religious stories, which provide a language for the interpretation of the social relations of reproduction in terms of women's duties to God. In addition there are scholarly stories from many disciplines: histories of childbirth, sociologies of pregnancy, philosophical considerations of abortion, biochemical accounts of the menstrual cycle, and many more. Finally, there are stories deployed in political struggle about law reform or service provision.

There is no single story about reproductive women: stories about women and procreation seem to run in all directions. The term story is used here to include a wide range of genres, from whispered gossip and cautionary tales to scientific reports and government policy documents. Each of these genres has a standard form that guides the reader through the evidence and arguments to the expected conclusions. The styles of argument and what counts as evidence vary according to genre. The political contests about the regulation of fertility are frequently contests about what counts as evidence and who is an authorised expert. In addition there are contests about the interpretation of the evidence, even when the evidence itself is agreed upon.

This book is about the terms of those contests: how they are constructed, who counts as an expert, which experience becomes evidence, who benefits from the particular outcome of the contest and where the contest is going in the immediate future. I argue that running beneath the surface in most of the public contests is the continual cultural construction, deconstruction and reconstruction of gender. The powerful representations of 'Woman as Mother' recur even in many feminist criticisms of medical practices or state policy about reproduction. While I recognise this process, I doubt if anyone can fully escape it because of the pervasiveness of motherly representations of women and the practical needs of political campaigns to speak to those current everyday understandings in order to avoid being totally marginalised. My concern with how to conduct a politics of reproduction that addresses changing issues and goes beyond the limitations of the slogans, symbols and thinking of the past thirty-five years drives my argument. I will examine the past, not to suggest activists knew better (or worse) then, but to explore some of the contradictions in their analysis and campaigning. There was no golden age and, as far as I can see, there is no golden age just over the horizon; reproductive politics is a changing but ongoing contest.

I develop an argument about a variety of contemporary meanings of fertility and reproduction. However, this is not an opportunity to gain a 'balanced view' of the strengths and weaknesses of the authorised 'sides' in the public debate. I do not provide an account of the 'right to life' arguments in their own terms as some US authors have (Luker 1984; Ginsberg 1989). On the other hand, anti-abortion rhetoric has contributed to the public debate in ways that would be impossible to ignore. Also missing from my argument is an adequate account of reproduction in the context of health care politics; there is no account of the politics of birthing, for example. Nor is there a measured account of disability issues and reproduction. Instead I refer to these areas only when they are a part of my current argument. Feminist language and arguments have shaped the contemporary politics of reproduction in contradictory ways. Women and men who would not call themselves feminist nevertheless use ideas and terms with feminist origins to think about fertility. Further, feminists do not agree among themselves about many issues. The politics of reproduction is not as straightforward as the demonstrations outside parliaments and clinics suggest.

During the late nineteenth and twentieth centuries, feminist campaigns have focused in various ways on the relationship between discourses of public law and government agencies and the personal lives of women. In answer to the objection that these personal matters had no place in politics, the radical Women's Liberation Movement asserted that 'the personal is political'. The assertion challenged women to use their individual stories as evidence of power relations in many social institutions including marriage, the medical profession and the law. The explosion of feminist writing is a testament to the enthusiasm with which many women took up the challenge. There was also an explosion of activism as new areas of injustice were identified. In the political struggles, the complexity of the many competing stories is condensed into a slogan or a symbol. The image of the slogan or symbol may be very abstract, as in 'A Woman's Right to Choose' which draws together the language of rights and choice from liberal democratic politics with an acknowledgment of the ways in which individual women's lives are connected to those of other people. The apparently concrete symbol of 'test-tube babies' combines a recognisable piece of laboratory glassware with small babies to create a disquieting image when used in connection with *in vitro* fertilisation (IVF) and related technologies. These technologies were once called the 'new reproductive technologies' (NRT), but are now more commonly called 'assisted reproduction technologies' (ART), though the baby in the test-tube continues to be used to represent the processes. Symbols and slogans rely on the cultural literacy of readers or viewers, but the meanings do not stand still. The political campaigns that use them change as the interpretations of the symbols and slogans change.

The slogans at the beginning of the chapters in this book are a device, like the banners of a street march or political demonstration; each is a condensation of many ideas and experiences, equally each seems to change meaning in different situations. Those complex and shifting meanings have been deployed by five major social groupings in reproductive politics: organised women, the agencies of the democratic state, the institutionalised medical profession, organised religion and coalitions of law reformers. This book is chiefly about the interaction of the first three, with the other two occupying a less prominent place in the argument. Feminism as a social movement has organised around slogans as the focus of campaigns calling for reproductive freedom for women. As one response to the demands raised by such campaigns, governments are expected to make public policy that will be acceptable to the majority of the adult population. At the same time, claims to scientific objectivity have made the medical profession seem more reliable as a disinterested source of information than are the clearly political women. In Australia the relationships among the groups have been complex and relatively undocumented. In addition, each group is divided, with most positions in a particular debate present within any particular social grouping. This book is an attempt to pull together the strands of analysis from a number of disciplines to enable us to better understand those complexities. I have come to think that insights from cultural studies need to be applied to the more apparently straightforward realm of political activity. At the same time, the importance of the material effects of power relations cannot be dismissed from understandings of the cultural meanings of fertility and human reproduction.

A story about the politics of reproduction

This is a political commentary interspersed with the previously published voices of individual women describing personal fertility stories. The personal stories first appeared as part of interventions in public debates and are reminders of the diverse experiences that inform feminist thinking about reproductive politics. Feminists have been campaigning for some version of women's rights to control fertility and the conditions of reproduction for over a century. Yet, there are laws regulating abortion as a part of the criminal law in every State in Australia, access to reliable birth control is frequently threatened by cuts to health funding, and the practice of ART is regulated more closely than most medical procedures. My account draws links between the various arenas of feminist engagement in the public debates about these issues and highlights some of the unresolved tensions in the feminist politics of reproduction.

Feminist campaigns engage with a large number of social institutions. Medical professionals and the health care delivery system are the targets of demands for services that recognise the physical and moral integrity of women. Calls for law reform have addressed the use of national or State laws to exercise control over women's sexual and reproductive lives through the criminalisation of abortion or limitation of access to contraception. Recent campaigns have expressed considerable ambivalence about new developments in technology, since most reproductive technology seems to have been developed and tested without much consultation with the ordinary women who would be the users. In national and international political arenas, arguments about the appropriate social roles for women have replaced eugenics in shaping the debates about the availability of birth control and abortion services for able-bodied women. However, eugenic concerns have re-emerged in arguments for pre-natal screening and some claims about the potential for embryo diagnosis to eliminate human defects (Sexton 1998).

At the same time feminist campaigns have been directed at the wider population to encourage women and men to take up new ideas about the place of procreation in the lives of women. In the face of a scientific tradition based on the notion of objective knowledge, feminist activism has sought to provide a recognition of women's experiences as a source of knowledge and self-determination. In addition to street demonstrations and formal public meetings, feminists have used traditional social movement methods such as small group discussion and self-education and have developed the speak-out, a large meeting of women giving testimony about a particular issue. As the Women's Liberation Movement gained media attention, the stories that had been shared with few if any friends became a part of the public record.

5

> *I can remember being taken to the labour ward. I can remember the pain and thinking how was I going to put up with it. The labour ward was reminiscent of a battlefield, with all these rows and rows of women screaming and crying. It was like a production line and there were lots of lights.*
>
> *. . . As the baby was being born they put a pillow on my chest so I couldn't see. I can remember hearing these other babies screaming and squealing and when my baby was born I was waiting for his cry. And when it came it was a very deep, resonant cry, not the normal high pitched wail of a newborn.* (Harkness 1991: 180–1)
>
> —Remembering the birth of a baby given up for adoption in 1965

The slogan 'abortion is a woman's right to choose' became one of the most well known feminist slogans, changing cultural and political understandings of abortion. It represented women as choosing citizens and significantly reshaped both public debates about abortion and women's personal reasoning about unexpected pregnancies. The appeal to rights has limitations within the liberal democratic political tradition, since the language of rights tends to be applied to individuals and to exclude a deeper discussion of the power relations within which the rights are exercised. Campaigns for reproductive rights have also used language from left struggles, analysing the broader social relations between women and doctors with concepts like exploitation and dominance. Personal sexual relations between men and women are frequently described in terms of the power relations they reflect from the wider set of inequalities experienced at work or in civil society.

The campaigns and debates reflect the tensions between these two sources of political language: one that focuses on individual action or agency and the other that emphasises the constraints of the social structure, particularly those of gender, class and race (Petchesky 1985: Introduction). In addition, the place of the debate in the wider political arenas has meant that reproductive politics also expresses the tension between political values of individual freedom and the maintenance of the social order. In spite of the tensions, access to abortion and contraceptive services is widely recognised as a key feminist demand throughout the world. The relatively clear analysis of contraception and abortion as important for women's well-being has not translated easily into an analysis of the newer technologies of IVF and related techniques. The newer technologies sometimes endanger the health of women and seem to reinforce motherhood as the major social role for women.

While there have been progressive challenges to legal and administrative regulation of reproduction, there has also been a change in conservative campaigns and language. Anti-feminists have referred to the rights of foetuses and embryos in their opposition to both abortion and ART, displacing the figure of a woman as a choosing citizen with the foetus as an endangered potential citizen. This appropriation of the language of rights has posed new problems for a feminist politics of reproduction. The woman citizen was able to appeal to her right to bodily integrity, but she also had a reproductive duty to the nation. Earlier feminists appealed to that duty as a justification for the right to vote. The 'ethic of care' was first developed in the context of understanding ethical elements of women's abortion decisions (Gilligan 1982). It has been used to deny women decision-making authority as a part of campaigns for 'foetal rights'.

Social movement interventions in abortion politics

It would be difficult to write a history of abortion in Australia from women's point of view because there are so few records of successful abortions. The existence of penalties for abortion in the Crimes Acts or Criminal Codes of the various colonies from 1861, when the colonies became responsible for their own legal systems, is an indication that the practice of abortion was well known. The crime statistics, for the most part, record abortions when the woman died, and hospital records indicate that sometimes women were infected or injured during the abortion (Allen 1990b; Siedlecky and Wyndham 1990). In spite of the law, there was not a high rate of arrest and conviction of abortionists during the period from 1880 to 1940 when the birth rate was steadily falling. Yet official inquiries and novels are evidence that abortion was a part of the lives of many Australian women from at least the last quarter of the nineteenth century. Oral histories and memoirs suggest that most women who sought and found abortions had

7

relatively safe operations (Bretherton and Mather 1997; Baird 1990; Berman and Childs 1972). Informal networks were used to refer women to various practitioners in the capital cities and rural centres, and corrupt police accepted bribes to keep abortion available even if illegal.

> *She explained to me what she was going to do, and I realised then what an abortion was to put a name to an action, yes and that I would lose the baby.*
> *. . . So what she actually did, she got soap, Velvet soap, and she grated that and used boiling water with Dettol maybe not Dettol, but something of that type of thing and had a syringe and inserted that into my womb until she could feel that she had penetrated. Then shortly, maybe six hours after that, I started labour pains. I actually remember walking into a car, and I got a big scar on my leg because I was so disorientated because of the pain and didn't know what to do, where to go. I finished up having the abortion—. I aborted at home, which was quite traumatic and very painful.* (Baird 1990)
>
> —Oral history account of an abortion in 1961

In Australia, abortion has become available without legislative reform except in South Australia, the Northern Territory, Australian Capital Territory and Western Australia. Abortion is regulated by the individual States directly as a part of the criminal law and indirectly through the regulation of the medical profession and support for public hospitals. At the same time, the provision of health care is shared with the Commonwealth government, which collects taxes, provides grants to the States and directly funds much health care through Medicare rebates and pharmaceutical benefits. This funding arrangement, part of the process called federalism, is a result of ongoing negotiations in the federal system of government which was devised when the colonies agreed to become a single independent country in 1901. The Commonwealth government collects income and many other taxes, and revenue is then shared among the States and the Commonwealth. The States have retained the authority to determine the criminal law within their boundaries. In the case of the provision of abortion services, federalism means that centrally collected health care funds may pay for abortions which are regulated by State criminal laws. It also means that each parliament can debate some, but not all, aspects of abortion service provision.

It has been in the States that the major campaigns for abortion law reform or repeal have been conducted. Campaigns were conducted after 1968 by the various state Abortion Law Reform Associations (ALRAs), which were offshoots of the Humanist Society and worked in cooperation with Councils for Civil Liberties. In South Australia, where the Abortion Act was first successfully reformed, activists and parliamentarians took the United Kingdom Abortion Act 1967 as the model, though ALRASA members wanted to make all terminations a matter between a woman and her doctor. While their stance and arguments seem limited today, it is worth remembering that members built popular support for abortion law reform, provided information to parliamentarians, kept an active eye on the parliamentary process and maintained a watching brief on the subsequent implementation of the act without the backup of a wider organised feminist community (Blewett 1975). Access to abortion was part of a broader vision of fertility control services, with many members active in the campaigns for public funding of Family Planning services (Siedlecky and Wyndham 1990).

In Victoria and New South Wales, highly publicised raids on abortion clinics resulted in acquittals for those charged and a changed interpretation of the law (see chapter 5). In Western Australia, ALRA was established in 1969 following the failure of a 1968 abortion law reform bill in the State parliament. An ALRAWA speaker on abortion law repeal participated in the inaugural meeting of Women's Liberation in Perth in May 1972. Between 1974 and 1998 abortion was available in Western Australia on the same terms as it is in Victoria and New South Wales, but without a WA court case or legislation (ALRAWA 1977). Unlike the other State ALRAs, the WA organisation continued to play an important role in reproductive politics after the emergence of Women's Liberation and has continued to welcome men as members.

The Women's Liberation Movement was just getting underway as the major Australian changes in abortion law were occurring, contributing a passion and changed language to later campaigns. The public demand shifted from law reform to law

9

repeal, a goal that still has not been met. At the same time as the legal situation of abortion was changing from totally illegal to ambiguously legal, the State and national governments were beginning to support birth control services. Many of the same activists were involved in advocacy for contraceptive and sex education and the establishment of birth control services. Within a decade the historical public opposition to birth control in Australia had been reversed, after years of traditional lobbying by small pressure groups and social change that could no longer be denied.

The support for social transformation that accompanied the Australian Labor Party victory in 1972 shifted the spotlight from moralising traditionalists to the everyday practices of women and men who were already trying to control their fertility. While some commentators argue that feminism is responsible for accessible contraception and abortion services, fertility control is more correctly seen as a part of wider social change in Australia, as is the broad acceptance of feminist ideas about women and work. The report of the Royal Commission on Human Relationships in the mid–1970s demonstrated the widespread popular articulation of the demand for reliable fertility control (Australia 1977: vol. 3). Australian feminists have been able to take advantage of a political culture that values both individual rights and community responsibility for the weakest members to campaign for fertility control services that are accessible to all.

The Women's Liberation Movement took up the political campaign to repeal the abortion law with the establishment of the Women's Abortion Action Campaign (WAAC) in several capital cities during the early 1970s. Levels of left sectarianism meant that a number of feminist abortion activist groups operated in several cities throughout the seventies. In some groups women argued strongly against formal connections with the developing abortion services in favour of a political campaign focused narrowly on law repeal. Unless workers from abortion clinics attended the political group meetings it was difficult for activists to keep up with the critique of medical service delivery and politicisation of women's health care being developed in the burgeoning women's services. WAAC and other Women's Liberation abortion groups operated as collectives with no formal leadership structures according to the ideals of the new movement, thus making it difficult to develop and extend analyses beyond the views of the most dominant members. When those members left, some groups collapsed and others hit a low point—but ultimately there has been a reshaping of abortion activism in Australia.

It is ironic that a low point in local activism came immediately after a major national success for feminist abortion politics. In late March 1979, the Australian House of Representatives defeated the private member's motion calling for legislation to deny medical benefits for abortion put by Stephen Lusher, a member of parliament from the Country Party, as the National Party was then called. During March reproductive rights activists rallied and demonstrated in cities and towns around the country. Although supporters of the motion tried to focus attention on the fate of unwanted foetuses, parliamentarians from both sides of the house made strong speeches for women's rights, reflecting on the risks in a society that allowed access to safe abortions only to those who could pay for private medical services. While some parliamentarians reproduced the 1960s arguments about inadequacies of the welfare system leading to abortion, others called attention to the inequalities between men and women. Members of the public were quoted in newspapers saying that abortion was 'a woman's choice' or 'a woman's right' to justify their opposition to the motion. For the first time the powerful Australian Medical Association made a public statement in favour of access to abortion. The defeat of the Lusher Motion seems to have established a new status quo for abortion in Australia. It solidified an ambiguous status for an ambiguous act: abortion remained formally regulated by the criminal law except in South Australia and later the two Territories, but it was a reimbursable item on the health benefits schedule. Yet, Australian women since the late 1970s have been closer to the radical claim for 'free abortion on demand' than women in most other liberal democracies.

My boyfriend dropped me off there. And I was in there and there was all these different types of women. Like I had this sort of image in my head that they would all be these young girls in a state of trauma and everything, and you got older women, younger women, you got all these kinds of women just sitting there calmly.

I woke up and I felt pretty bad but relieved at the

same time. Very painful but relieved at the same time. I was sitting next, lying next to a girl from Toowoomba and she was telling me all about her sad story about her boyfriend and it sounded pretty traumatic, but we were in pretty good spirits. (Ryan et al. 1994: 134–5)

—An account of a legal abortion in Queensland some time between 1985 and 1992

For a variety of reasons, further abortion law change through legislation seemed out of reach, and State governments that had not acknowledged even the ambiguous status of abortion continued to resist. In Brisbane, activists from Children By Choice, the counselling and referral service that grew out of ALRA, were able to take the lead during attacks on abortion rights by the Queensland government in the early eighties (Petroechevsky 1994). Tasmanian and South Australian activists had established strong feminist abortion groups by 1985. In Western Australia ALRA continued its work uninterrupted into the eighties, changing its name first to the Abortion Law Repeal Association, then to the Association for the Legal Right to Abortion. By the late 1990s apparently legal abortions were available in all States and Territories, although some women still had to travel long distances or interstate to find an appropriate service. Challenges to the ambiguous status of abortion have continued; the most recent occurred in 1998 in Western Australia. Two doctors were charged under the State Criminal Code with performing an unlawful abortion on a woman who had not made a complaint to the police. The political upheaval that followed the charges led to the introduction in Western Australia of the first bills to consider abortion in thirty years, including a private member's bill in the upper house to remove the abortion sections from the Criminal Code. Charges were dropped once the law was reformed.

Fertility seemed controllable by the 1980s; women who had never known sexual life without the pill and access to abortion were raising children of their own. NSW parliamentarians in 1988, arguing against a motion calling for the strict enforcement of the abortion sections of the Crimes Act, quoted a Family Planning Association document asserting that abortion was not a method of contraception, but rather was a necessary backup in case of method failure. They also appealed to the symbolism of the dirty 'backyard abortionist'; however, research findings suggest that many or even most women could find a doctor, nurse or skilled non-medical provider to perform an 'illegal' abortion before the middle of the century (Allen 1990b: 246–7; Baird 1990; Baird 1996). Unwanted pregnancy was sometimes represented as a moral failure, not because it revealed illicit sexual intercourse, but because it disclosed a failure in the rational use of birth control. This change in the popular perception of fertility control increased the demand for medically delivered 'effective' contraceptive methods (see chapters 4 and 5).

Feminists in women's services worked hard to make knowledge about contraceptive options available to women, but could challenge neither the dominance of the medical model of service delivery nor common-sense ideas about sexually expressed femininity and masculinity. There was no popularisation of the feminist critique of the cultural assumptions about heterosexuality. While there are many reasons for this, new thinking is constrained by the location of fertility control within contemporary health care systems. Feminists have had to engage with the medical model of health care delivery in order to gain public funding for women's health initiatives (Broom 1991). For the most part this engagement has strengthened their practical political analysis, but one cost has been the contraction of the analysis of what is at stake in debates about reproduction. Fertility control raises political issues far beyond the biomedical questions of the effective prevention of pregnancy or even the safe termination of unwelcome pregnancy. The cultural definitions of women as mothers or of women as a collection of unreliable reproductive organs (Martin 1987) cannot be challenged within a medically dominated health care system. Likewise, political challenges to the idea of women as decision-making citizens in the name of protection of the 'unborn' cannot be addressed simply by saying, 'let health workers make decisions about these matters'.

One effect of an underdeveloped analysis is that the next challenge is more difficult to meet. While reproductive rights activists were defending access to abortion by campaigning against legislative threats in Queensland and New South Wales and developing new services in Tasmania and South Australia, the terms of the public debate were changing (Ryan et al. 1994: 15–27, 41–87). Only a few years after the defeat of the Lusher Motion and widespread use of feminist language, newspapers were uncritically reporting attempts to protect 'unborn children' by preventing abortion. At the same time the publicity about assisted reproductive technologies changed some aspects of the experience of pregnancy. Ultrasound images of foetuses became 'baby's first picture' for many couples. As pre-natal screening became safer and more reliable, women were offered the 'choice' of abortion as a response to the diagnosis of a foetus with a serious defect. Yet, the mid-trimester abortion of a welcome foetus is a process very different from the termination of an eight-week unwanted pregnancy. The first Australian IVF baby was born in 1981, surrounded by claims that soon childlessness as a result of infertility would be a thing of the past. Medical science promised to solve all of women's concerns about fertility: too much or too little fertility could be adjusted and controlled.

Interventions in public policy about ART

The idea that fertility is in fact controllable for each woman, rather than controllable in the abstract, has had mixed consequences for both feminist politics and the lives of women. The idea of nearly perfect control has abstracted the physiological aspects of procreation from the wider social issues of sexual relationships, kinship, understandings of the social meanings of masculinity and femininity, and the power relations implicit in a technologically advanced culture. The underdeveloped links have led to an impoverishment of the debate by tending to condense complex arguments into one symbolic issue. This has contributed to contradictory mobilisations of the notion of a 'feminist' position in the public debate. Attacks on abortion rights continue to arouse political action but developments in assisted reproduction are greeted with confusion; it is hard to work out which questions to ask, much less useful answers to those questions.

The birth of IVF babies in Britain and Australia attracted little immediate interest among feminists active in the politics of reproduction. Wary questioning soon began appearing in small feminist publications, calling attention to the overblown claims and the ways that the rhetoric was fed by ideologies of womanhood. Interested professionals focused on medical, legal and ethical issues, calling on legislative bodies—standing in for 'society'—to fill the gaps in the existing law revealed by the technologies. The range of social issues now central to an analysis of assisted reproduction were seldom mentioned. Early statements that indicated any familiarity with feminist arguments referred to rights to have children and choices for women in the most simplistic formulations of human rights doctrines and liberal feminism. There was no recognition of the well-developed feminist critique of the medical profession which combined a gender analysis of professional power relations with a class analysis or political economy of technology.

How did it feel to hear the news that I was pregnant? Over the moon, ecstatic, elated, happy. And yes, to be honest, I guess a little frightened at first. People have often asked me did I find the program painful, did I find it intrusive? To be honest I never found the daily blood tests and injections painful. I handled them OK. I was probably luckier than some because we decided that it would be best for me to give up work before starting the program so although the waiting for the blood tests and injections was at times annoying, I never had that anxiety about being late for work.

. . . I wanted to spend at least two years with my daughter before starting the program again, and that's what we did.

But the second time around it took us six cycles to achieve another pregnancy . . . Twins! Our beautiful baby boys were born by Caesarean section.

When we first married and discussed, like most young couples, our hopes for a family, we decided we would like three children. Now, thanks to our wonderful doctor and the IVF we have the family we wanted. (Wood and Riley 1992: 40–2)

—An account of successful IVF treatment for infertility due to blocked fallopian tubes.

But feminists began their continuing engagement with what were then called the new reproductive technologies. I wrote one of the two Australian contributions to one of the first international collections of articles—*Test-Tube Women* (Arditti et al. 1984). These two contributions foreshadowed the divided focus between those engaging with questions of law reform and suggestions for

15

opening up the public debate and those calling attention to dangers for women as a group from the excesses of the new technologies. The latter position was reinforced by the extravagant claims made for IVF, an experimental procedure, by the medical entrepreneurs and the thoughtless futurology of many of their supporters. By 1984 numerous inquiries were being held around Australia with secular and religious feminists attending hearings, making submissions, sitting on panels and writing thoughtful articles for many publications. The Family Law Council included feminists with expertise in social welfare and social psychology on the committee appointed to investigate and report on the implications for the Commonwealth of the various State inquiries (Australia 1985).

The feminist perspective on the technologies gained social legitimacy in mid-1984 when Robyn Rowland resigned from a Monash Medical Centre research project about couples using donor insemination (DI) to achieve a pregnancy. The publicity surrounding Rowland's resignation opened public space for feminist questions. Policy makers began to address social issues originally raised by Rowland and other feminists as seriously as the issues raised by clergy, lawyers and philosophers. In submissions feminists pointed out the inadequacy of regulatory panels comprised of a majority of professional men making policy with direct effects on women's bodies and well-being. Today few regulatory committees with responsibility for reproduction and women's health have less than half their membership made up of women. On the other hand, it has become clear that feminists do not necessarily think alike about the details of policy; nor, in some cases, do they even share the same perspective on reproductive technologies.

Feminist positions were presented at a number of conferences as well as in print or as interventions in the policy processes beginning in the mid-1980s. In addition a number of women began research projects that sought to document the experiences of women using reproductive medicine in an attempt to achieve pregnancy. Several Australians attended the international conference that founded the organisation that became FINRRAGE (Feminist International Network of Resistance to Reproductive and Genetic Engineering) in Villinge, Sweden, in 1985. They also contributed to the 1985 *Women's Health in a Changing Society* conference in Adelaide (Kerby-Eaton and Davies 1986). Then in May 1986, several international members of FINRRAGE were guests at *Liberation or Loss: Women Act on the New Reproductive*

Technologies. At least three views were put by speakers at the conference: strong opposition to the technologies based on a radical feminist analysis of the male dominance of the medical profession and the dangers for women; wary engagement with attempts at regulation based on socialist feminist and the emerging cultural studies analyses of the ways power is mobilised; and support for the technologies in terms of feminist arguments about choice based in personal accounts of the pain of infertility. The position of strong opposition emerged in the conference resolutions.

> *I've been through three IVF cycles: two full ones and one with frozen embryos. In each case I had a successful embryo transfer. No one knows why it didn't work. I still have three frozen embryos in storage and if the next frozen cycle isn't successful I don't know if I will continue with the programme.*
> *. . . My greatest frustration in being involved with the IVF programme is the lack of information available to me. It also entails a great deal of stress—physically, emotionally, and financially. It's meant that my whole life —my work, my study and my marriage—is at a standstill until I become pregnant or give it up.*
> *. . . Is it worth it? I just don't know.* (Stuart 1989: 82, 88, 89)
>
> —Reflection on unsuccessful IVF treatment for infertility due to blocked fallopian tubes

This opposition came to be perceived for a time as the only feminist position and seemed to foreclose a wider debate within feminist groups about the meanings of reproductive technologies. At the same time a variety of views were debated in the public arena; these in turn required feminists to think through the issues in different ways. Equally, the vocal opponents provided a valuable response to the grandiose claims ⋅ of the reproductive scientists. Radio and television features, popular women's magazines and accessible books contributed to the debate, providing opportunities for many voices and juxtaposing opposing arguments within the same space and format. However, it was difficult to implement the oppositional resolutions through intervention in the Australian political and policy processes.

In reproductive rights as in other aspects of social policy, feminists have been active participants in the policy processes. In addition to their social movement roles of outside interveners and trenchant public critics of the inquiry processes and recommendations, feminists have been insiders in non-government organisations with interests in procreation, members of government departments, elected officials and members of committees of inquiry. In some cases outside critics became members of inquiries, being formally required to see the issues from another perspective. In other cases the insider feminists were able to introduce a stronger feminist argument into the final report than would have been likely had the committee merely reported on submissions.

Every state produced at least one report during the 1980s. The combination of feminist interventions is clearly evident in *Human Embryo Experimentation in Australia* (Australia 1986). Senators Rosemary Crowley and Olive Zakharov argued for a feminist approach to the issues raised by the debates of the Senate Select Committee on the Human Embryo Experimentation Bill 1985, in a minority report. The National Bioethics Consultative Committee (NBCC) was established in 1988 as the national body repeatedly recommended by inquiries into reproductive technologies. While the NBCC resulted from the intersection of a number of political forces in Australia, feminist lobbying helped to shape the committee and a number of female reproductive politics activists were appointed to it. The presence of women, even feminists, on committees did not mean that a unified 'woman's view' was put forward, however. This was a disappointment for some activists, but others saw it as a normalisation of the presence of the women on the committees. No one woman could be marginalised from the group because she represented the 'woman's view' among a group of professionals, but feminists were not necessarily assured of each other's support regardless of the issue.

It all began at the Monash Medical Centre, where she was born. I was allowed to sleep in Linda's room; my mother brought meals for me, although my appetite was

18

poor from excitement and exhaustion. Linda and I spent twenty-four hours a day together, and I found her constant availability for conversation and support to be ideal. I even took Linda many times to the special care nursery in a wheelchair, where she would sit next to me expressing milk while I fed Alice. She had unrestricted contact with the baby she gestated (as she always will), but said to me the day after Alice was born, 'I think she's nice, but I don't want her back'.

Watching Maggie learn to care for her new baby was a source of delight and amusement for me. It was a novelty to see her doing something at which I was more experienced than she was. Once Alice had hiccups, and Maggie said, 'Oh, Linda, what do I do?' I smiled condescendingly, and said with an air of experience, 'Nothing'. (Kirkman and Kirkman, 1988: 309, 333)

—From a book-length account of a surrogate motherhood arrangement between sisters

Reflections on rights, choice and control

The success of the feminist slogans about reproductive rights and choice and the popularisation of the idea that women should be able to control their bodies has had contradictory effects in debates about reproductive technologies. The language of rights and choice has been used to argue for access to new technology. So, for example, it is claimed that pre-natal diagnosis increases a woman's choices about pregnancy by giving her more knowledge about her foetus. Or some new medical techniques or drugs are offered on the grounds that women can be told information about the potential risks or benefits and then make an informed choice. Women can weigh the risks, of course, but clinicians sometimes used consent as a justification of poor medical practice. During the early years of IVF some clinics justified transferring four or more embryos into a woman's uterus to increase her chances of pregnancy on the grounds that she consented, thus putting her at risk of a high multiple pregnancy, early labour and very small newborns. This particular unconscionable choice is no longer offered to women at accredited clinics. The continuing critique of medical dominance and the insistence on respect for women certainly contributed to a political climate in which the worst abuses of power are less likely in Australia, if only by providing a secular language in which to express moral and social reservations.

Popular writing about reproductive technologies also drew on feminist language. Some infertile women used the feminist language of rights and choice to call for access to reproductive technologies. Some also argued that feminists should support their carefully thought-out choices to participate in infertility programs rather than criticise the abusive aspects of the treatment regimes. Magazine or newspaper debates with a feminist opponent of ART on one side and an infertile woman using feminist language on the other drew attention away from an analysis of the problematic assumptions about women implicit in some of the medical rhetoric. An account of the social shaping of motherhood as the only imaginable identity for most women too often seems like an accusation of 'brainwashing' or false consciousness as a response to an infertile woman's accounts of her efforts to become pregnant or her desire to rear a child. Sympathy for the personal unhappiness of the infertile woman made the structural analysis of social relations of reproductive medicine seem cold.

In Canada, feminists successfully took up the demands that women be central in policy making about reproductive technology. The national government established a Royal Commission on New Reproductive Technologies in 1989 with a large research budget, a woman chair and several feminist members, some of whom later left. The apparent promise of a woman-centred Royal Commission was transformed soon after it was established; the process and the final report better reflect the interests of medical scientists and politicians than the complex interests of women (Canada 1993; Basen et al. 1993/1994). The tensions and contradictions suggested by the mobilisation of feminist language to support questionable practices provide a challenge for the next decade of reproductive politics. Some commentators have suggested that feminists should give up the language of rights and choice because it is limited and can be used in misleading ways. I would argue instead that activists must find ways of extending the analysis of reproductive issues and of linking campaigns in ways that demonstrate the connections among the issues. This will mean accepting that reproductive politics will always be a process of contest because the very definition of womanhood is at stake.

The earlier discussion illustrates some of the sites of the contest. When doctors take up the rhetoric of choice, women may be offered unconscionable choices. The inappropriate reliance on choice in infertility treatment echoed frequent statements that new contraceptives would provide more choices for women. The importance of choice is asserted as if the fact of choice itself is a solution to the social problems arising from relationships between women and men, the limitations of contemporary medicine or the realisation that fertility is not always subject to rational control. Likewise, the 'choice' to abort a foetus with a disability is often offered as if the suggestion that no life is better than a life with a disability is completely unproblematic. People with disabilities disagree, though many also support access to abortion. The stories women tell about fertility suggest that working through problems related to reproduction and living with the consequences of a sequence of decisions is more involved than the rhetoric of choice suggests. However, the storytellers also celebrate their ability to make difficult decisions under conditions in which the best choice is not clear. There is a growing international literature that analyses such stories, reflecting on the diverse experiences and making the links among the different strands to articulate a global politics of reproduction (Corrêa and Reichmann 1994; Ginsberg and Rapp 1995).

One of the arguments for abandoning the language of reproductive choice treats choice as a consumer good rather than as a category for political or moral analysis. Since abortion or the use of a reproductive technology is seen as the only solution to a difficult problem, proponents of this view argue, it cannot be a real choice. Choices, it seems, are limited to the selection of one of several equivalent outcomes; they are not, as the liberal democratic political tradition has argued, expressions of personal liberty. Clearly no one lives in a state of complete freedom from constraint, yet each of us lives with the consequences of important acts. Liberal political philosophy has included discussions of the moral decision making in conditions of political or social constraint, usually in terms of civil disobedience or conscientious objection to military service, but contains few discussions of decision making about reproduction. Within the political and legal system in Australia, if women are denied the possibility of making decisions about their lives, then that responsibility is assigned elsewhere. No one imagines that the official denial of decision-making authority to women means that no women become pregnant unwillingly or that some women will not become infertile.

> *Personally, I have had three abortions, all of which at the time seemed the only viable alternative. I didn't have the courage to go through a pregnancy and have a baby without any support. For many years I have suffered severe anxiety, varying depths of depression and other effects. It is only since I recognised that I killed three of my children, actually giving them the dignity of human status that I have begun to find some peace.*
>
> *When society insists that what you are doing is the 'best' solution and refuses human status to your baby, you can't identify the grief and guilt inside because you're not 'supposed' to be feeling them. 'It was only a little bit of tissue after all.' May I assure you that the guilt can be overwhelming and the grief is as great, if not greater, than that of any woman who has lost a child at whatever stage of life.* (NSW, Legislative Council 1988: 1281)
>
> —From a letter quoted in a Parliamentary debate

Attempts to deny the legitimacy of women's decisions often lead to claims that women are exploited by the relations of reproduction. Feminists have pointed to the ways that coercive sexuality and lack of birth control exploit women's childbearing capacities and have been used to justify other forms of discrimination against women. Anti-feminists have argued that women are exploited by abortion itself. They say that open access to abortion makes it hard for women to continue accidental pregnancies; a man, they argue, can avoid the responsibility for his sexual activity by insisting that the woman terminate the pregnancy as a condition of continuing the relationship. In addition some opponents argue that abortion damages a central aspect of a woman's femininity by blocking her natural need to nurture life. This argument depends on a denial of the long history of irresponsibility by some men, the practice of fertility control by many women and the potential for exploitation of women implied by coerced pregnancy. There is also an implicit argument that the mixed and changing feelings that may follow an abortion are somehow worse than ambivalences and altered feelings in the years after marriage, childbirth or major job changes.

During the past decade the arguments about the potential for the exploitation of women by doctors have led some feminists to ask for public policy condemning various aspects of reproductive technologies, though it is unclear how the policy should be shaped. Feminist arguments concerning women's vulnerability to social and personal pressure about reproduction too often seem to demand the same forms of protectionist legislation as anti-feminist claims that the vulnerability is a part of women's nature. Thus the feminist arguments about the power relations of medicine, for example, are lost in popular coverage that locates reproductive women as both fragile and powerless, in a sense justifying decisions made on their behalf. One example of the contradictory effects of feminist arguments about women's vulnerability occurred during the parliamentary debate concerning the regulations on the importation of the chemical abortifacient RU486 in May 1996. Anti-abortionists were able to justify their opposition to the drug using feminist criticisms of the drug and the testing process. The health minister, representing the authority of the state, was required to 'protect' women from the power of pharmaceutical companies and the medical profession (Brough 1996b).

Since the struggle for the recognition of women's interests in social and health policy has not been won, it seems premature to call on an institution so implicated in the matter-of-fact subordination of women to protect them from other institutions. These contradictions are reminders of the complexity of reproductive politics. Campaigns need slogans and clear goals to be effective, but slogans may become substitutes for analysis and the goals of one campaign conflict with the goals of another. Further, changes in the social relations of reproduction affect feminist interventions in public debate about procreation. Repetition of slogans as a part of political activity does not mean that fertility is predictable. Women still become pregnant when they feel unable to undertake the responsibilities of childrearing. Women who want children find that they are unable to become pregnant without medical intervention. Feminists have argued for a politics based on women's experience. But all women do not have the same fertility experiences; nor do they recount similar experiences in the same ways.

Indeed, even when policy makers turn to women for assistance identifying health care needs, as did the Australian Department of Community Services and Health during the development of the National Women's Health Policy, abortion and *in vitro* fertilisation are the subjects of polarised views (Australia 1989: 4). There was widespread agreement among the women involved in the consultations for the National Women's Health Policy that there needed to be more easily accessible information about menstruation, fertility control and birth spacing, pregnancy care and childbirth, breastfeeding, post-natal care and menopause. Women also wanted health care services that were sensitive to their cultural practices and a variety of special needs. In general women recognised the need for flexible policies to meet a variety of experiences, but '[t]he question of whether and under what circumstances, abortions should be performed and financed [was] one on which there [was] no community consensus' (Australia 1989: 28). There was a range of views about IVF as well.

Feminism since the 1960s has been identified with political campaigns for legal abortion. One of the most well known slogans asserted that abortion is a woman's right to choose. The need for choices in health care and in other areas of women's lives is widely supported even by those who oppose easy access to abortion. It has come as a surprise to some people, then, that certain feminists argue against public support for IVF and related technologies on the grounds that those technologies exploit women. How can we explain the polarised views about abortion and IVF, polarisations that appear among feminists as they do among the broader population? In a sense this book is an explanation of the sources and effects of those differences. Before the more detailed discussion of the issues raised by feminist campaigns about fertility control I will discuss some of the ways that contemporary culture shapes female fertility.

Thinking about personal experience

The personal stories of unwanted pregnancy or infertility treatment quoted above illustrate the diversity of women's experience of fertility. The three accounts of abortion reveal that there is not a single response to the termination of pregnancy: individual women report experiencing 'pretty high spirits' or 'severe anxiety'. In rethinking what happened at the time of the abortion, one woman thought that she 'would lose the baby' whereas another was unable to accord her terminated foetuses 'human status' until some time later. The differences demonstrate the inadequacy of relying on some universalised version of women's experience as the basis of social analysis or policy making. The limited Australian research reporting women's abortion experiences points to the different circumstances in which women terminated their pregnancies as a significant contribution to their varied reactions. Women who felt pressured into the abortion by a lover, family or severely limited support reported more negative reactions than women who felt that they made the abortion decision themselves (Ryan et al. 1994: 6–7). Some of the women spoke about their annoyance that ambivalence was often not recognised as an ongoing response to the decision to terminate a pregnancy. They were able to resist others' versions of how they were 'supposed' to feel while also thinking they had made the 'best' or 'right' decision (Ryan et al. 1994: 132–3).

Those stories about how women are 'supposed' to feel help to shape women's experiences, however. The woman who expected that the clinic would be full of 'young girls in a state of trauma' was surprised to find a variety of 'ordinary' women like herself. On the other hand, the woman who was not 'supposed' to feel grief or guilt was left without a way to recognise herself as 'ordinary'. Feelings about new babies were 'supposed' to be differentiated according to a woman's marital status, and social practices reinforced the supposition. The joy and pleasure of seeing the 'beautiful baby boys' or the 'excitement' and 'delight' of caring for a newborn were denied to the woman who relinquished her baby. She was not allowed even to see the baby, she has only the memory of his voice to mark his birth. In addition there was a frequently reported fear that if a woman saw the baby, she would be unable to relinquish it. The idea that women somehow do not have a relationship with the baby until they see it is a denial of pregnancy as a bodily experience which is shaped by all the stories circulating in a culture.

In addition, these stories highlight the tensions between the desire to have or avoid a pregnancy and some undeniable physiological 'facts' of women's bodies. In spite of the language of fertility control, none of the women were able to 'control' their fertility by willpower alone. Each sought help in the face of uncontrollable fertility, whether too much or too little. The women's reflections on the experiences seem to be coloured by both the quality and the outcomes of the help. The woman for whom IVF was successful had a perspective on the unpleasant aspects of the treatment which was different from that of the woman with her life 'at a standstill' and still no baby. The pain of one abortion was mitigated by both feelings of relief and the sense of normality in the clinic. The stories remind us that women's experience is neither simple nor the outcome of a woman's individual thoughts and actions alone.

I have provided examples of very different experiences with fertility because I want to call into question the idea that an appeal to women's experiences provides sufficient evidence for political action or academic analysis. The power of many of the feminist challenges to the academic social science disciplines was the demand that a recognition of women's experiences would change the conventional analyses. The everyday lives of women had been treated too often as a background to the lives of men, which needed investigation and explanation (Smith 1987). However, in political activism there has been a temptation to take the experience of one person or of a particular group as representative of the experience of all women. Differences between women have been ignored or brushed aside in analyses that emphasise commonalties among women. Often these set up the unproblematic 'we' in opposition to 'them' (men), but of course, it is never as simple as that. Women differ from one another in many ways. The cultural meanings of fertility are central as determinants of the social status of women in the population and of specific women in their families or communities. Women who try to negotiate those meanings will have different personal circumstances as well, including age, civil status, class, health, religious practice, sexuality, caste, geographic location, disability, race, wealth, educational level. This list of possible factors influencing an experience suggests that the 'evidence of experience' is not transparent and that the individual woman both shapes her experiences and is shaped by them (cf. Scott 1992).

Unwelcome pregnancy or infertility is not just 'out there', waiting to be 'experienced' by women, but already exists in cultural practices: in the language that is available to speak of what has happened, in the subject positions available to the woman as she negotiates a fertility status that seems culturally inappropriate, and in the relevant social institutions. The meanings of the experiences have a social history as well as changing personal meanings within an individual woman's life. The 'unwed' mother of 1950 was not the same as the single parent of 1990 (Swain and Howe 1995). Of course, 'women' and 'mothers' are not transparent categories either, but are constructed and deconstructed by a variety of social practices including biomedicine, popular culture, and feminism (de Lauretis 1987). While women may agree that the work of mothering is important, they may disagree about how that importance should shape decision making about fertility, especially the decision to have an abortion (Cannold 1998).

In order to make sense of the seven stories threaded through this chapter, one needs knowledge of how women are constructed within the culture of late twentieth-century Australia. Discussions of 'culture' and the making of femininity and masculinity rely on examinations of particular ways of life and of intellectual and artistic practices in the reproduction of the contemporary male dominant social order. They provide an account of the constitution of human subjects as female or male within that particular gender order, with a lot of attention paid to social relations in the family, workplace and political institutions. Neither the gender order nor the dominant model of femininity and masculinity are static (Matthews 1984; Gilding 1991; Connell 1987; Connell 1995). A current approach to explaining how men and women are constituted emphasises popular culture including television, music, shopping, magazines and popular fiction in 'fashioning the feminine'; that is, as a source of the shared stories about how women are 'supposed' to act and feel (Johnson 1993; Douglas 1994). An additional source of those stories can be found in popular representations of the relationship between women and science, whether medical science (Martin 1987), workplace technologies (Cockburn 1985; Game and Pringle 1983) or reproductive technologies (Stanworth 1987). The terrain of technology as applied science is the site of a variety of struggles about the meaning of femininity and masculinity (Wajcman 1991; Haraway 1997).

The concept 'representation' is frequently used when discussing the images and stories told within cultural practices. Representation in this sense can be quite literal: the margarine or instant coffee 'mum' represents caring motherhood—that is, a real woman plays the part of an idealised role which is none the less recognisable as having some counterpart in less ideal everyday experience. On the other hand, she is a very particular kind of mum, married, white, and willing to wait on people well able to get their own crackers or instant coffee (Jakubowicz 1994: 74–8). She smiles and moves back out of the centre of the action once her role as carer is finished. Representations also can be fairly abstract—images of flowers and chocolates to represent giving or

27

feeling love. Or more oblique still, the use of sepia photography can suggest to the viewer that she or he is sophisticated and knowing—for instance, in soft drink or coffee ads.

These advertising images are simple, accessible and widely shared; here they provide an introduction to cultural studies which is both a theoretical exercise and a cultural criticism using theories of representation to try to explain how we understand our shared culture, including how boundaries are constructed around behaviour and feelings. Cultural studies acknowledges the active engagement with the act of viewing and listening as well as reading (Franklin et al. 1991; Grossberg et al. 1992). Women learn both the culture and how to represent themselves, and indeed how to misrepresent themselves, through stories portraying how women are 'supposed' to feel and what happens when they do not conform.

Critical discussions of the representations of women in advertising are common in newspapers, magazines and high school classrooms. There is no agreement on the political implications of such analyses, with some critics arguing for a higher level of censorship of public images and others arguing for the acceptance of the images on the grounds that viewers are capable of complex readings (Lumby 1997). However the critical analyses of representations of women through science and technology have not been popularised to the same extent. The early feminist criticism of the medicalisation of women's bodies emphasised the power that expert knowledge gave to medical men (McNeil 1987). It is still the case that popular accounts of birth control or reproductive technologies give a pre-eminent place to the voices of medical professionals. In the next chapter I'll discuss two strands of analysis of the social construction of women's bodies: examining first the self-disciplines of femininity, then the processes of medicalisation of women as reproductive bodies.

2 The Cultural Construction of Women's Bodies

From the early years of the Women's Liberation Movement, women's health activists emphasised the importance of embodiment to their politics, with the classic women's health handbook called *Our Bodies, Ourselves* to foreground the role of the body in a woman's sense of herself. Many feminist campaigns also emphasise the centrality of a woman's body: rape, domestic violence, sexual harassment as well as reproductive health care are evidence of contests over the right to define the meanings of women's bodies. Feminists asserted the right to dress for comfort and convenience rather than for the eyes of men. Women's health activists demanded an end to the patronising behaviour of much of the medical profession towards women who came seeking reproductive health care. Scholars documented the traditional disciplinary practices that devalued women by reducing them to bodies while men were abstracted to rational minds. In recent years the body itself has become the subject of inquiry in many disciplines after a period of concentration on social structural or individual intellectual or emotional issues. In part this reflects the work of the French scholar Michel Foucault, but the body had already been at the centre of feminist thought when his ideas began to be explored by a wide variety of scholars (Bordo 1993: 15–23).

This chapter has three parts. First, I will introduce some ways of thinking about women as culturally constituted bodies.

In the second part, I will examine several aspects of the constitution of women's bodies by medicalisation: the legitimacy of
medical knowledge, the use of medical interventions in reproduction, and the use of metaphors in the language of medical science.
Medicalisation has provided a scientific justification for occupational segregation and many social inequities. Then I will raise
some of the contradictory meanings of the slogan 'A Woman's
Body Is Her Own'. Does the notion of self-ownership also mean
that a woman can sell her body, its parts or its processes? If
not, is there a better way to express the demand for bodily
integrity?

A woman's body

During the past two decades the relationship between the images
of women and how women think about their bodies has become
a topic of public debate, particularly in terms of media, fashion
and health. Some commentators have argued that the thin
supermodels in some way encouraged young women to risk their
health through rigorous weight loss and exercise regimes. Others
pointed to the narrow ranges of body sizes and shapes represented
on popular television. Feminists discussed the effects of the
'tyranny of slenderness' on women's feelings about their bodies
from many perspectives. The examples from advertising and
women's magazines in the 1980s are reflected by similar texts in
the late 1990s, though the details of style and current cultural
references have changed. In *The Beauty Myth*, Naomi Wolf
(1990) had argued that a 'professional beauty qualification' had
been added to the skills and experience requirements in many
occupations in the United States during the 1980s, as a part of
the reaction against the successes of the feminist movement. She
did not make clear the exact connection between the contested
achievements of feminism and the emerging ideal of a thinner,
toned body that can wear high fashion without the help of shaping
underwear. Most of her evidence was drawn from the reports of
a few outrageous anti-discrimination cases in the US courts, rather
than being the findings of well-constructed social research. Certainly shorter, stockier women have not been excluded from
workplaces—whether the floors of factories or the floors of
legislatures—across Australia, nor have they in the United States.
In spite of its shortcomings, *The Beauty Myth* captured the anger
of many younger women caught in the contradictions of cultural

constructions of femininity and their own more feminist ambitions.

Taller, more conventionally glamorous women have not been
immune to media constructions that suggest that physical beauty
is at odds with intelligence and work competence. When I was
researching media accounts of IVF and related technologies
(Albury 1987), I was struck by the ways that the one female
scientist was represented. Linda Mohr developed the embryo
freezing process used in IVF programs and was featured in several
of the articles about the first 'frozen embryo' baby. Yet when
she gave a paper at an international professional conference about
the ethical aspects of her work, the newspaper coverage described
her as 'Tall and blonde, she looks as if she's just walked off the
set of Dallas', and used a large, fairly glamorous photograph of
her in street clothes (*SMH* 23.5.84). Two weeks later, when
ethical questions about the storage of embryos became news,
stories in which she was quoted were accompanied by a photograph of Linda Mohr wearing a white coat at work in a
laboratory. Male scientists were represented in several ways, of
course, but there was no contradiction between attractiveness and
intelligence.

For a long time, one of the dominant themes in feminist
analysis of the ways cultural practices construct gender was an
extension of the insight made by John Berger about nudes in
Western painting:

> One might simplify this by saying *men act* and *women appear*.
> Men look at women. Women watch themselves being looked
> at. This determines not only most relations between men and
> women but also the relation of women to themselves. The
> surveyor of woman in herself is male: the surveyed is female.
> Thus she turns herself into an object—and most particularly an
> object of vision: a sight. (1973: 46)

Feminist film theorists, starting from the work of Laura Mulvey
(1975) and E. Ann Kaplan (1983), have discussed the effects of
a 'male gaze' on visual representations of gender. A recent
Australian analysis includes a consideration of racial differences
as shaping the gendered gaze. It seems that in Australia, femininity has been white, leaving little place for Aboriginal or Asian
women (Brook 1997), though at times working class white women
have been able to achieve only a tenuous femininity (Finch 1993).
In addition feminist writers have considered two related questions—what happens when women 'look back' at the male

spectator, and what is the nature of female spectatorship (Gamman and Marshment 1988)? What happens when women are active watchers rather than simply seen? This question raises a huge array of problems about the nature of desire and pleasure which are beyond this discussion, or even this book.

Film theorist Teresa de Lauretis argued that an understanding of women within feminism should begin with an understanding of gender that does not elide so easily with common-sense notions of sexual difference. She suggested giving up certain common-sense ideas about what 'woman', 'women' or 'femininity' are. She argued for Michel Foucault's concept of a 'technology of sex' (Foucault 1979: 116) as the starting point for this different understanding. Foucault does not mean the same kind of technology discussed by critics of the effects of new technologies. The technology of sex is not mechanical or electronic. It is a set of shifting social practices (discourses) made up of words, professional practices, alliances between particular social groups, say church and state; in short a fully developed set of social relations that provides a structure, modes of socialisation, roles, a history, a context for political practice.

According to de Lauretis, gender, 'both as representation and self-representation, is the product of various social technologies, such as cinema, and of institutionalised discourses, epistemologies, and critical practices, as well as the practices of daily life' (1987: 2). She argued that going beyond Foucault, but not outside the possibilities he raised, enables one to think of 'gender as the product and process of a number of social technologies, of techno-social or biomedical apparati' (de Lauretis 1987: 3). In this theorisation, gender is a representation of a relation between one entity and other entities that are already constituted as a category through the relationship of belonging. The representation of gender is the process of the construction of this relation as well as being the product of it. In addition, historical women and men who are the social subjects of the representation also practise self-representation. By their practices of representing themselves as women and men, they take part in the social construction of gender.

Gender and working bodies

While the focus on representations of sexuality and reproductivity does not fully capture women's daily experiences, it does highlight the cultural practice of identifying women with their bodies. During the nineteenth and twentieth centuries, women's reproductive capacities have been used as justification for a number of social divisions between men and women. Further, class and racial differences among women have also been a part of these justifications. Middle class women were denied access to elite education and well-paid work on the grounds either that the physiological processes of their bodies weakened them for the tasks or that their reproductive organs would be damaged by mental labour (Ehrenreich and English 1979). At the same time, working class women did heavy physical work in factories, on farms and in the homes of middle and upper class people. Likewise, the indigenous women of Africa, Asia, North and South America, Australia and the Middle East were regarded as little more than animals, seemingly living in a 'natural' state.

A quick look at official information about women in paid work reveals that the effects of thinking of women as radically different from men have not disappeared (cf. Probert 1997). Today the Australian Bureau of Statistics collects workforce data according to whether female, but not male, workers are married and have children (Australia 1997c). The categories reflect the cultural assumptions about male and female identity: men are workers, so their personal situations are not a policy issue, but women are mothers who may be in paid work. This may be useful for planning child care policy, but also supports the assumption that children become a public policy concern only when their mothers spend part of the day away from home in paid work. The data about the sexual segregation of the workforce also echo cultural assumptions about women. Women are clustered in a few industries with about 60 per cent in wholesale and retail trades, community services, recreation and other personal services (Baxter et al. 1990). Writers have asked two interrelated sets of questions about these kinds of data. First, how can occupational segregation be explained, and second, where does all the unpaid work in households and communities that is done by women fit into an analysis of paid work?

Workforce segmentation has often been explained in terms of tradition, personal preferences or what were thought about as natural capacities or abilities (Mumford 1989). These explanations draw on an understanding of the unpaid work that women do as 'natural' or the result of practices existing since the 'dawn of time' and therefore very close to natural. By asserting that women are naturally caring, no further explanation is needed for the high number of women who are nurses, child care workers and primary school teachers, social workers, or other care workers. By asserting that women are good at detail and following instructions there is no need for more explanations about the high proportion of women who are clerical workers. The assumption that women are good at dealing with emotions explains the proportion of female sales assistants, counter staff and workers in the hospitality industries. These arguments have been strongly criticised by feminists and others who think about social and economic structural determinations of what appear to be individual choices.

Game and Pringle (1983) asked how women's occupations have been constructed as different from men's occupations. They reflected on the repeated use of binary divisions in definitions and some of the theorising about public and private spheres of life in a study of several industries. They found that the characteristics of men's and women's work were described differently across industries, but that men's work was more highly regarded. Whereas in trades and manufacturing industries men's work is heavy, dirty, technical and mobile and women's work is the opposite, in hospitals the division is justified in other ways because nursing is frequently heavy, dirty, technical and mobile. Here Game and Pringle paid attention to the relations of supervision and the power of knowledge claims. Male doctors supervise female nurses by claims to scientific medical knowledge and through the importation of the authority relations of the patriarchal family into the public world of work. In white collar work, the relations of supervision continue to differentiate male and female occupations. White collar men do light, clean, relatively non-technical work, but supervise trades- and unskilled men and all women. In the management literature, feminist authors point to the tendency to 'think manager, think male' as a real problem to be overcome in the struggle to change some of the workforce segregation. The office relationship between boss and secretary has resonances of the traditional relationship between husband and wife in terms of who manages emotions and who takes credit for the work of the pair (Pringle 1988). In addition, equally qualified male and female beginners are often channelled into what are perceived as gender-appropriate career tracks (Burton 1991).

The segmentation of the paid workforce is justified by reference to the unpaid work that women do. Yet that unpaid work is not counted as work and indeed was not referred to in the national accounts (Waring 1988). However, it has not always been this way. Women working in family businesses or on family farms were once counted according to the industry. The shift can be dated by looking at how data were collected by the census. The 1891 census called all women without paid jobs in the organised work sector, 'wives without gainful employment'. This means that the family income earned by the labour of husband and wife was counted as the husband's earnings only (Matthews 1984). In 1907 the Harvester Judgment in the industrial court ruled that the basic wage should support a male, his wife and three children in frugal comfort. Male wages were set at this amount in spite of the knowledge that many working men were unmarried. Women's wages were set at a lower amount because working women were assumed to be single and living with their parents; women were assumed to leave the workforce upon marriage and be supported by their husbands. This assumption prevailed in spite of the large number of single mothers and women supporting parents and sick or injured husbands, or wives of men who did not provide enough to meet the domestic costs (Ryan and Conlon 1989).

Recent research on unpaid work reinforces the common-sense view that women do most of the domestic work in a country like Australia (Bittman and Pixley 1997; Bittman 1991). Women cook, clean, raise children, do laundry, and emotionally support their husbands, parents and other relatives. Domestic work is not the only unpaid work that women do; women also do a significant amount of volunteer work in their communities. This ranges from informal child care between neighbours to undertaking formal training to be a part of a community support network for people with HIV/AIDS. Feminists have argued that there is too much reliance on the unpaid community work of women in the provision of social services, but non-government organisations are being forced to rely on more rather than fewer volunteers (Baldock 1988). Many part-time community workers also have a volunteer component in their jobs because it is seldom possible to fit all the work into the paid hours; men who do community work face similar problems. The relegation of a greater proportion of unpaid work to women rests on similar assumptions to those supporting the segmentation of the paid workforce: the presumed characteristics of women and the undervaluing of emotional connection. Women and men do not simply bring their existing sense of being feminine or masculine to work, but find that the

35

work experience reinforces other cultural assumptions about the meanings of gender.

Self-discipline and female bodies

Although there has been some discussion of the gendered meaning of work, feminists in cultural studies have devoted more attention to perceptions and experiences of the body as a site of cultural production. In explaining the contemporary processes of the production of gender, feminist writers from many academic traditions have drawn on and argued with insights from the work of philosopher and historian Michel Foucault (de Lauretis 1987; Smart 1989; Bartky 1990; Sawicki 1991; McNay 1992; Bordo 1993). He developed the concept of a disciplinary power that is creative and productive—making 'docile bodies' through a series of calibrated social practices. Foucault (1978) argued that modern institutions exert discipline in ways that increase the utility of the body, through disciplines of time, posture and action. In the end the subjects of such actions also subject themselves to the discipline; that is, they internally police their attitudes and behaviour. Using examples of the practices of schools, prisons, armies and factories from the eighteenth century, he demonstrated that power can be thought of as a grid of small disciplinary practices that produce modern bodies. He argued that this was a new way of exercising power through the body of individuals and the body of the population, which he called bio-power. It does not operate from the top down on the model of the king over his subjects, but everywhere through regional and local mechanisms on the model of capillary action (Foucault 1980).

One of the weaknesses of Foucault's account is his inattention to differences of gender. That is, docile female bodies have not been disciplined in the same ways as docile male bodies. Those three exemplar institutions of the late eighteenth and early to mid-nineteenth centuries—the prison, the school and the army—were male institutions. The history of the making of female bodies would be different. Sandra Bartky began her sketch of the contours of that history by highlighting three types of bodily practice: (a) those that aim to produce a body of a certain size and general configuration; (b) those that bring forth from this body a specific repertoire of gestures, postures and movements; and (c) those directed towards the display of this body as an ornamented surface (1990: 65). Each of these groups has designated experts and recognisable public representations.

Today advertising provides a series of condensed representations of feminine and masculine bodies. The representations reflect a range of stories that are circulating in a particular society, drawing in the potential consumer with appeals to sexual desirability, nostalgic yearnings, cheeky humour, social status and more. In an exploration of the meanings of hunger for men and women, Susan Bordo (1993) demonstrated some of the ways advertising in the United States reflects differences of gender and race as a part of the public disciplining of bodies. Later in the same book she explored some of the practices that have been used by women and sometimes against women to produce slender bodies. She argued that female bodies can be read as a 'text of femininity', a text that changes over time (the nineteenth century hysteric was not the same as a late twentieth century anorectic) but which is still an expression of the cultural demands for feminine appearance and behaviour.

If the body practices of femininity constitute a discipline, who are the disciplinarians? There are obvious experts in the three aspects of bodily practice described by Bartky: nutritionists, doctors, fashion editors, exercise instructors, advertising writers, hairdressers, beauty consultants, and a variety of advisers on deportment. Yet these experts can gain their status only if people pay attention to their advice. Women have to be willing to first accept the cultural constructions of femininity and to undertake the practices that the experts recommend. Hence women try to gain weight in one era and lose it in another, raise and lower skirt hemlines, buy shifting fashion colours and alter hair and make-up styles and colours frequently with the changing representations of the feminine body. These changes in ornamentation and general shape are applied to an already disciplined body. Most women try to adopt some of the accepted gestures, postures and movements that represent femininity. Many of these are so deeply engrained that it is difficult to sustain changes like sitting with legs apart when wearing trousers, making large physical gestures or ignoring the implicit demand that women smile or use placatory expressions in response to strangers, sometimes even those using abusive language (Bartky 1990). Women subject themselves to surveillance and self-discipline.

To say that women are self-disciplining is not a criticism because it is hard to imagine how a woman could live successfully within her culture and not embody some of what is considered femininity. Men embody the masculinities of their culture, too (cf. Connell 1995). There are many ways to express femininity during any historical time, although some may be more valued than others. At the same time, it is clear that some women seem to carry some of the practices 'too far'. The discussions of anorexia nervosa are shadowed with this idea of going too far, usually in terms of a woman having a misperception of her size and so continuing the practices of diet and exercise beyond the needs for health or beauty. In a suggestive discussion of anorexia, Susan Bordo (1993) considered the cultural value of control as part of an explanation of how young women can carry the search for slenderness beyond the conventional demands for feminine appearance. The fear of loss of control is strong in contemporary culture, yet few situations are within the control of individuals. The ability to continue the disciplines of diet and exercise is a demonstration of successful control over one area of life.

Notions of the cultural importance of control are important for understandings of fertility for women. Modern contraceptives are strongly promoted as highly reliable in protecting both women and the population as a whole from the dangers of uncontrolled fertility. I will argue in chapter 4 that pregnancy is often regarded as a moral failure of control and personal responsibility rather than as a failure of the contraceptive method or plain bad luck. In addition, women who find that they are infertile report feeling a loss of their femininity and betrayed by their inability to control their bodies. Appropriate fertility is a part of the cultural expectations about femininity as is the expectation of personal control. In the past, pregnancy demonstrated a single woman's lack of sexual self-control. Today, in Western countries many people accept sexually experienced single women, but now expect that women will avoid unplanned pregnancies. Most women willingly adopt the self-discipline of contraceptive use, but women did not establish the contemporary disciplines of fertility control. Medical professionals are the experts in human fertility, recognised by governments and individuals alike.

Medicalisation of reproductive bodies

Claims based on the authority of medical knowledge have been a part of the process of the spread of medical power within society and, more particularly, within the health care system. The promulgation of that knowledge by the medical profession has provided the language in which we speak of bodies, and the practices that interrogate and report bodily experience. Experiences that are not recorded in medical books or scientific journals, but which women report as health related, are dismissed as 'anecdotal' and therefore less important. The experience has to be 'medicalised' in order to be recognised; that is, it must be turned into a problem that is capable of being addressed in a medical way. This has meant that bodily experience must be treated as a form of illness or a potentially pathological condition in order to be worthy of study. Someone has to ask the questions and collect the answers for experiences to become data and be subjected to scientific analysis. The medical language and descriptions then come to dominate the discussion of those particular experiences, and the parts of the experience that do not fit easily into the abstracted medical model are discounted.

Sociologists have explained the process of medicalisation and its effects using various theoretical perspectives (cf. Turner 1987). Schools, employers and even courts accept doctors' certificates for absence from ordinary or even extraordinary obligations. Although medical science became an authorised source of knowledge about bodies by the early twentieth century, social studies of the medical profession were as slow to theorise the body as other areas of social theory. Feminists analysed the medicalisation of women's bodies, combining insights from the women's movement and the radical science movements in the late 1960s. They began with a critique of medical dominance in most aspects of procreation. Very few pregnant women are sick, yet the medical monitoring of pregnancy and the practice of giving birth in hospital means that most are treated as if they have a potentially pathological condition. When women want to avoid pregnancy and participate in heterosexual intercourse, they must visit a medical practitioner for the most reliable methods of contraception. Feminist critics of the medical profession have argued that the high level of medicalisation of women's health has led to women being regarded as prone to illness, or even to femininity being pathological. The medical profession has taken on an aura of masculinity and responsibility for interventions designed to restore women to health (Ehrenreich and English 1979; Broom 1991). The masculine culture of the profession has survived the entry of women and the changed behaviour of some male practitioners.

It is possible to get some sense of how important the medicalisation of procreation is for women in urbanised Western countries by engaging in a 'thought experiment'. What would it mean for men's lives if they had to consult doctors about their sexual and reproductive functions when nothing was 'wrong'—no disease symptoms, no problems with erection or ejaculation, no concerns about sperm counts? What if that consultation included blood pressure checks, a physical examination of penis, testicles and prostate, a urine analysis, and perhaps a fitting for the correct size of condom? What if health promotion campaigns regularly suggested that this 'men's health' visit, which was preventive and thus in addition to visits for illness or injury, should occur every year or two from the time the young man began sexual activity until his death? It may be that today, there is too little attention to men's reproductive and sexual health; however, full medicalisation could be a part of a process that defined men's bodies as a site of pathology. It is more difficult to imagine women being entrusted with the knowledge and skills necessary to examine and treat men's bodies in the way men were assumed to have the ability to treat women.

The institutional power relations implicit in all aspects of health care service have also come in for considerable scrutiny. Area health authorities, hospitals and universities or other training institutions are organised on bureaucratic lines; registration boards are hierarchical and set down specific criteria that must be satisfied before anyone is allowed to practise whether as an ambulance officer, nurse or neurosurgeon. Sociologists working within the intellectual traditions of both Max Weber and Karl Marx have argued that the rationality of 'scientific' knowledge has become the model for good and efficient decision making in bureaucracy as well as a major component in the claims of medical professionals in their struggle to dominate health care (Friedson 1970; Johnson 1972). Evan Willis (1983) provides an account of the development of 'medical dominance' in Australia, relating the activities of the medical profession here to similar activities in other countries. The community health movement and the rise of self-help groups have challenged particular aspects of medical dominance, but also work within the broad medical framework in order to gain both government funding and recognition as health care providers (Broom 1991; Weeks 1994).

Another group of sociologists and social historians have developed a critical perspective in directions suggested by Michel Foucault. Foucault's work on bodies was a part of his exploration of what he called the 'how' of power. How the model of natural science came to dominate Western thinking, how it shaped the institutions within Western societies and how it has provided methods for knowledge production which also produce power relations, even at the most micro levels of society. In his study of the beginnings of modern clinical medicine, Foucault wrote about the development of the 'medical gaze'. The medical gaze is a systematic way of looking at and seeing bodies which assumes a normal body with a variety of possible pathologies. Each pathology has a set of distinctive symptoms. The job of the doctor is to examine the patient using both physical senses and a form of questioning that will produce the medical 'history'. It is a method of distinguishing the important from the incidental in the process of diagnosis and then monitoring the effects of therapeutic intervention (Foucault 1975).

The rest of this chapter is about some of the ways in which the medical gaze has come to organise women's bodies and to define them as reproductive. Pregnancy and childbirth are today so shaped by the medical gaze, the social process is so medicalised, that it is hard to think of these processes outside of medical language and practices, what is called, following Foucault, 'medical discourse'. Going to the doctor or the clinic opens the pregnant woman to medical definition and to the possibility of a range of medical interventions. Women are recruited as willing subjects of this medical gaze, though they are not necessarily passive, as the history of changes in obstetric care demonstrates (Arney 1982).

Interventions in bodily processes

The noticeable physiological processes that separate women's bodies from men's have become points of medical intervention. Many interventions carry benefits for individual women as well as potential benefits for the medical profession. There is a large literature analysing the effects of those interventions, ranging from accounts that emphasise the dangers women faced in childbirth before medical intervention (Shorter 1984) to accounts that focus on abuses of power by doctors (Corea 1977). While these accounts are compelling reading, they tend to underestimate the interaction of the factors involved in changing practices of reproductive health care; in particular they fail to acknowledge the impact of the demands of women on the practices of the medical profession. Women as an undifferentiated group have not been unwitting dupes of powerful men, nor have medical professionals altruistically brought comfort and safety to women.

During the nineteenth and early twentieth centuries informed women wanted access to the benefits of science during pregnancy and childbearing (Arney 1982; Leavitt 1986). One outcome of this interplay between hopes, claims, demands and changing services has been the integration of women as reproductive bodies into medical practice. Rather than retell the many histories of this process here, I will begin with a discussion of the forms the interventions can take today.

One of the effects of these interventions is regulation; that is, setting and monitoring the range of acceptable variation in body functioning. When the unacceptable variation is regarded as an abnormality or pathology, then interventions to make women's bodies conform to the 'normal' can be attempted. This process raises the question of how 'normal' is constituted and how the effects are lived out by women. The marketing of the contraceptive pill in 28-day packs, complete with inert tablets to take in order to maintain the discipline of daily medication, is one example. Any length of pill-taking regime could have been chosen, since the hormones suppress ovulation, but many women during the early trials were concerned at their failure to menstruate (Oudshoorn 1994: 120). The researchers then incorporated the 'average' cycle length into the medical regime, creating an experience of 'normal regularity' for millions of women. Many pill takers are unaware of the length of cycle or the kind of period they would have until they change methods of contraception or try to become pregnant.

In addition, medicalisation has meant increased surveillance of bodily processes both by health professionals and by women. Changing standards of ante-natal care are a good example. Ann Oakley (1984) traced the changes in ante-natal care in Britain from the early twentieth century when care for pregnant women was seen as a way to reduce infant and maternal mortality and morbidity and thus to increase the healthy population. While midwives continued to be central in the care of women who remained healthy during pregnancy, medical education began to include ante-natal care in a serious way by the mid-1930s. The post-war introduction of the National Health System (NHS) changed the shape of ante-natal care, shifting the supervision of pregnant women from midwives to general practitioners. Women began attending practitioners for ante-natal care earlier in their pregnancies, and more data about them were regularly recorded— blood pressure, weight, urine, blood tests (Oakley 1984: 149). The development of ultrasound imaging of the foetus during the late 1960s and early 1970s again transformed ante-natal care. The focus on the health of the pregnant woman was thereafter shared with a focus on the foetus as a separate being. Oakley argued that the history of the care of pregnant women can be read as an instance of the social control of women, in which the regulation of women's lives by the medical profession was sanctioned by the state. The apparent alliance between women and doctors to achieve healthy pregnancies and safe childbirth included a strong imperative for pregnant women 'to solicit, and pay attention to, medical advice' (Oakley 1984: 257).

I have organised the interventions into a table. I have not included every intervention nor indicated the effects of the differential rates of intervention that mean that some women have too little intervention while others have too much. Class, race, geography, marital status and, in some countries, insurance status have noticeable effects on the level of intervention for any individual woman. Notice that all aspects of the reproductive cycle have been medicalised, including the production and use of sanitary pads and tampons which are sometimes advertised as 'designed by a gynaecologist'. The so-called 'new' technologies for assisted reproduction fit into a pattern of intervention that shapes all women's experience of the reproductive aspects of their lives whether they are seeking a particular intervention or not. In this sense, women as a group, have been medicalised as reproductive beings.

Some of these interventions have been incorporated into women's daily lives in fairly matter-of-fact ways, but others come as a surprise and women often find them unnecessarily intrusive. Birth control is a form of medicalisation that most women accept as unproblematic. Most methods that act in or on the female body require a medical consultation and some level of monitoring to ensure that the woman's general health remains good. Certainly the fertility control that medically delivered methods offer is welcomed by many women since it allows them to participate in heterosexual relationships and plan their lives with less chance of unpredictable childbearing. I will discuss birth control in more detail in chapter 4. Although medical intervention to control fertility seems commonplace to many in Australia today, older women and men remember when only some married women could get birth control from doctors and very few abortions were openly performed (Siedlecky and Wyndham 1990).

Childbirth may include more interventions than the pregnant woman had planned when there is a standard time set for the

Table 2.1   Interventions in Human Reproduction

Physiological process (woman's body)	Reproductive technologies (fertility and infertility)	'New' assisted reproductive technologies (infertility)
Ovulation	Hormonal contraception (pill, injection, implant)	Fertility drugs; Ovum collection
Fertilisation	Barrier methods of contraception (condom, diaphragm, cap); Spermicides; 'Morning after' pill; Sterilisation	Donor insemination (DI); *In vitro* fertilisation (IVF); Gamete intra-fallopian transfer (GIFT); Micro-injection of sperm
Implantation	Intra-uterine contraceptive device (IUCD or IUD)	Embryo transfer
Menstruation	Drugs for premenstrual syndrome (PMS) and period pain; Personal hygiene products	
Pregnancy		
1st trimester	Pregnancy test; Ante-natal care; Early abortion; Chorionic villus sampling for foetal diagnosis; Hormonal support for early pregnancy	
2nd trimester	Ultrasound; Amniocentesis for foetal diagnosis; Mid-term abortion	
3rd trimester	Foetal surgery; Pre-term caesarian section	
Labour	Induction; IV fluids and drugs; Foetal monitors	
Birth	Episiotomy; Instrumental delivery; caesarian section	
Neo-natal care	Drugs to prevent haemorrhage or to suppress lactation; Special care nurseries; Bottle feeding	

various stages of labour. Some women have used a variety of tactics to avoid similar interventions during a second pregnancy, including staying at home during a second labour to avoid another caesarian being performed because the labour was 'too long' (Martin 1987: 141–2). The less rigid standard in Australia today means that the clock does not determine how a woman will give birth. While tests and standardisation of procedures may have increased interventions in Australia, most are done with the consent of the birthing woman (Libesman and Sripathy 1996). There have been some alarming cases in the United States in which hospitals sought court orders to require a woman to follow 'doctor's orders'. Some of these cases have had very distressing outcomes, while others seem minor in retrospect because healthy babies were born while the court was sitting (Daniels 1993). While poor black women are more at risk of court-ordered intervention in the United States, even white middle class women are not immune to the reconstructions of pregnancy that question the bodily integrity of women (Bordo 1993; Daniels 1993).

Assisted reproductive technology is by definition a series of medical interventions as has been amply documented by feminist critics of infertility programs since the early 1980s (Arditti et al. 1984; Stanworth 1987; Spallone and Steinberg 1987; Klein 1989a; McNeil et al. 1990; Basen et al. 1993; Basen et al. 1994). Many of the tests for infertility are physically or emotionally invasive. The drugs used to induce ovulation have immediate side effects, and may have long-term effects on the woman's body and unknown effects on the baby she may later bear. Egg collection and embryo transfer are also physically invasive. In addition women who become pregnant in infertility programs frequently are subject to greater medical surveillance during their pregnancies and also have a higher rate of premature births and thus babies in special care nurseries.

The publicity given to the range of interventions affecting uncomplicated pregnancy, infertility and small or disabled newborns contributes to many women's perceptions of their bodies as problematic. Some supporters of assisted reproduction seem to welcome increased intervention even for fertile people in the name of increasing the level of rational control in procreation (Singer and Wells 1984). Announcements of technical innovations frequently compare potential 'success rates' with pregnancy rates achieved by fertile couples, as if a series of medical treatments were the equivalent of several months of unprotected intercourse at home. The interventions have come to be the measure of the performance of reproductive bodies; even healthy fertile women can fall short of the standard.

The language of medical science

One of the effects of the medicalisation of procreation is the widespread acceptance of medical language for talking about all aspects of reproduction including menstrual periods and menopause. For example, pregnancy is counted from the date of the last menstrual period, not from the date of implantation or of the sexual intercourse that was likely to have begun that particular pregnancy; the objectively observable became the marker, even though the woman was certainly not pregnant on the first day of her last period. The pregnancy itself is divided into trimesters, objective time, not time as marked by the woman's experience of pregnancy which may include the duration of 'morning sickness', 'quickening'—the time the woman feels the foetus move—or the time when everyday clothes no longer fit. Subjective time will differ from woman to woman and pregnancy to pregnancy.

The social shaping of medical definitions of women and women's bodies can be observed in many types of writing from medical textbooks to popular magazines and advice manuals. In 1972, sociologists Diana Scully and Pauline Bart published a study of textbooks then in use in US medical schools. They argued that the books 'revealed a persistent bias toward greater concern with the patient's husband than with the patient herself. Women are consistently described as anatomically destined to reproduce, nurture and keep their husbands happy' (Scully and Bart 1972: 283). You may say, ah but things are different today, that sort of criticism has had some effect. To a degree it has, of course, but when Koutroulis replicated the study using the texts used in Australian medical schools she found that:

> [t]he texts reveal pervasive stereotypes and sexist role-portrayals of women, consistent with the findings of Scully and Bart. As the subject matter of the texts, women are presented in the stereotypical roles and activities of wife, mother and house-keeper/homemaker. . . . There was considerable 'medicalisa-tion', and the description as pathology, of socially-based problems such as the stresses associated with caring for young children, particularly of women in the paid workforce who were seen as primarily, and often solely, responsible for their children's well-being and the stability of the marriage. (1990: 81–2)

The medical books reflected the same assumptions as the ABS categories about workforce participation.

In part this lack of change reflects the pervasive ideas about the social roles of women and men. The extent of the unexamined use of social ideas in scientific explanation can been seen in a comparison of writing about male and female contributions to conception. An anthropologist researching medicalisation found that the dominant cultural attitudes about men and women were present in medical textbook discussions of the physiological process of reproduction. The processes of the male body were appreciated in a way female processes were not:

> The mechanisms which guide the *remarkable* cellular transformation from spermatid to mature sperm remain uncertain . . . Perhaps the most *amazing* characteristic of spermatogenesis is its *sheer magnitude*: the normal human male may manufacture several hundred million sperm per day. [Emphasis added by Martin.] (Martin 1987: 48)

The same text that discussed the process of sperm development as a 'remarkable' feat of 'manufacture' described menstruation in terms of failed production characterised by 'regression', 'profound constriction', 'disintegration' and a menstrual flow consisting of 'debris' (Martin 1987: 49). In the description, all aspects of female functioning were related to reproduction, with menstruation portrayed as a mark of failed reproductive functioning, regardless of the woman's wishes or active attempts to prevent conception. After all, to a woman using contraception, menstruation is a sign of success. Menopause was described as a pathology, a hormonal deficiency disease, rather than as a part of the natural history of the female reproductive system.

Medical scientists and biologists are members of the same culture as people without scientific training, so they reach for the same range of metaphors to tell the story of what they observe during their research. The pervasive metaphors of passive women and active men are obvious in the scientific stories about fertilisation. Sports metaphors have been used to describe ejaculation and fertilisation in terms of a race among the competitive and active sperm for the opportunity to dive into the passive and waiting egg. Even if the sperm are not portrayed as practising for the Olympics, images of struggle and danger are present in descriptions of the process of fertilisation. Though the popular science accounts are more familiar, similar images shape the reports in science journals (E. Martin 1991). Here is the account from the seventh edition of the popular women's health book, *Everywoman*:

> Of the millions of spermatozoa deposited in the vicinity of the cervix, only a few thousand manage to negotiate the twisting mucus tunnels of its canal to reach the cavity of the uterus. Of these only a few hundred get through the narrow cornu of the uterus to enter the oviduct, and only a few dozen swim up along the oviduct, against the current made by the moving fronds of its lining, to reach the ovum. Only one penetrates

> through [the] tough, glistening, transparent 'shell' (the zona
> pellucida) which surrounds the egg. Once the spermatozoon has
> penetrated the 'shell' of the egg, it alters the zona in some way,
> so that no other spermatozoa are able to penetrate it.
> (Llewellyn-Jones 1996: 14–15)

The diagram that illustrates the process emphasises the dangers
and competitive aspects of fertilisation. There are illustrations of
the 'hazards of the journey' in the woman's cervix, uterus and
fallopian tubes, and a depiction of the 'winning spermatozoon'
and several 'losing spermatozoa' (Llewellyn-Jones 1996: 16).

These are claims that suit cultural beliefs about men and
report very little information about sperm cells. The meaning of
sperm shape, number and mobility is still contested (Pfeffer
1993). Far from the story of the Darwinian struggle of single-
minded individual spermatozoa, some researchers argue that the
sperm move in circles, not straight lines, and tend to diffuse in
all directions once released from a man's body. The shape and
activity of the female organs guide sperm to the egg (Pfeffer
1985: 40). In addition, researchers in infertility clinics have
discovered that the passage through the woman's genital tract
changes the sperm and allows them to fertilise an egg. The
process, called 'capacitation', changes the chemical activity of
sperm as a result of contact with the woman's body fluid, and
has to be imitated by the infertility practitioners (Wood and Riley
1992: 59).

Other researchers into the action of sperm and egg at
fertilisation have discovered that the competitive story is incomplete or misleading. The tail of the sperm makes weak movements
which fling the head from side to side, not forward, and cannot
break the chemical bonds that form the zona pellucida. In many
species, it seems that the egg 'chooses' and 'envelops' a sperm
rather than the sperm forcefully 'penetrating' the egg. Yet the
scientists describing their work fell back on images of aggressive
and dangerous females, entrapping males like spiders in webs
rather than using a metaphor that allows communication and
shared activity between egg and sperm (E. Martin 1991: 498–9).

The account of the Billings Method of fertility control using
periodic abstinence provides a less competition-based account.
The method itself relies on a woman being able to recognise
'fertile-type' cervical mucus which

> is essential in maintaining the fertilising capacity of the sperm.
> It enables sperm movement by providing guiding channels and

a protective environment for them; it sustains them nutritionally during their journey to the Fallopian tubes, and it captures damaged sperm. (Billings and Westmore 1992: 24)

In the accompanying diagram of the process of fertilisation, far from posing a 'hazard of the journey' the mucus is portrayed as a 'biological valve' 'forming pathways and protection for sperm', with the result that 'about 200 normal sperm cells reach the egg' of the about 300 million 'mixture of normal, old, immature and abnormal sperm cells' in the ejaculate (Billings and Westmore 1992: 37). In this account, a different female stereotype is brought into play, however. Neither passive, nor aggressive, the female body acts as a nurturing and protective mother to 'nurture' the sperm before there is a baby to nurture.

It may seem that the use of gendered metaphors for fertilisation is not too surprising. The metaphors usually reflect conservative gender stereotypes with origins in modern European thought rather than the diversity of human experience. Indeed, other aspects of the social relations between men and women in the nineteenth century are expressed in medical language used to discuss infertility. 'Hostile' cervical mucus refuses passage of the husband's sperm (Pfeffer 1993: 55), or 'incompatibility' in the sexual relationship is reflected in infertility with the responsibility for creating fertile attitudes handed to women (Pfeffer 1993: 130). Stereotyped characteristics of women and men are revealed in the metaphors used to describe the activity of the immune system, with some cells represented as militaristic and masculine while others are feminine or homosexual; that is, able to be penetrated (Waldby 1996; Martin 1994).

It is possible to tell a different story, however, one in which the female body facilitates the activity of sperm. A large number of cooperative sperm (the seminal collective, so to speak) gather around the egg after being encouraged and guided in their action by the fluids and movement in the female reproductive system. The egg is moving along the fallopian tube to meet the group of sperm. Each member of the collective releases a small amount of a chemical that will open the protective coating of the egg (the zona pellucida) just long enough for the egg to incorporate a single sperm. Once a sperm is enclosed in the egg, the zona pellucida closes again in order to protect the now fertilising egg. Indeed, the size of the sperm collective should not be too large—according to infertility specialists, the use of a larger number of sperm for fertilisation *in vitro* can lead to too many

49

sperm passing through the zona pellucida and thus to irregular fertilisation in about 3 per cent of the embryos formed this way (Wood and Riley 1992: 60). It may well be that as many irregular fertilisations occur in women's bodies and are shed rather than implanted. One's surprise at this alternative story demonstrates the power of the dominant metaphors in the language of reproductive science. The apparently objective story of the physiology of reproduction is shaped by the same assumptions that shape other aspects of women's public and domestic lives.

Owning bodies?

The assertion by a woman that 'her body is her own' is a refusal to become an object; it is a demand to be taken seriously as a subject, a social actor. When feminists assert that a woman possesses her body they are making a number of overlapping claims including, firstly, that each woman, and no one else, should have the final say over her body. At the same time they are recognising that this claim is made among a competing group of counter claims for authority over women's bodies. Indeed much of the feminist analysis and politics explored in the remaining chapters is a challenge to the competing claims by fathers, husbands, doctors and protectors of public morality.

One of the ways that women claim authority over their bodies is by appealing to an analogy with the ownership of property. The analogy of bodies with property has a long history in liberal democratic thought, beginning with John Locke in the seventeenth century asserting that a person's property rights over things develops from a pre-existing right to the 'property of his own person'. The person then acquires rights to other forms of property by means of mixing the 'labour of his body' with the common resources provided in nature. Locke used his formulation to justify the extension of political liberty to the great majority of men. The strong argument against slavery comes from a notion of self-ownership: once all humans were recognised as equally persons regardless of colour or ethnic origin, they could not be bought and sold as chattels. Yet within traditional liberal theory there was a reluctance to recognise self-ownership by women (Pateman 1988). Marriage was an institution that seemed to transfer the ownership of women from their fathers to their husbands. This ownership extended from control over the woman's sexual expression to possession of any children she might bear. It is no surprise that nineteenth century feminists campaigned for changes to laws of marriage and divorce including custody of children, and for the recognition of a woman's right to set conditions on her sexual experience within marriage.

The Women's Liberation Movement used the notion of self-ownership and female autonomy as the basis of the early campaigns for sexual and reproductive rights. They argued that autonomy meant reproductive choice for women, including the right to terminate a pregnancy, but in the heat of the political campaigns did not think about many of the theoretical problems with the underlying analogy of the body as property (see chapter 5). Some political philosophers seem to treat the body in the same way as other property, arguing that more than moral authority or autonomy over one's body is implied by self-ownership (cf. Nozick 1974). Susan Moller Okin (1989) poses one problem for this approach when she notes that according to the traditional Lockean view that the mixing of one's labour implies ownership, women own their children, and by extension all humans, because women grow children with the labour of their bodies. Other problems with this interpretation are highlighted by the debates about the meanings for women of assisted reproductive technologies, especially egg or embryo donation and surrogacy. If bodies and body parts are property in the same way that cars or coats are property, then the selling of semen, eggs, embryos or reproductive services such as gestation should pose no problems. Yet there seems to be more to these actions than the simple case of property exchange, in part because procreation makes babies. Babies are not like cars or coats— rather, they soon gain consciousness and as young adults claim autonomy themselves.

Rosalind Petchesky suggested that the Lockean paradigm of self-ownership is not the most appropriate for thinking about feminist demands for bodily integrity. She began her analysis with the concept of self-possession drawn from the ideas of the Levellers, seventeenth century political activists against the enclosure of common land in England. Activists regularly faced arbitrary arrest and imprisonment for not having marriage licenses as well as for sedition. Their claim to self-ownership was not a formal abstraction but, 'it was an oppositional stance against interference by public authorities in one's sexual and bodily life' (Petchesky 1995: 392). Leveller women made demands in the name of the community, as well as on their own individual behalf, against invasion by the state. This was a demand to control the boundaries of their communities and bodies, not a claim about buying and selling. Similar claims about the control of boundaries appear in the writing of many third world women. The sense that women's bodies are their own is the basis of claims for an equitable share of resources for women: food, housing, education, access to market work, a clean environment, freedom from threats and violence, as well as high-quality reproductive health care including contraception and abortion (Petchesky 1995: 402–4; Corrêa and Reichmann 1994; Kabeer 1994).

In this chapter I have explored some of the ways that the medicalisation of reproductive bodies has contributed to the social construction of women's bodies. Those constructions then shape the language available for women seeking to make sense of their bodily experiences. However, women's subjectivity is not completely constituted in relation to medical discourses, and many cultural practices of femininity are at odds with a narrow definition of women as reproductive. The claim that women's bodies are their own throws up the demand for women to make the decisions about the experiences that shape their lives. In the next chapter I explore the struggles over state regulation in reproductive politics, especially the ways that feminist ideas have contributed to the recognition of women as experts in their own lives.

3 State, Morality and Contests Over Expertise

This slogan identifies some of the parties involved in the struggle over decision making about fertility and childbearing—clergy, state agents whether legislators or department officers, and individual women. It also serves as a reminder of the different ways these interested parties are organised and the contests among them. Organised religions have claimed a special capacity to make moral arguments and hence to provide guidance about moral decision making, though they do not always agree with each other. They also have a network of local congregations and national and international bodies with hierarchies, recognised spokesmen and the resources for undertaking prolonged political campaigns. The state seems unified but is comprised of legislative bodies, bureaucratic agencies and judicial officers. These contribute to the regulation of fertility in contradictory ways. Women have organised to challenge conservative moral dominance and to intervene in state policies. These organisations have ranged from formally structured interest groups that undertook long education and lobbying campaigns, to informal coalitions that came together to act during a crisis and then dissolved. Like the religious organisations and the state agencies, the women's groups have not always agreed with each other. The three parties have engaged in contests about one of the recurring themes in liberal democratic politics—to what extent should the state enforce morality?

This chapter examines the contests among proponents of the

available meanings of womanhood and fertility in Australia. The civil liberties position, achieved during the late 1960s, reduced the role of the state in the enforcement of morals. That reduction has been challenged both by feminists who have raised new ethical concerns and by those who deplore what they see as a move towards permissive morality. The slogan itself has been used by feminists since the 1970s as a part of the campaign to change abortion laws and increase access to contraception. It originated during the time when women began to be recognised as experts in their own lives by many agencies of the Australian state. That recognition has not meant that the struggle to gain public acceptance of women's decision making is over, however; old meanings of fertility, womanhood and expert knowledge are regularly reasserted.

Law and morality

For many centuries religious institutions promulgated doctrines that asserted pregnancy and childbearing as the divine plan for women's lives. Procreation was the justification for sexual expression in the Christian tradition. Sexual desire was itself viewed with suspicion, first as a distraction from spiritual duties and later as a distraction from hard work. At the same time women sought to limit childbearing either privately or with their partners (McLaren 1990). The Judaeo-Christian arguments about procreation, the meaning of marriage and the hierarchical relationship among fathers, mothers and children were written into a variety of Western laws regulating marriage, divorce, the status of children, property rights, inheritance and what counted as sexual crime (Smart 1989; Graycar and Morgan 1990; Kirkby 1995). Other religious traditions have also influenced legislation in countries where they are predominant and have structured women's lives by regulating sexuality and reproduction. I have not discussed them here because these ideas are not yet prominent in Australian public debates, though they are important in the lives of some Australian women and men.

During the 1920s, with the growth of secularism in Great Britain, civil libertarians joined sex reformers to argue for a separation of the morality based in the Judaeo-Christian tradition and the criminal law relating to a number of sexually related activities (Weeks 1981). The civil libertarian view has been articulated in a number of government inquiries since 1957 when the Wolfenden Committee into homosexuality and prostitution in Great Britain concluded that there was a limit to state regulation of sexuality because while there might be a place for protecting citizens from offensive or injurious behaviour, '[T]here must remain a realm of private morality and immorality which is, in crude and brief terms, not the law's business' (quoted in Hart 1963: 14–15).

The civil libertarian view is in direct opposition to a significant stream of legal thought that holds that one of the important roles for law is the enforcement of moral values within a society. The debate during the 1950s and 1960s in relation to homosexuality, prostitution and censorship of sexually explicit material and abortion turned on interpretations of John Stuart Mill's 1859 essay *On Liberty*, in which Mill set out the grounds for interference in the private lives of citizens (Hart 1963; Devlin 1965). The reforms of those decades reflect the civil libertarian position of Mill himself, who argued:

> That the only purpose for which power can be rightfully exercised over any member of a civilised community, against his will, is to prevent harm to others. His own good, either physical or moral, is not sufficient warrant . . . Over himself, over his own body and mind, the individual is sovereign. (Mill 1859/1956: 13)

Mill included both women and men in the protections from paternalism and despotism provided by this principle. Those who argued against this view generally asserted that the presence of immoral activity is harmful to the community as a whole, especially to those who have not yet firmly established their moral values.

The short period of law reform in the United Kingdom, Australia and the United States indicated, not the end of the debate, but rather a change in the balance of forces and indeed, we can see now, marked the beginning of new forms of political intervention about sexuality and morality more generally. 'Sexual politics' was identified by the Women's and Gay Liberation Movements as a realm of ethical debate that had previously been regarded as the preserve of experts. The new analyses challenged a range of normative discourses which had valorised a single heterosexual family form as natural and all other social–sexual practices as deviant and threatening to the good order of society. The unmediated voice of the people in question seldom appeared even in accounts by experts who argued for law reform (cf. Wilson 1971; Callahan 1970).

The liberal Roman Catholic ethicist Daniel Callahan, for example, began his important analysis of abortion law and policy from a consideration of the medical 'indications' for abortion and worked through different legal regulatory regimes around the world in the 1960s in an attempt to establish a consensus-based moral policy. Such a beginning effectively accepted medical definitions of normal and pathological conditions in women and foetuses, and acknowledged the profession's claims to expertise about the bodies and lives of women. The seldom explicit definition of what was normal for women included chastity before marriage to a man who was a reliable breadwinner. While the couple thus formed might use contraception to space their children, there was no doubt in Australia, as elsewhere, that each pregnancy would be welcomed and the child cared for at home unless there were overwhelmingly bad circumstances (Siedlecky and Wyndham 1990). Yet, Callahan acknowledged in the late 1960s that the majority of women gaining abortions in all the legal regimes he studied were married and trying to limit family size or cope with adverse socio-economic circumstances. He thought that unmarried women resorted to illegal abortions because of the social stigma of 'illegitimacy' (Callahan 1970: 292–4).

While married Australian women were expected to welcome babies, '[t]he mother without a marriage certificate and the child without a male provider existed in a separate space, the stigma attached to their deviance/defiance used to reinforce morality in the community as a whole' (Swain and Howe 1995: 1). In the United States, white and black pregnant single women were thought to be deviant too: young whites were 'seeking love' thus expressing a psychological problem, but young black women were acting out strong biological and sexual urges which indicated a 'lack of psyche' (Solinger 1992). In 1971 Paul Wilson combined an account of abortion law and practice along with homosexuality and divorce to argue for law reform in the regulation of sexual behaviour. He offered psychological explanations of unwanted pregnancy rather than a sociological explanation of the limited availability of contraceptives during the 1960s in Australia, especially for unmarried women. Nor did he discuss the social conditions that meant that sexual intercourse was not always approached with rationality and planning (Wilson 1971: 30–32). Wilson had interviewed women who had successfully sought illegal abortions but he did not report their views about the moral or social issues surrounding unwanted pregnancies.

The conventional social and political practice of silence by those who sought abortions was such that Madeline Simms could describe her surprise at meeting a woman who admitted to having had an illegal abortion, at a meeting of the British Abortion Law Reform Association in 1962 (Hindell and Simms 1971: 114). Some of the US activists had publicly discussed their own abortions as a part of the argument for law repeal in particular states (Lader 1973), but it is unclear what effect they had on the trickle of reform legislation that preceded the 1973 Supreme Court decision known as *Roe v. Wade*. Some of the early Women's Liberation actions were public 'speak-outs' by women describing the personal humiliations and dangers of illegal abortions. The feminist assertion that the personal was political made such testimony the raw data for political analysis.

The view that the state should regulate morality lost the dominance that it had previously enjoyed, but did not disappear. In the United States the Supreme Court decision also marked a change in the politics of opponents of abortion law reform, drawing in community-based activists, many of whom were mothers of relatively large families of young children, rather than professional people (Luker 1984). It came at a time when many previously unexamined assumptions about the social order were undergoing profound change. It is worth remembering the number of challenges to the relatively unquestioned status quo that appeared on the news and current events programs on network television: the civil rights movement, the anti-war movement, the development of the 'counter-culture', and a variety of sexual liberation movements. This outburst of 'permissiveness' began during a period of economic growth and continued as the long post-World War II boom was beginning to go bust. Abortion and homosexuality became symbols, for some in the United States, of the loss of moral values and national pride.

In Australia, during the 1970s and 1980s right-wing politics seemed to have a weaker grip on the national imagination. Civil rights for Aboriginal people, the end to participation in the war in Vietnam, the recognition of sexual minorities, and the acknowledgment of women's skills and ambitions beyond the family all became a part of the national political debate. I discuss some of the limitations to these achievements in this book, but the climate of moral politics has been better for heterosexual women, gay men and lesbians here, the long delay in reforming Tasmania's anti-homosexual-practice laws notwithstanding. Abortion still remains a part of the criminal law, but is widely available, and mainstream party politicians have not made sexual morality central to their electoral appeal. Since the late 1970s, Senator Brian Harradine has made legislative interventions, but these did not end Medicare funding of abortions or health funding for organisations that offer abortion advice in Australia (Siedlecky and Wyndham 1990: 96). During the 1980s and early 1990s he also made interventions in attempts to regulate infertility treatments, especially to prohibit embryo experimentation.

The 1996 electoral victory by the Liberal–National Party coalition altered the apparent political consensus about abortion services. Neither major party held a clear majority in the Senate; Senator Harradine and one other senator held the balance of power, their votes being necessary for the new government to pass its legislative program. The government seemed to be willing to make policies that coincided with some of Senator Harradine's beliefs, including cutting overseas aid for many programs that offered birth control services as a part of its first budget (Brough 1996b). Senator Harradine was also able to mobilise bipartisan support for a bill that required the minister for health to directly approve the importation of certain drugs that could be used for abortion (currently RU486) and to table that recommendation in the parliament (Brough 1996a; Tingle 1996). The effect was to further politicise medical abortion by removing it from the standard regulation of experimental drugs, which are imported with the approval of an officer in the Therapeutic Goods Branch of the Department of Health. The National Health Medical Research Council (NHMRC) tabled, rather than endorsed, the report and recommendations of its expert panel on the termination of pregnancy services which was subject to considerable internal debate in late 1996 (Brough 1996c; Pitt 1997). Then in mid-1997 publication of the report was further delayed because the NHMRC withdrew its logo from the cover (Horin 1997). It was finally published as a discussion paper (Australia 1997a) and again withdrawn. Senator Harradine's views about the report and abortion in general were again canvassed in the media.

Senator Harradine has been persistent in his campaign to regulate fertility-related services in Australia, but he has been successful in mobilising effective support only when the government needs his vote. Brian Harradine, an Independent senator from Tasmania, is an example of a politician who was more common during the 1950s and 1960s. He is a conservative Roman

Catholic with strong trade union links (he was an organiser in the Federated Clerks Union) who was once a member of the Australian Labor Party. He was expelled from the ALP in 1975 after years of party infighting and stood as an Independent in the December 1975 election after the dismissal of the Whitlam Labor government. He combines a commitment to social justice for the underprivileged with an overwhelming belief in the importance of the conservative Catholic position on sexual morality and family values (Marr 1997).

This combination of beliefs was dominant in the NSW Labor Party during the 1950s and 1960s, after conservative Catholic ALP politicians in some other States had split to form the Democratic Labor Party (DLP). Karen Coleman argues that the dominance of the right in New South Wales is an explanation for the form of abortion politics in the State during the 1960s and 1970s (1988). During the early 1970s the ALP moved to a position nationally in which issues of sexual morality became issues for a 'conscience' vote rather than a vote tied to party policy. The Catholics who remained in the party after the split could vote against legislation counter to their religious beliefs and not risk expulsion. In New South Wales the strongest public proponents of a conservative Christian family-values position are the Protestant members of the Christian Democratic Party (formerly the Call to Australia Party). Leaders of mainstream parties in recent years who have expressed personal disapproval of abortion also have a commitment to the separation of church and state in a pluralist society. Legislation should not enforce sectarian morality.

There are no doubt many reasons for the relative unwillingness of major parties to elevate the elimination of abortion services to a central plank in an election platform, including compulsory voting and the preferential ballot, but I will suggest two others that call attention to different national approaches to using the state to enforce morality. The robust tradition of economic debate in politics means that Australians, who are concerned about their personal futures during a time of economic restructuring, blame government policies, big business or international markets. They do not displace their financial anxiety onto issues of sexual morality as seemed to happen in the United States. The United States has no shared language of class politics, so those who feel disenfranchised by growing income differentials may 'have turned to the realm of morality to express class resentments' (Fernandez-Kelly 1992: 253–4). Men hurting from the effects of severe economic and social dislocation have blamed the social change on independent and professional women. The open availability of abortion thus became the symbolic representation of the threats to masculine identity based on providing financial security for women and children. As the economy has recovered, the support for violent anti-abortion protests has decreased (Ginsberg 1998). Australian men seem to be working through the challenges to old forms of masculine identities in other ways, even though they are not necessarily any more open to the claims of feminists (Connell 1995). It may be that the recurrent 'immigration debate', with the representation of recent immigrants as competitors with unemployed Australians, serves a role similar to the anti-feminism expressed in the United States.

Second, the moral discourse of politics in Australia is more strongly marked by concerns for social justice and government intervention when the market forces cast individuals out. Unemployment in a time of economic restructuring is not regarded as a moral failure, so may be less of a threat to personal identity than in the United States where self-reliance and individualism are more marked political values. In addition, the Australian public moral discourse is more secular, without the recurrent reference to a relatively conservative Christianity. The apparent influence of the conservative religious, family-values Lyons Forum within the coalition parliamentary parties may signal a change in this pattern of debate. However, the major policy changes signalled by the Howard-led coalition government are economic, with industrial and tax reform, not social morality, high on the agenda.

Contesting moral thinking

The discussion of the need for regulation of financial institutions does not raise the same passions as the calls for the regulation of sexual morality. Public morality is based on the duty to obey certain laws and regulations that govern particular activities. People may disagree about the precise level of regulation necessary to achieve a productive balance between the needs of the market and the protection of vulnerable members of society, but they seldom frame their arguments as if the very survival of the social order is at stake. Yet, some of the rhetoric of the 'moral right' in democratic countries in response to the rapid social change of the past forty years suggests just that.

It may also be that personal morality, which is so often collapsed into sexual behaviour, is viewed as appropriate to the private realm of family life, a part of who we are, rather than what we do. Public life is regulated by rules that are thought of as rational, detached from individual personalities; personal life is regulated by the recognition of personalities and their specific needs (Poole 1991: 45–64). A good mother is, by definition, a woman who treats her children differently from the way she treats other children. Women who work as family-day-care mothers find the need to treat their children the same as the other children in the group to be contradictory (Nelson 1994). The rational moral position of good (child care) worker is in tension with the moral identity of being a good mother. Men have been expected to live with this double experience of morality as a rational worker and a good family man, but according to liberal moral and political theory women have not because they have been protected from public life. So the use of the politicised language of rights to discuss personal morality seems like a challenge to the social order that has divided the private world of family life and personal identity from the dehumanising world of work.

The act of making a moral judgment based on balancing competing principles or rights claims always raises some problems. Sometimes the balance is easy to assert and widely accepted. For example, no one would argue that the right to free speech includes a right to shout 'fire!' in a crowded theatre. However, some people who oppose racist abuse are not willing to infringe the right to free speech by enacting criminal racial vilification legislation. The clear public dangers of shouting 'fire!' override individual liberties, but there is much less agreement about the social dangers of public racist talk. If public rights debates are sometimes hard to resolve, then claims for rights in the private realm of sexuality and family life have proved even more difficult. There is also little agreement about how to balance a woman's demand for the democratic right to personal autonomy in reproductive decision making with the demand that all humans, including foetuses, have a right to life.

In discussions about abortion, the difficulty in achieving agreement about moral judgments arises from the way the question is framed. While democratic political theory suggests that the autonomy of citizens means that each citizen has control over his/her body as if it were a possession, that understanding has been different according to the sex of the citizen. Male citizens have autonomy over their bodies, but for several centuries both theory and practice held that men also exercised control over the bodies of women through marriage or fatherhood (Pateman 1988;

Okin 1979). Indeed the very fact of women's biological and emotional connection to their children was a disqualification to full autonomy; that is, women would be unable to exercise the level of objectivity required by autonomous moral decision makers. As with other aspects of the account of radical differences between men and women, this account of moral differences rests on unexamined definitions—in this case, that autonomy means independence or self-sufficiency. The public man of liberal theory does not self-sufficiently raise his own hens or grind his own wheat even if he prepares his own breakfast, nor does he live without emotional ties. He lives in a household with an adult woman and some children at the very least (cf. Rawls 1971), yet these living arrangements are not assumed to impinge on his objectivity. There is little discussion of that lack of self-sufficiency at all. This refusal to acknowledge the interconnected lives of relatively privileged men may be an effect of their ability to define what is important and what is not. When the work of maintaining daily life is devalued, so too are the efforts of the people who do that work. In different ways privileged women, working class women and men, and women and men from the subordinated ethnic groups do work that makes the apparently autonomous life of privileged men possible (Tronto 1993).

Until the 1970s most discussions about sexual morality and political rights were attempts to determine the boundaries of the liberal principles. What kind of harm should the state seek to prevent? For example, did prohibition of homosexual acts protect the vulnerable in the community or did it make criminals of people who were simply living their personal lives, even if those lives were objectionable to some other members of the community? Many of the debates of the 1950s and 1960s were resolved in civil liberties terms. For legislative purposes, the principles of liberalism were accepted as having priority over moral objections based in religious traditions. Objections have been made to the individualism of this liberal language because of its class and racial basis and the inequitable social order it upholds (Young 1990; Phillips 1993; Tronto 1993; Yeatman 1994). Feminist political philosophers have developed sophisticated criticisms of the assumptions of the rational autonomous individual and his masculinity (see above and Lloyd 1984; Pateman 1988; Gatens 1991). In a related stream of thinking, feminist philosophers and psychologists have considered the importance of connectedness and dependency in the lives of all humans. After all, even the most independent man was once a helpless baby who was nurtured towards autonomy. This recognition has contributed to the development of an alternative ethic of care.

Carol Gilligan coined the term 'the ethic of care' to describe a characteristic of women's moral reasoning that differed from a more principle-based moral reasoning that social psychologists had argued was characteristic of the moral development of men. Gilligan found that women who had abortions did not arrive at the decision by simply balancing their right to autonomy and the foetus's right to life, but rather thought about their lives and choices in terms of a network of social connections (1982). While there has been considerable debate about Gilligan's methods and conclusions about moral development (Tronto 1993), the idea that women tend to emphasise connectedness with others is widely accepted. Tronto uses it as a basis for speculation about the characteristics of a social order based on connection and care rather than individual autonomy. One problem with many uses of the notion of the ethic of care has been the slippage from a recognition that women have more highly developed caring skills because of social power relations to a belief that women are 'naturally' more caring than men. The latter position recapitulates conventional views about women.

Quite separately, social policy scholars in Britain began to describe the caring work of women and the way that the state was able to rely on women's sense of duty to members of kin networks in order to cut back on community services (Finch and Groves 1983). Many studies have put the analysis of women's caring work in the context of the conventional sexual division of labour and the culturally constituted power relations of domestic life that feminists have been analysing for the past century (Finch 1989). Assumptions about women's interest in care and connectedness by social policy makers in times of financial stringency and so-called economic rationalism have contributed to a combination of funding cuts, decreased independence for those in need of care, and guilt on the part of women and men who cannot replace the missing services for their old relatives, disabled children or each other—not exactly what a social ethic of care seems to suggest.

The state and population

The rise of the liberal democratic state was accompanied by changing ideas about the definition of the nation and the role of government. The condition of the people was increasingly important and the development of social sciences in the nineteenth century, especially statistics, made it possible to record the population and its well-being. Modern warfare required the mobilisation of the whole population, not just a standing army, so the health of young men became a matter of concern. As the welfare state developed, governments had to feel certain that only eligible citizens received the benefits. The interest in population was not limited to legislation but spread throughout the concerns of government agencies. In many countries statistics bureaus were opened to collect information that was to provide scientific evidence on which to base economic and social planning. All of this state activity was not the result of the good intentions of those who happened to be public officials at the time, but rather was a response to a complex politics of nationalism. In Australia, nationalism helped shape not only federation, but also the White Australia Policy which aimed at the reproduction of a British population in the Pacific. In addition, many liberal reform movements challenged the new national governments to improve the conditions of poor and disadvantaged sections of the population. Many aspects of family and sexual life thus came to be regulated by various state agencies.

One way to understand the apparently contradictory interest of the liberal state in the personal reproductive concerns of individual citizens is through the work of Michel Foucault on power. I introduced Foucault's ideas about self-discipline and some feminist interpretations of the concept of that discipline making 'docile bodies' in chapter 2. He argued that the family can be seen as the 'crystal' in the deployment of sexuality. An idealised or normative version of family life was used in a number of discourses to connect the wider concerns about populations with the bodily practices of individuals. Concerns about the health or size of the population, or sections of the population, were frequently collapsed into concerns about the sexual morality of particular individuals. The vigour of the middle classes was at risk from the fragile or inadequate mother; the morally corrupting servant who taught youths to masturbate; the couple who used birth control rather than procreate or abstain from sexual intercourse; and by the end of the nineteenth century, the perverse adult who pursued pleasure rather than sexual morality. Experts in medicine and population developed and gained authority to speak about sexuality and morality (Foucault 1979). Foucault argued that these experts became a part of a new type of power over life which he called bio-power. Bio-power had two main foci: one was centred on the individual body and sought to discipline it; the other was centred on the species body or population and sought to regulate it (Foucault 1979: 139). These foci gain particular importance in discussions of sex because 'sex was a means of access both to the life of the body and the life of the species' (Foucault 1979: 146). Bodies could be disciplined in terms of sexual practice, but the social body could be investigated and regulated using the new methods of statistical assessment and survey research. Previously private practices became the subject of public scrutiny and concern.

While Foucault's account is very suggestive, he did not explore extensively the gendered forms of bio-power. Certainly, during the nineteenth century, sexuality was deployed differently in the constitution of feminine rather than masculine subjectivity. While feminists and purity campaigners in Britain did argue that male sexuality could be controlled by an act of will, few disputed the notion that male heterosexual desire was in some way natural (Bland 1995; Weeks 1986). Female desire was widely regarded as readily controllable by willpower and, in most women, more closely tied to reproduction than to sexual activity. In addition, Foucault suggested that we divert our gaze from the activity of the state in the regulation of sexuality and look at more local sites of power and knowledge; medicine is one. This is of course useful advice, since state activity is not solely responsible for the regulation of women and fertility. However, state agencies have been deeply implicated in a variety of codifications of the meanings of sexual practices.

The role of state agencies has made them a major target of feminist activists since the 1960s, yet the agencies have not spoken with one voice. Rosalind Petchesky, in an attempt to explain the contradictions in US interventions in contraceptive and abortion practice, argued that the state has had three purposes in intervening in fertility. The three aims reflect different aspects of the liberal democratic state: an interest in the size and health of populations; a concern with setting the boundaries of women's control of female sexuality; and an overwhelming interest in maintaining its own legitimacy (Petchesky 1985: 117). Attention to the continuing concern with legitimacy helps to avoid an analysis of government interventions that relies on a simple gesture towards male domination or offers a complex analysis of discourses which loses sight of aspects of politics far from the arenas of the deployment of bio-power. The three purposes that

Petchesky identified need not be limited to an analysis of the overall shape of population and fertility policies. Keeping in mind the different ways in which they can be balanced against each other according to the goals and practices of a particular agency helps make sense of the often dramatic conflicts between agencies. In addition, there are factional battles over preselection in all the major parties and the unseemly scramble for 'popular' policy angles in the run-up to any election.

The willingness of the coalition government in the late 1990s to highlight Senator Harradine's concerns has been about gaining his vote in the Senate as much as it is about a concerted effort to set boundaries around women's actions. One measure of the legitimacy of an Australian government is its ability to pass its legislative program through both the House of Representatives where it has a majority and the Senate. The Liberal–National Party coalition was unwilling to negotiate with other parties in the Senate and thus risk significant change to its legislation on matters like the partial sale of Telstra. In a sense the breakdown of the consensus on fertility control has been the result of pressing political needs by those in government rather than of a commitment to Harradine's views.

The state contributes to debates on fertility control in a number of ways. Institutions of the state control the agenda and venues of political debate, regulate welfare and business practice and exercise judicial functions. The legislative and law enforcement aspects are highlighted when police roll up in front of clinics and seize thousands of files as the Queensland police did in 1985 (Loane 1985); when women are pursued through courts in an attempt to stop a 'lawful' abortion (*SMH* 31.3.1983); when police take bribes rather than raid clinics (Wainer 1972; Allen 1990b); or when State governments allow hours of time for a private member's motion against the availability of abortion (Albury 1989). Since the middle of the last century legislatures in capitalist countries also have aided the medical profession in its struggle to become the single legitimate authority on health and illness.

Many analysts have argued that the agencies of the welfare state promote a particular form of family life: a nuclear family of heterosexual married couple and dependent children, financially supported by the man (Bryson 1993; Baldock and Cass 1988; Donzelot 1979; Wilson 1977). In Australia, welfare services have the model family 'built into them' and until very recently the model was white and either middle class or 'respectable' working class. Unemployment benefits were structured on the assumption that men should be able to provide for their families, with married men attracting a higher rate than single people, rather than both unemployed partners receiving benefits in their own right. This rests on the same assumptions that formed the basis of the Harvester Judgment (1907) which granted a family wage for men and a lesser wage for women (Ryan and Conlon 1989).

Nineteenth century social surveys recorded not only over-crowding and unsafe play spaces for children, but also the moral judgments of the working class women by the middle class surveyors (Finch 1993). Standards of cleanliness, child care and, later, sexual propriety that were regarded as correct in middle class households with their servants and separate bedrooms became the benchmark against which the poor were measured in parliamentary debates and in the beginnings of welfare services. At the same time, the white male officials and settlers also judged Aboriginal women and men against the same middle class stand-ards, setting in place the opinions that were to shape the social policies that attacked Aboriginal family and community life throughout the remainder of the nineteenth and much of the twentieth centuries (Grimshaw and May 1994). In the nineteenth century poor white women and men were not invited to speak to parliamentary inquiries, so their understandings of life were not a part of the public record until some time during the twentieth century. The interpretations of Aboriginal people were entirely absent from the public record as the system of Aboriginal Protection Boards and missions was established. Children were taken away from their mothers and communities, hypothetically to be assimilated into white Australian society (Read 1983; Cummings 1990; van Krieken 1991: 96–7; Australia 1997b). Aboriginal people were less likely than poor whites to meet the middle class standard for housekeeping and child care.

Female wards of the state have sometimes been subjected to fertility control methods chosen for the convenience of the caretakers rather than with consideration for the health or deci-sion-making powers of the girls. There is a history of young women being charged with being in 'moral danger' or 'exposed' for having a sexual relationship before the statutory age of consent. These young women became caught up in the juvenile justice system as a result of their autonomous sexual behaviour (Carrington 1993). Women receiving a supporting parent's benefit are subjected to surveillance by the Department of Social Security to make sure that they do not have a male lover who would be automatically assumed to be providing financial support. These and other welfare practices are premised on and provide support for assumptions about the role of women in the contemporary social order (Baldock and Cass 1988).

Middle class white women occupy a contradictory position in any analysis of the experiences of women caught up in the regulatory mechanisms of state welfare provision. They were instrumental in establishing charitable and early state welfare institutions in the late nineteenth century and were important in the early twentieth century baby health and home science movements to teach women how to be housewives and mothers (Gilding 1991; Reiger 1985). White women were the employers of Aboriginal servants and frequently treated their employees according to the unthinking racism of the time (Huggins 1994). At the same time as they were the model for other groups of women, middle class women were also regulated by a system that assumed that women belonged at home, dependent on a male wage for their well-being. Feminists who wrote accounts of the lives of women in Australia during the early to mid 1970s emphasised the relative powerlessness even of women who worked in state welfare or education agencies (cf. Summers 1994), though it is less likely that welfare beneficiaries or working class parents in a confrontation with a teacher would think so.

The state agencies do not speak with one voice and state policies change over time. The National Women's Health Policy (Australia 1989) identified 'sex role stereotyping' as a major health issue for women. Women in paid work may receive a child care subsidy. The actions of Commonwealth and some State governments since the Liberal–National Party coalition victory in the 1996 election have exposed the continuing contest about such policy directions. The calls for a return to the 'family values' of some less complex past demonstrate fears about women's resistance to the disciplines that produce docile female bodies but are also an attack on the social changes that have followed the policies that recognise and promote equality between women and men. Those policies were developed in response to the politics of the women's movement that began in the 1960s, so political counter demands are not a surprise.

The Women's Liberation Movement

The political demand that women should make decisions about their lives did not mean that there was a clear understanding of

how those decisions should be made. Developing that understanding began by criticising the disembodied nature of liberal
ideas of citizenship and by initiating political campaigns that put
women's sexual and reproductive bodies on the political agenda.
Behind the differences about how to change the agenda there
has been a determination that there will be no return to the 'good
old days' when laws reinforced male control over the activities
of women in the name of a natural order or a greater social
good. In Australia, the campaigns have been particularly successful in the areas of workforce conditions and some aspects of
physical and sexual violence. In addition, governments have
responded to the demands by establishing women's units to review
many aspects of public policy. While change is incomplete in
these areas, reform of the regulation of reproduction has barely
begun.

In Australia, as in other Western democracies, the Women's
Liberation Movement developed along with movements against
the US-led war in Vietnam, and supporting solidarity with
decolonising struggles and civil rights for racial minorities
(Burgmann 1993). These and other new social movements are
characterised by fluidity, with relatively informal groups of people
organising around a particular issue. The groups direct their
activities both towards affected communities to encourage more
participants and towards the established political institutions
(parties, government bodies and unions) to alter policy. With no
formal organisational structure existing, there is no easy way to
'join' a social movement, nor any easy way for past activists to
pass on their knowledge. The movements change over time,
interacting with new political campaigns, changes in government
policy, changing social and economic circumstances and the
insights of new members. While activists in the Australian
Women's Liberation Movement developed analyses in dialogue
with papers and ideas from overseas it is important to remember
that Australian feminism became distinctive in a number of ways
that reflect Australian political culture in the 1970s and 1980s
(Eisenstein 1991).

Few of the new feminist activists had been a part of the
women's organisations that had been established at the turn of
the century and continued after the vote was achieved. Many
were ignorant of the existing organisations of the women's peace
movement, equal pay and married women's right to work campaigning groups, small groups lobbying for birth control and
abortion law reform and the more publicly acceptable Country

Women's Association or the YWCA. Beginning in 1969, the Women's Liberation Movement (WLM) grew up first in university suburbs with early participation by trade union activists and members of left parties. The Women's Electoral Lobby (WEL) began in Melbourne in 1972 in order to survey and publish the views of candidates in the federal election. The survey was successful in putting feminist issues on the political agenda. While WEL was related to Women's Liberation at first, they were quickly perceived as very different. There were many discussions about the merits of reform—working with established political parties as WEL did—or revolution—challenging the established social and political institutions as WLM aimed to do—as the most appropriate basis for achieving feminist goals (Mercer et al. 1975; Reade 1994). These heated differences seem less significant in the 1990s, but they provide an indication of the previous political experience and commitments of the activists in the early 1970s.

Women's Liberationists frequently had backgrounds in the left and/or the anti-war movement. They were critical of the sexism of the male leaders and the apparent reduction of women to the traditional role of 'auxiliaries' who typed reports, did the mailings, and kept households together while men made decisions and developed theory (Burgmann 1993; Curthoys 1992; Curthoys 1994). The language of the anti-war and anti-colonial struggles was extended to discussions of women's oppression and exploitation. Many early members of WEL had been active in the Australian Council for Civil Liberties, abortion law reform, political parties or community organisations (Reade 1994). As the organisation developed, members were more comfortable working in standard pressure group ways. They analysed issues, wrote submissions and lobbied politicians on specific issues before the parliaments, and their spokeswomen made themselves available to the press as 'experts' in a way that women's liberationists were reluctant to do. The Whitlam government responded to many feminist demands, appointing Elizabeth Reid as the prime minister's adviser on women's affairs, establishing a range of women's services and supporting activities during the United Nations' International Women's Year (1975). WEL was the source of many developments in women's policy and the springboard into public service positions or political preselection for many women during the 1970s (Sawer 1990). The Office of the Status of Women in Commonwealth government and a variety of State public service offices to review policy related to women have been some of the most visible responses to the feminist demands of the early 1970s (Sawer and Groves 1994; Eisenstein 1996).

Although there were differences about how the goals should be achieved, both the WLM and WEL shared a set of demands: equal pay, equal employment opportunity, equal access to education, free contraceptive services, abortion on demand, appropriate child care services open twenty-four hours a day and an end to sex-role stereotyping and sexism wherever they occurred (Sawer 1990; Burgmann 1993). One of the first major campaigns was for access to safe and inexpensive abortion. In addition, feminists mounted a critique of the medical profession which led to the establishment of women's health centres (Broom 1991) and the development of a national women's health policy (Australia 1989). Feminists in trade unions, Commonwealth, State and local governments and public services, educational institutions from preschools to universities, the professions and community organisations have worked to turn these and later demands into implementable policies.

Feminists reflected on the political campaigns and argued about tactics and theoretical perspectives. The combination of activism and scholarship was the foundation of what is today called women's studies and feminist theory. During the early 1970s three main theoretical perspectives were debated: liberal, radical and socialist (or Marxist) feminism. They were so closely linked to forms of political action and choices of political issues that Verity Burgmann refers to them, not as theoretical positions at all, but as ideological divisions (1993: 82). Certainly, the names of the positions came to be used as terms of political abuse as well as categories of analysis. Nevertheless, many accounts of feminist thought written during the 1980s treat them as theoretical categories, often with little reference to the political origins or uses of the terms. As international feminist theory has developed, the categories of the 1970s have become increasingly limited and most texts also add psychoanalytic and postmodern approaches to gender relations (Weedon 1987; Connell 1987; Tong 1989; Walby 1989). Throughout the 1980s feminists grappled with issues of ethnic and cultural difference that were seen to challenge the assumed universals of women's experience (Ramazanoglu 1989; hooks 1990; Mohanty 1991; Anthias and Yuval-Davis 1993; Pettman 1992; Clough 1994; Evans 1997). Feminist scholarship has both challenged and changed the humanities and social sciences and mounted a strong challenge to the claimed objectivity and gender neutrality of the sciences and technology. Indeed, the range of literature is so great that it is no longer possible to refer to a handful of central texts as it was twenty years ago. Readers are well advised to use electronic indexing tools in libraries.

In political campaigns and academic conferences in English-speaking countries women of colour argued that too frequently the concerns of the apparently unitary 'all women' were in fact the concerns of relatively privileged white women and not meaningful to women subordinated by race and class. The desire of some white feminists to set the conditions for negotiations to 'resolve' or 'deal with' difference led women of colour to challenge the racism of white women. Many white feminists also recognised that racism was present in the women's movement as it was elsewhere and tried, often unsuccessfully, to be more inclusive in their activities and campaigns. There have been continuing reflections on racism in Australian feminism at least since the mid-1970s; more concerned at first about Aboriginal–white relations, and then about the inclusion of women migrants with non-English-speaking backgrounds (Sykes 1975; Burgmann 1984; Flick 1990; J. Martin 1991; Pettman 1992; Huggins 1994; Murdolo 1996; Kilic 1997). However, as Ang (1995) points out, attempts at 'inclusion' continue to highlight the fact that one group has the power to determine the central ideas or space, while others do not.

The simple addition of a category 'black feminism' to the established categories of liberal, radical and socialist feminisms suggested that questions of race and racism were the province of 'others', not whites. However, it is possible to take black feminist thought seriously as a source of women's knowledge about social relations and so challenge white analyses of a shared past and to recognise it as marked by racialised power relations (Collins 1991). Collins argued that the knowledge gained by African-American women working as domestics in white households provides a unique 'outsider-within' stance with a 'distinct view of the contradictions between the dominant group's actions and ideologies' (Collins 1991: 11).

Some women of colour have argued for the use of the term 'third world women' as an inclusive term to represent themselves (Trinh 1989; Mohanty 1991). Although 'third world' calls to mind negative stereotypes of powerlessness and poverty, the term also serves as a reminder of both the political power relations of colonisation and the power relations of racial subordination within colonising countries. Instead of asserting a 'natural' unity among diverse women, it signifies political alliances formed in a 'common context of struggle' against those power relations rather than focusing on colour or racial identifications (Mohanty 1991: 7). White women can make alliances over specific issues and are also challenged to explore how they have benefited from the power relations that form the context of a particular struggle (cf. Bass 1998). In the struggles that constitute the politics of reproduction this means a shift from concerns about 'fertility rates' and representations of women as victims to a focus on the sexual and reproductive health needs expressed by third world women (Mohanty 1991; Corrêa and Reichmann 1994). The nuanced analyses of the more recent feminism reveal the fiercely debated differences between liberal, radical and socialist feminisms of the 1970s to be little more than a reflection of the political perspectives of white women within the liberal democratic political tradition.

Feminism, fertility control and women's voices

The research process of the Royal Commission on Human Relationships in the mid-1970s marked a change in the discourse of expertise—women were accepted as experts in their own lives, no longer as simply the objects of knowledge. Several parliamentary debates about abortion during the 1970s and 1980s demonstrate both the changing context of the assertion of female autonomy and the changing ground of the challenges. According to the developing feminist analysis of reproduction, adequate and appropriate contraception was necessary for heterosexual women to engage in self-determined sexual exploration. But doctors, clergy and male partners were no longer to be the arbiters of 'adequate and appropriate'. It was no longer good enough for the 'usual experts' to be rounded up to provide an account of female sexuality. In addition to social workers, clergy, medical men, psychologists and psychiatrists, criminologists or even sexologists, women have been called upon to provide testimony of their experiences. The analysis of women's testimony also changed and it was no longer reshaped to explain women's words within the framework of the received opinions of authorised experts.

Once feminists began writing about sexual politics, abortion gained a central place in thinking about heterosexual experience for women. For feminists, unlike many other experts, the answer to the question, 'who needs access to abortion?' ceased to be a list of disadvantaged women whose lives were in some way deficient (too young and unloved, too old, married to a drunk, too poor) and became obvious—women who have sexual intercourse with men (Greenwood and Young 1976). With that understanding came a number of accounts that interpreted women's self-reported experiences of abortion and/or their views on sexuality, motherhood and the gendered social order (Franke 1978; Luker 1984; Ginsberg 1989). While it is important to remember that women as well as the 'experts' of the past speak in their own interests and as members of their particular culture, these accounts reveal women as moral and social agents, actively constructing and reconstructing their lives.

A striking example of official acceptance of the shift to the recognition of women as experts of their own lives was the Royal Commission on Human Relationships, which used the phone-in as a research method to gain information about 'unwanted pregnancy' and abortion. The responses from the phone-in were reported along with written submissions, commissioned reports and publications in the *Final Report* (Australia 1977, vol. 3: 113 ff.). Analysis of these and other data suggested that 'pregnancies are most likely to be unwanted when they occur to married women with more than two children and to young single women' (Australia 1977, vol. 3: 115). These responses were used differently from the submissions by women to the previous inquiries into population and fertility.

During the New South Wales Royal Commission on the Decline in the Birth-rate in 1903–04 and the 1944 National Health and Medical Research Council (NHMRC) inquiry into the decline of the birth rate, evidence in written submissions and oral testimony was used most often to illustrate the commissioners's opinions about women as natural mothers instead of reporting what women themselves thought. In 1903–04 the commissioners frequently led medical and clerical witnesses in testimony about the 'true' reasons for family limitation. They do not seem to have sought out the views of women about bearing and rearing children. They dismissed economic causes even in the wake of the 1890s depression and offered instead the following, all of which had the common element of selfishness:

i. An unwillingness to submit to the strain and worry of children;
ii. A dislike of the interference with pleasure and comfort involved in child-bearing and child-rearing;

iii. A desire to avoid the actual physical discomfort of gestation, parturition, and lactation; and
iv. A love of luxury and of social pleasures, which is increasing. (Hicks 1978: 23–4)

As a part of the Labor government's planning for post-war reconstruction, the NHMRC was asked to inquire into reasons for the fall in the birth rate. The council established six expert panels to examine various aspects of the question and invited written submissions from interested groups and from women who were limiting their family size (Cass 1988: 171). In its report the inquiry specifically contradicted the previous claims that selfishness was the main factor in the declining birth rate, stating that the evidence suggested that 'the decreasing dependence of women' and feelings of insecurity were responsible for the growth in the use of birth control (Cass 1988: 171). The report also included lengthy quotations from some of the 1400 letters written by women to the inquiry. Cass points out that the letters have been selected to emphasise 'the struggle to maintain a decent standard of living upon the basic wage level' (Cass 1988: 175). The report recommended a variety of social welfare policies to increase women's sense of economic security; it did not question women's willingness to raise as many children as they could financially afford.

By 1977 the desire to limit births was accepted and the experiences of women when their attempts failed were more important for the development of a national public policy. Recommendations reflected women's stated needs, and many have been implemented without reference to the Royal Commission report. The Fraser-led coalition government in 1977 had a hard time accepting the findings of an inquiry established by a Labor government. During the 1980s phone-ins became a standard part of the methodology for research into policy needs for vulnerable groups of people. By the 1990s the Commonwealth Department of Health and Human Services was willing to fund research that asked women about their experiences of abortion under different legal regimes (Ryan et al. 1994).

While the increasing presence of feminist contributions to public policy helps explain the growing recognition of the evidence of experience, the power of the appeal to such evidence can also be observed in later parliamentary debates about abortion. During the 1979 Commonwealth House of Representatives debate that defeated a private member's motion to deny public funding for abortions that were not a 'medical necessity', only one MP spoke of personal experience with a medical situation in which abortion might be offered today, but was not then. He spoke in an emotional way, providing evidence of how deeply he honoured life rather than an argument about the motion (Australia, House of Representatives 1979: 1119). A few others spoke of experiences from their professional practice as doctors and Bill Hayden from his experience as a police officer. By and large the speakers relied on published material and moral visions of a just society to shape their arguments.

In 1988, in the New South Wales Legislative Council debate on the Bignold Motion—which asserted the 'right to life' as a fundamental human right and called on the government to strictly enforce the letter of the sections of the NSW Crimes Act that regulate abortion—members relied neither on emotional grandstanding nor on experience gained in a professional capacity. In addition to published information about fertility control and abortion being presented, two women MLCs reported their own experiences with the possibility of abortion during wanted pregnancies. Two male members spoke of their gratitude towards the birth mothers of their adopted children. Other participants in the debate spoke of the experiences of personal friends, or read letters in which constituents appealed to personal experience as the basis of their views. The Hon. Marie Bignold, for example, read from a letter from a member of 'Women Exploited by Abortion' in support of her motion. The writer authorised her insights as 'the voice of experience'; she and her group felt they had abortions without being fully informed about either 'the reality of the unborn baby being a human life' or any real alternatives to abortion (NSW, Legislative Council 1988: 1281–1282). However, no member of the Legislative Council discussed a personal involvement with premarital pregnancy and its outcome or the search for an abortion pre-1971; the floor of the Legislative Council did not become a 'speak-out'.

The government approaches to the challenges of assisted reproductive technologies (ART) initially were at first the formation of expert committees and intellectual struggles with the legacy of the 1960s debates about the relationships between law and morality, but the more open definition of public consultation meant that feminists were soon intervening. While the Christian religion has lost some of its old authority over the bodies and behaviour of women to the medical profession, religious values continue to inform most contemporary ethical discussion of reproductive technologies, even if only as the basis for the definition of terms. For instance, the first and most seriously recognised opponents of IVF from an ethical perspective were clergymen or representatives of a religious perspective (Overduin and Fleming 1982; Nichols and Hogan 1984). Feminists did not have the authority of religious thinkers, though there was an existing body of feminist ethical argument about reproduction: especially abortion, access to birth control and a range of issues about childbirth. Eventually interventions by activists and feminists in official positions could not be ignored.

The Australian Senate Select Committee formed in response to Senator Harradine's Human Embryo Experimentation Bill, 1985 accepted the liberal democratic legal framework that regarded protection from harm as the only justification for interference in the freedom of others. Within this framework they asked, 'What is the respect due to the embryo?' (Australia 1986: xiii). The committee then used a strictly biological definition of the human embryo: 'the entity which exists from the completion of the fusion of egg and sperm: that is, from the sequence of events described as fertilisation' (Australia 1986: 9). Much of the discussion of scientific information in the report is an effort to determine if there is a significant 'marker event' at which the fused egg and sperm become an entity that is due the respect of a breathing human being. The majority report argued that there is no such event, and therefore full human dignity and, by extension, human rights, should be recognised from fertilisation, a conclusion interestingly congruent with the Roman Catholic views of Senator Harradine.

Senators Rosemary Crowley and Olive Zakharov in a dissenting report argued that the development of an embryo fertilised *in vitro* is totally dependent on the willingness of a woman to take it into her uterus and thus regarded implantation as a significant marker event. Their view was informed by the feminist politics of reproduction, and they went on to argue that women and men in infertility programs were the appropriate decision makers about embryos they might want to have implanted just as women are the appropriate decision makers for foetuses already in their bodies. This Senate Select Committee Report was one of the first official reports to include an overtly feminist argument in a discussion of the role of regulation in infertility services, though the Family Law Council's (Australia 1985) report was also informed by feminist insights.

Feminist arguments about fertility and ART were taken more

seriously in the mid-1990s than they were in the early 1980s, and some seem to have become a part of common sense. But the challenging nature of those objections are often diluted in official discussions of the principles that should guide any regulation of reproductive technologies. In the early 1990s the Canadian government held a Royal Commission on New Reproductive Technologies to 'inquire into and report on current and potential medical and scientific developments related to new reproductive technologies, considering in particular their social, ethical, health, research, legal and economic implications and the public interest, recommending what policies and safeguards should be applied' (Canada 1993: 3). The Royal Commission was a response to feminist political interventions and began its work with a commitment to foregrounding the impact of the technologies on women (Eichler 1993). In addition, the commissioners set the final report within the framework of the ethic of care and eight guiding principles. Yet, in spite of this beginning and an expressed understanding of the ethic of care as an approach that recognises human connectedness rather than regarding people as 'individuals first and foremost', the moral stance used in the final report is collapsed into the notion that those who are authorised to make interventions in human lives and relationships should apply the medical principle of 'non-maleficence (do no harm)' (Canada 1993: 52–3). The shadow of the religious understandings of the origins of human life and of professional ethics seems to overpower the possibilities of a different kind of moral thought. The recommendations offer a case study in disciplining of bodies by normalisation and surveillance in the manner discussed by Foucault: a range of health and education outreach programs to protect fertility are suggested for the whole Canadian population.

The contemporary women's movement has been successful both at shifting the public agenda to incorporate issues that are important to women and at including the voices of women in policy making. The shift has not been uncontested, however. The previously unexamined assumptions about the 'natures' of men and women and the value of the social order based on male dominance continue to inform the thinking of many people. In addition, both feminist theory and feminist practice have demonstrated that feminists themselves have shared and reproduced relations of dominance based on race and class. Nevertheless the vision of women making their own decisions about reproduction has gained international recognition and support. Docile female bodies are harder to find. In the next chapter I will examine the tensions between feminist and medical visions of female sexuality and fertility control. While feminists consider the meanings of heterosexuality for women a matter for debate, even the most women-centred medical advice is based on conventional cultural understandings of female and male desire and sexual practice.

4 Sexual Politics and Contraceptive Choice

The struggle for access to reliable and safe contraception seems to have been won. Of course, there are still health risks associated with some forms of birth control and some methods allow more unwanted pregnancies than users find acceptable. But the transformation in popular and professional attitudes over the course of the past century has been enormous. During the first half of the century birth control advocates had to struggle against moral opposition based on a combination of beliefs about the 'natural' biological function of women as reproductive, which came from both medical practitioners who based their arguments on 'science' and religious leaders who based their opposition on the Bible and 'God's law'. Feminists feared that birth control would benefit men only, making it impossible for women to control their own sexual experiences if the danger of unwanted pregnancy was eliminated (Gordon 1982). There was an undercurrent of suspicion that birth control would lead to immorality on the part of women because they could indulge in sexual intercourse without 'consequences'. Trade unionists and some socialist activists expressed concerns that birth control for working class people would serve the interests of the bosses because the ability to make choices about family size would remove one of the justifications for higher wages. Nationalists in many countries, Australia included, were afraid that birth control would be used by people in the culturally dominant classes—white, middle class, native-born (not indigenous), educated, Protestant—and that thus they would be 'outbred' by the subordinate groups and/or by colonialised people (Hicks 1978; Allen 1982).

The body of 'woman' recurs as a link between the individual and the population and highlights one of the tensions that are always present in any extended discussion of fertility control. Fertility is at the same time a concern of individuals and a social concern (Weeks 1981; Gordon 1976). Women have preferences about the number and timing of births. Those personal preferences may be at odds with the preferences of their male partners, their families, religious leaders and political leaders of their nation, or at odds with at least some of these others. This tension underlies most of the popular writing about birth control. Discussions of the methods of contraception often include a short discussion of world population, yet in Australia very few women or couples make their childbearing decisions in light of concerns with the size of the world population. Rather they think about their economic situation, their beliefs about what makes good family life, their social and spiritual values whether religious or secular. These considerations are often mixed together with notions of adult femininity and masculinity, a sense of following an expected life plan shared by peers and, of course, luck.

Personal decision making took place in the context of a changing public debate about the nation, family life and fertility control. There were, of course many contributors to the changes; however, I want to focus on the medical profession because the medical profession in the past used 'science' to oppose birth control, but is now the authorised source of reliable birth control and contraceptive advice. Today, many young, heterosexual women assert that they make their own decisions about birth control, yet the choices available to them are constrained by health professionals, notions of acceptable risk and the dynamics of their sexual relationships. It would be simplistic to suggest that women should avoid medically delivered birth control or that popular ideas about sexual pleasure are a male conspiracy. However, I suggest that the availability of birth control is as contradictory today as it was a hundred years ago, though in different ways. The 'politics' or power relations of birth control is a politics of expert knowledge as well as a politics of service delivery. This chapter is an exploration of some of those constraints and contradictions. I will discuss heterosexuality in the context of analyses of sexuality that develop the insights of feminist and gay and lesbian activists and scholars. The second part of the chapter is a critical account of the medical discourses that dominate the popular advice literature about contraception. While some feminist challenges to previous conceptions of female sexuality and sexual responsibility have been incorporated in advice books, few of the radical challenges to common-sense views of heterosex are addressed. Fertility control is a case study of the contradiction between the demand for choice of methods of birth control and the discourses that shape and limit those choices.

Desires and devices

Women and men in industrialised countries today are trying to control their fertility within that social order, not in a separate and private place that they have constructed for themselves. In addition to the broader political and economic conditions, there are prescriptive assumptions about the appropriate social roles of women and men. Women are described principally in relation to fertility: Are they mothers? Will they be mothers? Can they be mothers? Contraception has not challenged the basic equation of womanhood with motherhood though it has altered the conditions under which women are mothers. Rational planning of each birth, apparently within the realm of possibility for everyone, has given new meaning to 'accidental' pregnancies and to 'infertility'. In addition, some women have been able to remain childless without giving up heterosexual activity while others have found that their attempt to delay childbearing has destroyed their fertility; the promises of high-technology contraception look very different to these two groups living as women who are not-mothers (there is not even a neutral, much less even a positive, term for such a life). Just as motherhood has remained unchallenged, so have the power relations implicit in heterosexuality remained unchallenged by high-technology contraception.

One of the most intractable areas of feminist activism has been human sexuality. It has been important to challenge the expert speaking position of doctors, psychologists and clergy in discussions of women's experiences of sex. The first few years of the Women's Liberation Movement were politically exciting. No topic was off limits for discussion, no expert too important to be questioned. Regarding sexuality especially, the personal was political. Many of the 'founding mothers' of the movement wrote trenchant criticisms of expert descriptions of female sexuality which defined these descriptions both as lacking and in the service of a dominating male sexuality. While many writers in the 1980s developed strong critiques of the research and politics of so-called sex radicals such as Kinsey, Masters and Johnson and their popularisers (Coveney et al. 1984; Jackson 1987; Jeffreys 1990), feminists in the late 1960s and early 1970s were able to use the findings as evidence against 'pop' Freudianism. In the frequently reprinted article, 'The Myth of the Vaginal Orgasm', Anne Koedt (1972) cited the sexuality research by Masters and Johnson to debunk the Freudian definitions of women as frigid if they did not have 'vaginal' instead of 'clitoral' orgasms. She argued that the continued emphasis on vaginal orgasms was an outcome of a combination of male preference for vaginal penetration, the social control of women and male fears that female sexual pleasure without penetration would mean an end to female sexual availability to men. Many activists argued that the social restrictions on women's sexual knowledge and experience were central to any explanation of women's subordination to men. Their work was quickly available in Australia and widely discussed in the local Women's Liberation groups along with similar British writing. Many of the key articles in the debates that have followed that early feminist challenge to conventional heterosexuality are reprinted in an anthology edited by Stevi Jackson and Sue Scott (1996).

In both small group 'consciousness raising' and larger 'speak-out' movements women encouraged all women to tell of their personal experiences with men and to develop a political analysis of male dominance. A sense of solidarity among women and a commitment to political action on behalf of women were the desired outcomes of these meetings. Women in the groups discovered that domestic violence and rape were more common than crime statistics indicated. Many women experienced psychological or economic manipulation in marriage or love relationships. Abortion and unwanted pregnancies were facts of heterosexual life (the pill had been available only since 1960 and was often restricted to married women). Lesbians were the women next door, in classrooms and at work, not an exotic species of 'deviant', though it is important to note that many heterosexual women were also afraid that any publicity to lesbians in the movement would give feminism a bad name. From these small group discussions and public meetings arose many of today's familiar women's services: rape crisis centres, abortion referral agencies and clinics, women's refuges, women's help and information lines and a proliferation of support services. The funding of many of these services has become a part of government health and human service provision, although the relationship between feminist service providers and the state funders is often filled with tension (Stevens 1995; Weeks 1994; Brennan 1994; Broom 1991; McFerren 1990). The demands of feminists have been integrated into government service delivery, though conservative governments fund services that emphasise 'family' interests rather than women's rights.

It is interesting that the feminist critique of heterosexuality has been both incorporated into the public discussion of sex and at the same time transformed in a way that makes it less challenging. In the 1990s when sexual practices are described in considerable detail in women's magazines and health promotion literature, it is difficult to remember just how new this authorised public discussion of sex is. It is not that sex was not discussed, but that it was most often discussed in euphemisms and well-known stereotypes. Most discussions of male and female sexual responses took place within what Connell and Dowsett (1992) call 'nativist' discourses. Nativism is frequently called 'essentialism' and is based on the assumption that certain sexual activities and desires are natural to humans. Most commonly nativist discussions of sex assume that male sexuality is assertive or even aggressive. Female sexuality in this view is passive, or at least women are slower to respond to sexual arousal than men.

In Australia government campaigns against sexual violence have challenged the idea that men are 'naturally' aggressive by separating notions of sexual urges from abuse of power. Pamphlets frequently use the technique of contrasting 'myths' of rape or sexual abuse with the 'facts': the idea that women 'provoke' men with sexy clothing is denied and the belief that women often say 'no' to a sexual overture but really mean 'yes' refuted. But the pamphlets do not address common-sense notions about masculine sexuality directly. Discussions of sexual activity in popular magazines like *Cleo* or *Cosmopolitan* seem to incorporate the ideas of the feminist writers of the early 1970s by arguing for women's sexual pleasure. At the same time they rely on the common-sense notions of nativism to discuss differences between male and female sexuality. In both informative articles accompanied by photos or drawings and advice columns the issues are framed in terms of generalisations about 'most men' and 'most women'.

The popular accounts reflect similar tensions in feminist

writing about sexuality. Women experience sexuality as an obligation (Matthews 1992) as well as a source of both 'pleasure and danger' (Vance 1984), sometimes at the same time. Throughout the 1970s women wrote articles about how to masturbate to encourage women to explore sexual pleasure in comfort. The skills thus learned were then able to be shared with a partner: 'tell him what feels good'. Physical and social explanations of some women's lesser enjoyment of sex replaced previous psychological ones. Better touching (what she liked), more pleasant atmosphere (candles, soft music), more time and more open communication between partners were offered as remedies for an unsatisfactory sexual relationship instead of therapy to encourage the woman to accept her 'femininity' (Barbach 1976). The advice to change personal practices does not address the sources of sexual inequality beyond the individual couple, however. While equal pay has not been seen as a precondition for sexual pleasure for women, feminists have highlighted social and economic inequalities as a major contributor to sexual danger for women.

Side by side with writing about the possibilities for sexual pleasure, feminists campaigned against the sexual abuse of women. Campaigns to raise public consciousness about rape resulted in rape crisis centres, marches against rape in war, government-funded sexual assault services, rape law reform and an increasing body of feminist jurisprudence. During the 1990s there have been repeated outcries in the Australian media when judges have suggested that a particular sexual assault was not serious or that a husband is entitled to use force on his wife. Men also kill wives and ex-wives who try to escape violent or abusive relationships. For some men, including judges, it seems to be difficult to accept that women are able to express independent views. At the same time we have seen the use of rape as a weapon of war in the former Yugoslavia, just as it has been used in other interstate and civil wars and by torturers from many regimes (Pettman 1996: 100–4). The bodies of women represent the boundaries of nations and national honour. Men justify the sexual attacks on women in terms of injuries to 'enemy' men—getting 'their' women. In addition, feminists have named unwelcomed sexual approaches in public places like work or shops as sexual harassment. Men can use comments or actions to sexualise women colleagues, to enact the cultural notions of male sexuality as uncontrollable or aggressive and of men as socially dominant.

Once feminists moved beyond challenging the dominant

notions of female sexual passivity to a consideration of the wider social meanings of sexuality the analysis did not become easier. It has been difficult to develop an analysis of sexuality that takes into account the diversity of women's sexual experiences. Campaigns against sexual abuses—rape, child sexual assault, domestic violence, and pornography—have sometimes fallen into a rhetoric that rests on an essentially violent or abusive masculine sexuality. This has narrowed the space for an analysis of the social construction of masculine heterosexuality since it seems to preclude any articulation of pleasure in personal relationships between women and men without some expression of violence. It has also made it difficult to develop a political analysis of the conditions for sexual relationships between men and women that is not based on a form of 'sexual desire which eroticises power difference' (Jeffreys 1990: 2).

In 1980 Adrienne Rich offered one path out of this impasse in a now classic article about female sexuality. In 'Compulsory Heterosexuality and Lesbian Existence' she argued that far from being a personal choice or preference for women, 'heterosexuality, like motherhood, needs to be recognized and studied as a *political institution*' (Rich 1980: 637, original italics). The inequalities of the workforce and domestic life can thus be regarded as a part of institutional heterosexuality since they combine to limit women's independence from men. When women are paid low wages and child care is difficult to obtain, then marriage is a logical precondition for childbirth and childrearing, and once the children are born, these same conditions make it difficult for a woman to leave an unsatisfactory marriage without economic hardship. Further, she argues, following Catharine MacKinnon (1979), the sexualisation of women at work demonstrates the way in which economic imperatives are shaped by sexual demands. As more recent writers would put it, masculinity and femininity are constructed at work through the sexualisation of the relationships among workers of different biological sexes (Pringle 1988). Sexuality cannot be confined to what people do in their personal time in bed as many people analysing sexuality before the sexual liberation movements suggested.

Rich suggested that it is important to consider the existence of 'woman-identified experience' throughout history as a part of a lesbian continuum of resistance to compulsory heterosexuality (1980: 648). Some writers criticised her combination of intense friendships between women with sexual relationships between women, but the concept of a lesbian continuum does two things in the argument. It provides a way to identify the heterosexually oriented assumptions of most aspects of acceptable social life by calling attention to forms of lesbian existence, and it provides a way to discuss the 'double-life' of women (Rich 1980: 654). When living a double-life, a woman seems to acquiesce to the institutionalised aspects of heterosexuality which focus on male interests and at the same time develops networks of women friends for emotional support. At the end of the article Rich calls for further research on heterosexuality as an institution and on the double-life of women. These two challenges have been taken up in various ways by a wide range of researchers from economists to film critics.

At the same time, for many years writers about sexual relations between men and women continued to ask and answer what Rich argued was the 'wrong question'. 'Are we then to condemn all heterosexual relationships, including those which are least oppressive?' (Rich 1980: 659). It was the institution of heterosexuality that needed analysis in order to understand the ways in which women's choices have been constrained. The insight that heterosexuality was an institution contributed to a complex literature that analysed the contradictions in individual lives between the experience of those constraints and the emotional and physical pleasures of heterosexual relationships. At the same time in political campaigns, the analysis of the economic and cultural institution of heterosexuality was collapsed into a set of erotic practices between different sex partners. The combined campaigns against sexual violence and the commercial exploitation of sexuality served to reduce discussion of heterosexuality to a rhetorical mode that emphasised the dangers and seemed to reduce the pleasures to forms of false consciousness on the part of women who continued to express sexual desire for men. Of course, there is no point in denying that some men abuse some women and children sexually; however, for feminists to seem to argue that all heterosexual desire or practice is abusive is to fall into the very set of definitions they set out to challenge—the masculine domination of human sexuality.

Public discussion of heterosexuality has remained within the traditional discourses that have supported male dominance, in part because there has been little space in which to discuss the possibility of a feminist heterosexual practice that also challenges the institution of heterosexuality. Conservatives with religious or secular moral approaches have continued to argue for the centrality of female heterosexual submission within marriage as a core value of the social order. Science in the guise of sociobiology was brought to the defence of a 'natural' male sexual aggression based in one argument on the number and activity of sperm. Since the arguments of vocal feminists about heterosexuality seem to suggest that male sexuality is necessarily aggressive and impervious to change, there is a gap in the public discourse about sexuality.

There is no easy way to open popular assumptions about male heterosexual practices to social or cultural analysis in the way that feminism and gay liberation have opened the assumptions about female sexuality (straight or lesbian) and gay male sexuality to scrutiny. While feminists and gay writers have critically evaluated the misleading descriptions of female and homosexual male sexual feelings and practices in the writings of psychoanalysts, sexologists and popular sex advice books, there has been no similar criticism of the construction of male heterosexuality that was also supported by these same shapers of the normal and the perverse. Jonathan Ned Katz, informed by gay and feminist writing about sexuality, published the first lengthy study about the 'invention' of hetero-sexuality in 1995. He interrogated the works of the same psycho-analysts, sexologists, sex advisers and political activists to discover how heterosexual pleasure replaced procreation as the norm for adult sexual expression.

The Women's Liberation Movement built on the civil-liber-ties-based demand that laws regulating the availability of birth control and abortion should be reformed, with a distinctively feminist analysis in the 1970s and 1980s. The analysis attempted to combine insights into sexuality with a broader critique of social structures and processes that constrained women's lives. While earlier waves of radicalism had included strands of sex reform, the 1960s and 1970s represented a time of popularisation of sexual liberation with political claims made by women and by homosexuals. The claims challenged the apparent naturalness of male dominant heterosexuality from a number of directions. Women challenged the belief that female sexuality was based in reproduction rather than physical pleasure. Gay men and lesbians challenged the privileging of heterosexuality in civil and political institutions which turned them into deviants or criminals (Rubin 1984; Weeks 1985).

The developments in the sexuality debates existed side by side with a changing movement to provide birth control services to all women. Campaigns linked to heterosexuality such as the demands for safe contraception have been entered by medical and public health professionals who have uncritically relied upon the dominant models of sexuality rather than expanding the challenges. Birth control advocates offer moral and practical advice to individuals in educational or clinical settings. In these settings, far removed from the complexities of daily life, birth control needs are discussed in the technical language that assumes the dominant model of procreative heterosexuality. In the clinic it is common to assume that avoidance of pregnancy is always the client's first priority and it is therefore easy to assign blame for 'failure' (unplanned pregnancy).

Your choice

Popular advice books are a readily accessible source of information about birth control, childbirth and relatively common health issues. When I first began investigating popular advice about contraception there were six readily available contraceptive advice books on sale in newsagents as well as in general bookshops (Albury 1990). Five were written by Australians, with four published locally. The authority of the medical profession was important in these books, explicitly because the authors were doctors or connected to medical institutions and implicitly because the scientific claims of the medical discourse were accepted uncritically (Billings and Westmore 1988; Dunn and Leeton 1982; Kane and Porter 1988; Kovacs and Westmore 1986; Lanson 1983; Llewellyn-Jones 1986).

By 1997 some of these books had been revised and reissued. Those advice books had been joined by a collection of more general gynaecological information and advice books written by Australians and published locally; all except one cost $20.00 or under. One or more of these books are currently available in general bookshops and on the shelves of some newsagents. These books reveal the impact of the feminist women's health movement on the delivery of reproductive health care; the discourses of expertise have changed in tone, at least. They are written in a clear and accessible manner, frequently addressing the reader as 'you'. All except one have a doctor as a main author, though a journalist or technical writer may be a co-author (Billings and Westmore 1992; Grimwade et al. 1995; Llewellyn-Jones 1996; Mackenzie 1994; Macquarie 1994). The *Australian Women's Health Handbook* has a team of medical advisers and reminds readers that it is not a substitute for medical advice (Kelly 1994).

89

In the general books the authors begin by describing the levels of ignorance about female body processes and the confusions that may arise for women who act on incorrect information. They say that the information in the books will enable women to share in the responsibility for their gynaecological health. Accurate information is described as necessary for making a variety of health-related decisions. In particular, the authors insist that women or couples should make contraceptive decisions on the basis of up-to-date information. The books address a woman who is interested in making an informed choice about the method of contraception she will use in her heterosexual relationship; her negotiation of sexuality in the relationship is largely unexplored. Lesbianism is virtually absent from all texts. All of these books relied on the medical authority of the authors, with only two providing easy access to the medical literature, while two books refer readers to other books written for non-specialists and two suggest no alternative sources of information. Interestingly, some of the books that were available during the 1980s are on the reference lists in more recent books. *Everywoman* appears on several lists as does the feminist *The New Our Bodies, Ourselves* (Boston Women's Health Book Collective 1985). The newer books reiterate the importance of good information even before visiting the doctor, 'so that together they can make the best decision' (Grimwade et al. 1995: 152).

Making choices

As these books describe methods of birth control they also suggest the grounds on which women or couples should make choices among them. All are based on the model of rational decision making that has widespread publicity as the method of choice for decisions ranging from defence spending to personal career planning (cf. Stone 1988). One of the 1980s books devotes a chapter to 'how to choose' that is a case study of this form of rational decision making, which the authors call 'the vigilant approach' (Kovacs and Westmore 1986: 93). Quotations from the more recent books demonstrate that this approach continues to be unchallenged.

- Identify objectives. 'While sex can certainly lead to babies, making babies is not the only reason for having sex. Many

people have sex just for pleasure—or a host of other reasons.'
(Kelly 1994: 40)

- Identify alternative courses of action for achieving objectives.
  'The more you know about all the methods—how they work,
  their efficacy, possible side effects, advantages and disadvantages—the easier it will be for you to choose a method likely
  to suit you.' (Mackenzie 1994: 149)
- Predict and evaluate the possible consequences of each alternative. 'You need to weigh up the pros and cons.' (Grimwade
  et al. 1995: 150)
- Select the alternative that maximises the attainment of objectives. 'Though some methods suit some people very well,
  there's not yet a method that's suitable for everybody and
  it's uncommon for a single method to suit the same person
  throughout her or his reproductive life.' (Mackenzie 1994:
  149)

The emphasis on the effectiveness of the methods serves to
make a high priority of the single objective of prevention of
pregnancy through the use of a particular method of birth control.
Of course women have other objectives as well—maintaining a
relationship, staying healthy, protecting fertility, having an exciting
sexual adventure, and feeling good about themselves, to name a
few. The books recognise some of these other objectives in the
discussions of the advantages and disadvantages of the methods,
usually described in terms of whether they will interfere with the
spontaneity of sex, possible side effects, reversibility and perceptions of motivation or messiness.

Most of the authors describe the activity of choice as a
balancing of the various considerations against each other. Effectiveness, side effects and the effects on sexual expression are frequently cited as elements in the equation. While many
authors recognise that a woman's choice will change with the
changing circumstances in her life, little discussion is devoted to
aspects of the woman's life beyond fertility and her relationship with her partner. Workforce participation, financial obligations, needs of children or elderly parents, and housing
conditions may affect decisions about fertility or the possibilities
for sexual expression, but all are ignored. Further, the effects
of particular disabilities on contraceptive choice are ignored.
In general the couple is assumed to be able-bodied and no
further advice or references are suggested for those who are
not. Very little attention is given to men making independent

decisions about controlling their fertility. This may be an effect of the assumed target audience for women's health advice books—women. Nevertheless, it puts men in a contradictory position regarding fertility control: the man is in the background, but a necessary actor. Two pairs constitute the social world: the contracepting heterosexual couple and the woman and her doctor. It is the woman who moves between the pairs.

The similarity of the discussion in books written over a decade apart reveals that there is a genre of 'contraceptive teaching'. They are more like medical books than other more psychological self-help literature. For example Kane and Porter (1988) introduce the methods in the context of a description of the physiology of human reproduction, with the methods as interventions in the process to avoid the procreative outcome of heterosexual practices. Other more general books often introduce the birth control section with a short comment on the dangers of overpopulation before returning to the presentation of alternatives for individual Australians. No link is suggested between global population figures and Australian fertility rates, but this comment has the effect of setting up a tension between the situation at home in which people exercise choice and a presumably different and threatening situation elsewhere. Each method is then presented in a chapter that reviews the background, safety, effectiveness, acceptability and availability of the method. A summary then evaluates the method and highlights considerations for decision making in the form of advantages and disadvantages grouped around reliability, side effects and effects on sexual expression using an implicit version of the procreative heterosexuality model of the 'sex act'. This pattern is continued by the books available in the mid-1990s, with either a series of chapters or sections of a single chapter describing the methods: hormonal contraception (pills and injections), intra-uterine devices (IUDs), barrier methods (condoms, diaphragms and sponges), fertility awareness methods and sterilisation. Some of the recent books include abortion in the birth control section.

While individual women or couples are urged to choose a method, the medical profession is presented as the most reliable source of information. This position was articulated most clearly in the 1980s by Dunn and Leeton in a discussion of side effects of the pill, with the mass media condemned for providing information that is 'often biased and misleading'. 'The best way of obtaining contraceptive advice is to ask a qualified health professional, who should be informed, sympathetic and unbiased' (Dunn and Leeton 1982: 29). No guidance is offered by these or other authors on how to decide among conflicting medical opinions, on how to judge how informed or unbiased the professional adviser might be, nor on what to do if the professional does not take the client's concerns seriously, which happens all too frequently regarding contraception (Pollack 1984). Although Grimwade et al. (1995) seem to suggest that doctors do not have the time to answer many questions, other recent writers continue to assert that doctors are most likely to have the best knowledge about birth control methods. Mackenzie acknowledges that the attitudes and beliefs of the contraception providers can influence the views of users, but goes on to comment on accounts in the news media:

> News reports about contraception may be sensational and misleading. If you hear something that worries you, check with your doctor, the Family Planning Association or another reliable information source to make sure that the report was accurate and balanced. (1994: 149)

There is a slippage between women as patients who attend doctors for treatment and women as consumers who attend doctors to buy a product. And unlike the provision of other consumer advice, there are few disinterested, that is, non-medical, sources of information recommended. Most alternative sources are regarded with suspicion.

Preventing pregnancy

Central to the presentation of information about methods is the assumption that one of the first things that a contraceptive user wants to know is how effectively the method will prevent pregnancy. It is puzzling that the 1980s books effectively separate the discussion of birth control from any discussion of abortion, though all except Billings and Westmore argue that abortion can provide a backup for failed contraception. For a number of years studies have demonstrated that the pill may be more risky than pregnancy for particular women and that barrier method contraceptives combined with early abortion in case of pregnancy are safest for all women (Petchesky 1985: 182–8). The usual consideration of the effectiveness of the methods only in comparison with using no method, rather than in comparison with the health risks of the methods including the risks of early abortion as a backup, may serve to increase women's distress and the sense of personal failure when an unwanted pregnancy does occur. The choices available are seldom as stark as the choice between any specific method and no method at all. A more complex discussion of the reasoning of individuals who use contraceptives might provide openings for women to think through some of their feelings about terminating a pregnancy. Abortion might be a result of the use of a marginally less 'effective' but otherwise safer method of preventing pregnancy.

By the 1990s, Llewellyn-Jones said that he included abortion in the birth control chapter because 'even in the most sophisticated societies, induced abortion remains an important method of birth control for women who have an unintended pregnancy, either because they do not use a contraceptive or do not follow the directions for use' (1996: 97). This assertion that unintended pregnancies are the result of women's failures contradicts Llewellyn-Jones' later discussion of the failure rates of the different methods and his openness to the possibility that 'the man uses contraceptive measures' as the couple's choice (1996: 98). There is an ambivalence that suggests that an unwanted pregnancy or an abortion is a sign of moral irresponsibility or failed rationality.

There is another kind of contraceptive failure that receives scant attention in these books. Healthy women who want to delay a birth may find that the chosen method causes illness or infertility. Both of these outcomes put considerable strain on a woman and on her relationships with her partner, family and friends. The implication in the advice books, that every woman should contracept as if she and her partner are super fertile, denies the knowledge accumulated in infertility clinics. In addition, hormonal contraceptives and IUDs provide no protection against sexually transmitted diseases (STDs) for either partner. This is particularly important for women since the diseases that are most likely, gonorrhoea and chlamydia, are often symptomless until the infection and threat to fertility, is well advanced. The low risk of HIV infection for most heterosexual Australians is not a function of heterosexuality, as the incidence of HIV infection among heterosexuals in Africa and Southeast Asia demonstrates, but rather a combination of socio-economic factors.

While the authors mentioned STDs briefly in the discussion of the advantages of condoms in the 1980s, by the mid-1990s the risks of infection for health and fertility are given more credence. Young women are encouraged to use both the pill and condoms until they are in monogamous relationships, and STDs are usually described in a separate chapter. In a striking change from the previous decade, Macquarie (1994) fully explains the use of a condom twice, once in the chapter on contraception and again following her discussion of infections, as well as providing a short discussion of alternatives to penis-in-vagina intercourse.

The risks from infection following the insertion of an IUD are dealt with ambivalently: either the risks are minimised or the fault is ascribed to the lifestyle of the woman rather than to the presence of a foreign body in her uterus, the habits of her partner or poor medical practice. Dunn and Leeton put it bluntly:

> In most cases of infection, it is found that the infection was already present and was aggravated by the IUD. The risk of infection in an uninfected uterus is rare, being less than 2 per 1000 women. Those women whose lifestyles expose them to infection, particularly to sexually transmitted diseases, are more likely to experience this problem. (1982: 42)

Years of discussion by women's health and health promotion activists are reflected by the mid-1990s when Llewellyn-Jones acknowledged that the male partner could increase a woman's risks of serious infection while using an IUD (1996: 126). Grimwade and Mackenzie note that a non-monogamous partner is a contra-indication for the use of an IUD; the problem for the woman is that she may not know about her partner's behaviour. The authors offer no advice about how a woman might approach this question with her partner.

Billings and Westmore approached the problems of disease and infertility somewhat differently in 1992, repeating their approach from the 1980s. Since they were interested in promoting a non-technological method, the risks of infection as a result of the IUD were presented straightforwardly (Billings and Westmore 1992: 180), the risks of the pill to fertility and feelings of well-being were taken seriously (1992: 175–6), but the protective potential of condoms was not accepted (1992: 84). They discussed the risks to fertility and health in a chapter on 'Learning about fertility in adolescence' and concluded that 'a one-to-one relationship between a healthy man and a healthy woman preserves the health of the couple and that of their children' (1992: 84). This is certainly true, but their recommendation of chastity for everyone until marriage is made against a social climate that encourages sexual self-expression. True love does not protect anyone from disease or from the long-term consequences of past diseases. This approach does have the advantage of placing the responsibility for future health and well-being on both men and women rather than blaming a woman for her past 'lifestyle' when it is obvious that at least one man was involved or that a doctor misdiagnosed or ignored her early reports of symptoms.

The books recommend rational decision making about contraception. Yet culturally, the steps of rational decision making seem out of place as a description of the process of sexual choice and sexual expression. The advice seems at odds with both the nativist constructions of sexuality as an unstoppable force and the feminist analyses of the gender power relations at work even in intimate situations. It is impossible to predict and evaluate the consequences of each alternative and then choose in a way that maximises the previously identified objectives, if for no other reason than that sex with a partner is not a solitary experience. In addition, the power of sexual experience for many is the sensation of being carried beyond rationality; the ability to express oneself without recourse to language and reason. This view of sexuality creates a tension with the demand for rationality in contraception especially since it is the 'nature' of the activity that creates the risk of pregnancy. However the books do not discuss birth control or safer sex in relation to erotic practices. The advice books resolve the tension between rationality and eroticism through discussions of the potential for 'spontaneity' as an advantage of a particular method of contraception.

Being spontaneous

The authors of the birth control advice books assume rather than describe the sexual activities of heterosexual couples. However, the combination of the emphasis on effectiveness and the repeated comments about spontaneity in connection with various methods are suggestive of what is assumed. In addition, the more general books described sexuality in terms of physiological changes using the Masters and Johnson model. They assume that these changes are heterosexually specific and significantly different for women and men.

> Orgasm during coitus for women in contrast to orgasm for the vast majority of men is not a one, two, three push-button affair. It is a complex process that can be affected by a multitude of factors, some obvious, some obscure. (Lanson 1983: 204)

This description seems like an artefact of an earlier time compared with the 1990s books which offer accounts of sexual practice in more popular language, recognise that women are desiring, know that men have more than three 'buttons'. Nevertheless, most authors assume unproblematically (though probably correctly) that penis-in-vagina intercourse is the central sexual practice for most heterosexual couples.

These assumptions about human sexuality are present in the accounts of birth control methods as well. Repeatedly one reads that the pill and IUD do not interfere with spontaneity whereas the interruption of sex play or spontaneity is a disadvantage of barrier methods. During the mid-1980s couples were given permission to reject condoms based on popular understandings of male sexuality and sexual practice. The biggest disadvantage of using condoms is that 'a condom must be placed on an erect penis' (Dunn and Leeton 1982: 5). This disadvantage can be overcome, however, 'if the woman puts the condom on to the man's erect penis during love-play' (Llewellyn-Jones 1986: 115). The other 'disadvantage' is subject to less agreement: the condom 'tends to lessen sexual sensation' [for men] (Lanson 1983: 271), or 'the assumed disadvantage that the condom reduces sexual pleasure is untrue' (Llewellyn-Jones 1986: 115).

The greater emphasis on safer sex in the 1990s has meant that most of these objections are no longer given such weight, though they may be discussed as ideas or problems to be overcome. Many authors recommend that women have their own supply of condoms and Macquarie (1994) argues that women have the 'choice' to refuse to have sex with a man who will not use one. Llewellyn-Jones is more positive about condom use in the seventh edition because of AIDS and a greater understanding of the long-term effects of STDs:

> In fact it can be stated that if a woman enters a sexual relationship with a man, she should insist that he uses a condom until she is certain that he has not been infected with wart virus, chlamydia or any other sexually transmitted disease. (1996: 101)

Both of these authors seem to require a higher degree of rationality from women than men at the beginning of a sexual relationship. Neither author alludes to the ways that culturally expected expressions of masculine or feminine sexual behaviour might make this difficult, nor do they mention the added complications for both partners of alcohol or drug use. All of these factors may be present as partners first get to know each other or when individuals have sexual adventures. While some sub-groups may be comfortable with matter-of-fact-condom use (Morrissey 1996), others may feel awkward and resist the advice.

The disruptive aspect of diaphragm use was said to be overcome during the 1980s by the woman inserting it each evening; by the 1990s authors suggested that she could keep it by the bedside or insert it when intercourse was expected. This is a recognition that sexual intercourse is not something that happens to women and it indicates a shift towards an understanding of male sexuality as open to reason and negotiation, rather than as a force of nature like a cyclone or earthquake. While natural (fertility awareness) methods are successful at preventing pregnancy only if a couple abstains from coitus when a woman is fertile and thus mean 'that you can't always have intercourse when you feel like it . . . Weighed against this are the many days when lovemaking can be completely spontaneous, free from drugs and devices, and from any doubt about your state of fertility' (Billings and Westmore 1992: 57). It is interesting that only Billings and Westmore acknowledge the lack of spontaneity involved in using drugs and IUDs as opposed to the barrier methods. It is hard to avoid the conclusion that some fantasy of male spontaneity based on the idea that sex is a force of nature is being protected. The fantasy seems to be male because women are asked to use the medically delivered methods, apply the barriers or be aware of their fertility status, in short, to protect them both.

'Spontaneity' seems to have several related meanings when applied to sexual expression: whenever you feel like it, without inhibition, without 'interruption', and more vaguely, free and open. In the discussions of birth control these meanings are elided and serve to create a potential resolution to the tension suggested by rational sexuality. Birth control is offered to make spontaneous sex more possible by removing the fear of conception. At the same time, birth control undercuts the notion of spontaneous sex by requiring rational decision making and careful implementation of the decisions through the consistent use of the chosen method. That tension is partially resolved by placing 'spontaneous' sexual expression within the Masters and Johnson model of procreative heterosexuality with its privileging of the able-bodied male sexual experience and male ejaculation inside a woman's vagina as the definition of 'the sex act'. The penis and its pleasures are thus central, with erection to be obtained and maintained, inhibition and thus frustration to be avoided, skin touching skin to enhance sensation. The narrowing of the range of possible sexual practices then makes the articulation of the objectives of birth control easier.

'I've had enough'—sterilisation

Permanent contraception is offered by tubal ligation for women and vasectomy for men. For people who have struggled with various methods of fertility control for years, sterilisation offers a welcome relief from the worry of unintended pregnancy or small but annoying side effects of particular contraceptives. At the same time it is clear that the idea of sterilisation itself, and its growing popularity, fit into the dominant values about sexuality and fertility control. Sterilisation offers unlimited spontaneity, a high level of effectiveness in the prevention of pregnancy, the total separation of sexual expression and procreation, one-visit medical delivery rather than user control over a lengthy period of time. But sterilisation does not provide any protection from STDs and does not affect the fertility of the unsterilised partner. In addition to the complications that some women experience following tubal ligation (Turney 1993), the main drawback of sterilisation is the final nature of the procedure.

People's lives change and with those changes there may be a reconsideration of decisions about fertility. New microsurgery techniques are more often successful in rejoining the vas than in rejoining fallopian tubes, but the subsequent pregnancy rate is not high enough to call any form of sterilisation reversible. The ideology of rational planning and individual responsibility coupled with notions about the importance of sexual spontaneity and no accidental pregnancies may push couples into decisions about sterilisation that do not take enough account of the possibility of change. According to the rational planning model, a couple make decisions about the number of children they want at an appropriate time in their relationship and then act on this plan. Hilary Thomas reviewed thirty years of the *British Medical Journal* and found that doctors had preconceived assumptions about the contraceptive needs of women at various stages of their reproductive life cycle. The stages were described not in the context of a life of changing experiences, but as 'discrete phenomena' (Thomas 1985: 60–2). Sterilisation fits into this model as the logical response following the birth of the last planned child.

Llewellyn-Jones (1996) and Mackenzie (1994) begin their sections on sterilisation with comments about couples wanting permanent contraception once their families are complete. One popular article about vasectomy and vasectomy reversal demonstrates that interpretations of 'complete' differ during the course of people's lives. The article discusses the possibility of failure to conceive following a reversal, but also suggests IVF using sperm removed through a needle as an alternative to reversal for some men (Greenland 1997).

While most women and men report satisfaction with their sterilisations, some express serious regrets. Regret is more common among women who changed partners or suffered the death of a child after the sterilisation (Church and Geller 1990: 15). This indicates that the sense of a complete family should be considered in the context of relationships with a partner and children rather than as a stage in one's life. It is frequently difficult for women and men to imagine the details of life in ten years' time or to predict responses to divorce and remarriage or the death of a child. The international literature identifies youth, marriage of less than five years, small families at the time of the procedure, a feeling of no control over the decision to be sterilised and opposition by the husband as characteristics of women who later regret sterilisation (Church and Geller 1990). Similar reasons are expressed by men who later regret vasectomy (Liskin, Benoit and Blackburn 1992: 13). Most writers about fertility control recommend careful thought by individuals and couples before the procedure. Fertility control providers are encouraged to offer high-quality counselling, to allow time for decision making, and to ensure that sterilisation is chosen without pressure or coercion. It is the permanence of the procedure that makes the 'choice' of sterilisation different from the other contraceptive choices.

The discussions of sterilisation, whether for medical or popular audiences, focus on the advantages of sterilisation as a method of pregnancy prevention and on the relative safety of the operation. But even pregnancy prevention is dependent on the continuing fidelity of the couple. A woman whose partner has a vasectomy must use contraceptive measures with a different partner; a man whose partner has a tubal ligation could impregnate a different woman. Either way, a pregnancy outside the relationship would affect the sterilised partner as well. Of course, the man and woman also continue to face the same risks of sexually transmitted disease with new partners or if one partner brings a disease back from a sexual adventure. The 'success' of sterilisation is dependent on monogamous heterosexuality and completed families.

The potential health risks of sterilisation are frequently minimised in the popular literature. For example Mackenzie simply asserts, '[t]here are no side effects' before discussing some of the reported long-term effects of sterilisation for women (1994: 199). She does briefly discuss the possible risks of the procedure itself in terms of the usual risks of abdominal surgery—infection and bleeding—though she does not mention risks associated with anaesthesia. Lyn Turney (1993) reviewed the medical literature on tubal ligation and found a series of effects, some of which could develop as late as eight years after surgery. She asked '[h]ow safe is safe enough?' and argued that the medical literature indicates that assertions of the safety of female sterilisation are unfounded. Yet for many women, even with knowledge of the possibility of later physical symptoms, contemporary methods of tubal ligation are 'safe enough' in terms of all the relationships and risks in their lives.

From birth control to safer sex

The use of contraceptives may be more ambiguous than the analyses of male or medical domination suggest. For example, the pill is often criticised because it removes any responsibility for fertility control from men. Yet, before the pill, men as a group were not avid contraceptors; women in many countries embraced the pill with enthusiasm as personal protection against previous method failure and male irresponsibility. Whatever is true today, the medical profession was a reluctant participant in the struggle for accessible fertility control (Gordon 1976; Reed 1978; Siedlecky and Wyndham 1990). It was difficult for single women to obtain medically supplied contraception (diaphragms, then pills) until the early 1970s in Australia. Medical spokesmen argued that the risk of pregnancy kept women chaste until marriage and that reliable contraception would allow men to enjoy sex without any potential consequences (Siedlecky and Wyndham 1990). This form of protection failed the thousands of women who had illegal abortions, became single mothers and married because of pregnancy. Through the 1960s and into the 1970s some doctors refused birth control to childless married women on the grounds that motherhood was the point of marriage. Feminists struggled to enlarge access to fertility control and then to include women's experiences and sensibilities in the delivery of fertility services. The Family Planning Association, numerous women's health services, and the approach of many recent contraceptive advice books are institutional responses to that work.

The importance of effectiveness in the prevention of pregnancy rather than effectiveness in protecting health and fertility (often called 'safety') is explained by the assumed model of sexuality. Campaigns to prevent the spread of HIV infection seem to follow the same pattern. Condoms rather than alternative sexual practices are the main, if not exclusive, focus of the slogans addressed to heterosexuals. In the campaign characterised by the slogan, 'Tell Him, If It's Not On It's Not On', women were expected to regulate male sexual practice with the implication that failure to do so is a form of irresponsibility even though the man may be assumed to be the vector of disease. Masculine heterosexuality occupies a privileged place even in health promotion campaigns (Waldby 1996: 10–13). This is a replay of the century of advice to women to take full responsibility for contraception even though men are enthusiastic participants in the activities that lead to pregnancy. While it is true that women are likely to suffer the consequences of unsafe sex, whether pregnancy or disease, this approach allows men to avoid responsibility for their actions in exposing their female partners to danger. Indeed, single pregnant women have been subject to several regimes of psychological interrogation and diagnosis while their male partners have disappeared from view (Solinger 1992; Luker 1975). In addition these directions to take responsibility must be carried out alone during a sexual encounter in circumstances that a vast body of literature suggests are unequal. They assume a relationship with exactly the level of care and commitment that might make them less necessary, a relationship in which the man respects his partner's wishes and in which there is some degree of communication about sex. Women in a relatively less powerful position are expected to take responsibility for the consequences of the activities of two people; activities that are conventionally directed by the wishes of the man.

The resolution of the tension between popular perceptions of sexuality as unfettered by rationality and the medical advice that pregnancy prevention should be the primary objective of every heterosexual sexual encounter appears in these books as an individual responsibility for the choice and use of a reliable method of birth control. Since the sexual practices of the couples are assumed to be those that carry the highest likelihood of pregnancy, the woman is the partner who will get pregnant. It is further assumed that she will take responsibility not only for avoiding unwanted pregnancy and infection, but also for protecting the spontaneous image of sexuality. In a sense, then, women bear the weight of the tension to be both rational and spontaneous; to be prepared at all times to avoid conception and yet to act without interruption or inhibition. In spite of changes during the past decade, the advice still sounds suspiciously like a new version of the old requirement that women have to be responsible because men are not reliable.

Looking back over the discussion of fertility control, it is possible to see two themes that run in contradictory ways below the surface. The first is the apparent desire on the part of birth control advocates to minimise the effects of social relations in their promotion of effective contraceptive methods. They seem to assume that everyone shares the same perspective on reproduction with the same set of priorities about fertility control and the same definition and experience of sexuality. This reflects the medical literature that is organised in terms of stages in a life cycle as if the model that explains diseases also explains relationships. The second is the unexplained ambivalence towards the role of abortion in fertility control, though this is contested in Australia. In the next chapter I will take up the contests about abortion.

5   Abortion Politics and Australian Governments

This is perhaps the best known of the contemporary feminist slogans. While many people call for choices for women, this particular choice remains highly contested. Abortion is both a necessary service for many women and also the source of mixed feelings. Those mixed feelings are translated into contradictory public policy. In Australia abortion is still included in the Crimes Act or Criminal Code in most States, though the laws have been interpreted in judicial decisions in several jurisdictions to permit abortions by medical practitioners. Information is widely available to women through public information and referral services as well as through many doctors and health centres. Public hospitals resist providing abortions but the procedure is rebatable under Medicare. In this chapter I will first discuss the struggles for reform or repeal of abortion laws in Australia and the sources of the legal and political debate that most influences Australian political discourse—the United States and the United Kingdom. Then I will examine the tensions that arise from the feminist demand that women make abortion decisions. In particular I will explore the interest the state has in this aspect of reproductive health care.

Most scholarly accounts of abortion politics begin in a similar way: a discussion of the power the issue has to polarise opinion or an attempt to grapple with the complexity of the issue by referring to the types of arguments involved (usually social,

104

medical, ethical, religious and legal, with strong thematic links between the arguments), followed by the assertion that the 'central' or 'fundamental' question involved in the abortion debates is the definition of the beginning of human life. This assertion has served to shape the debates in particular ways. It simplifies the issue by displacing the shifting array of questions onto the definition of the beginning of human life, and thus reduces the policy discussions to a search for 'the' definition, suggesting that once the apparently scientific question is answered, the appropriate policy response will be clear. This strategy serves to define abortion as something that is done to foetuses, not as a part of the social and physical experience of a woman. A narrowed focus on the foetus renders the woman invisible; the pregnant or potentially pregnant woman disappears as a social agent, a citizen or a person—she becomes an object of knowledge for experts. As the pregnant woman disappears so does the challenge of taking seriously the differences in the lives of men and women in public policy; a challenge that would call into question the usefulness of much liberal democratic rhetoric, especially the vexed notion of choice.

When abortion is debated in parliament similar effects are produced. Participants in the debates marshal the various arguments in support of their view of the best public policy outcome. The question 'best for whom?' shapes the focus of specific arguments. Like the more scholarly accounts which point to the multifaceted nature of abortion policy as an issue, parliamentary debates highlight the range of groups involved in abortion policy. Taxpayers, 'the nation' as a moral entity, foetuses as future citizens, medical practitioners, legislators and women feature in various ways in the parliamentary debates in Australia. Various government publications, ranging from official statistics to reports of inquiries or Royal Commissions are also the outcome of struggles over the meaning of abortion. Different national political contexts produce specific approaches to abortion. Therefore events in one country cannot be assumed to be predictors of events in another. In spite of similarities in vocabulary, the US experience is not a template of things to come in Australia. While I draw on the international literature, this chapter is an analysis of abortion politics in Australia and so emphasises feminist engagement with legislatures and bureaucracies regarding attempts to regulate abortion and campaigns to expand access to abortion as a part of reproductive health care.

Researchers in the field of cultural studies have provided a different way to read the parliamentary and scholarly debates about the issues raised by abortion (Science and Technology Subgroup 1991). Instead of reading for a definitive analysis of the moral or policy issues it is possible to read for a series of analytic gaps created and reinforced by selective use of information about abortion. This pattern of information and gaps then serves to construct images of the act and of the people connected with abortion. For example, in spite of a repeated use of the biological facts of embryology to assert the status of the foetus as deserving 'human rights', two important 'biological facts' are ignored: first, a foetus does not spontaneously appear in a woman's uterus, rather it is produced as a result of sexual activity (even in the instance of IVF, semen is supplied by masturbation within the context of an ongoing sexual relationship); and second, a foetus is not an independent individual, but is totally dependent on a functioning female body. In addition the developing foetus is not simply 'carried' within the woman's body but rather exists in a complex biological relationship and is attached to her body by its placenta. The woman's body is *pregnant*—hormones circulate, the centre of balance alters, skin texture changes, new tissue is produced to support both the pregnancy and lactation following birth. This complex biology gains meaning from the social life and relationships of the woman. Those meanings cannot be inferred from a knowledge of reproductive biology. Instead, questions must be asked about how that woman actively constructs a life as a pregnant woman: is she married or single; how does she feel about her body and sexual expression; is this her first pregnancy or fifth; was it easy to become pregnant and sustain the pregnancy or not; does her job offer maternity leave; is her partner (if any) employed; what is her vision of family life; and, centrally in discussions of abortion, does she want to be pregnant?

In the public debates the analysis of her social context is frequently expressed in abstract and often gender-neutral truisms about moral or religious 'values', economic 'situations', social 'pressures' or health 'conditions'. When particulars are introduced it is usually as a specific 'case history' to justify a particular element in the argument. In these examples the pregnant woman is portrayed as unable to be a proper mother for some reason that might be alleviated by an abortion. In either case, the pregnant woman as an active social agent disappears and becomes visible only as an object of knowledge—an overburdened mother, an unwed teenager, a woman with a defective foetus, a sexual risk taker, a misguided or selfish woman—about whom experts can debate. Strangely, the heterosexual intercourse necessary to begin the pregnancy has totally disappeared except for the unmarried woman and the 'risk taker' in which cases the burden of responsibility for the prior sexual act seems to rest on the woman. The social power relations of heterosexuality discussed in the previous chapter have been replaced by the social power relations of expertise. However, the erasure of specific women and their sexual partners has not resolved, nor particularly clarified, the issue. Over the past century, not only definitions of abortion, but also the agenda for debate, and even the authorised participants, have been matters of controversy. Two recent Australian studies illustrate how the inclusion of women's experiences and opinions has the potential to change the shape of the debate. Women who have had abortions do not focus on the issues raised in the policy literature. Those who oppose easy access to abortion begin with concerns about the foetus, but address 'hard cases' from the perspective of the pregnant woman's life (Ryan et al. 1994; Cannold 1998). The inclusion of women's views opens the field of policy debate to include questions of health service delivery, male – female power relations, the availability of child care and better pay for women.

Repeal all abortion laws!

The demand for legislative repeal of the abortion sections of the criminal law calls attention to one site of the public campaigns about abortion. The crime of abortion sets out punishment for those who attempt to 'procure a miscarriage', and sometimes, for the woman seeking an abortion (Cica 1991; Ryan et al. 1994). The authority of the state is deployed in order to criminalise an act that is regarded as immoral by some individuals. Although illegality and immorality are intertwined in the history of Western jurisprudence, the practice of abortion raises more difficulties for public policy than acts between consenting parties such as homosexual sex or prostitution. Nevertheless, during the 1950s and 1960s civil libertarians gained considerable support for law reform based on the interpretation of the role of the state that intervenes only to prevent harm (see chapter 3). Civil libertarians thought of women as being citizens and thus able to express their interests and to make moral decisions about their own lives. Arguments were presented in terms of rights: either a right to privacy—that is, non-interference in their sexual lives—or the right to equality with men as the recognition of citizenship implied. While the limitations of rights-based claims have been discussed by feminists from many perspectives (Himmelweit 1988; MacKinnon 1989; Poovey 1992), arguments about rights continue to have high political recognition in liberal democracies.

Opponents of the civil libertarian view argued that the woman is not making a decision about her own body and mind alone; the foetus as a potential person is also involved. Indeed, abortion is intended to end the pregnancy and so profoundly harms the foetus. However, no foetus has standing in law until it is born because of established definitions of legal, not moral, personhood; therefore, an aborted foetus cannot ever be a 'person' in law. This raises two questions: what is the meaning of the inclusion of abortion in the laws about crimes against the person since 1803, and what interest does the contemporary state have in maintaining anti-abortion laws? While the questions are related, I will provide a short answer to the first and explore the second in greater depth.

Historical meanings of abortion laws

It is possible to approach the question of 'why criminalise abortion?' from two directions. Some legal writers suggest that originally the pregnant woman was being protected (Williams 1957; Brookes 1988). In the decades before antisepsis and pure food and drug regulation, women in the burgeoning industrial cities might have approached unscrupulous strangers for remedies for unwanted pregnancies that threatened their ability to earn a living. Their attempts to preserve their livelihoods might have led to death or disability. Later in the nineteenth century, the medical profession lobbied for laws against abortion as a part of their campaign against alternative health practitioners (Brookes 1988; Mohr 1978). One part of this campaign was the argument that women's perception of the foetus as alive and thus a potential child only after 'quickening' was wrong because women were self-interested. Medicine offered a 'true' scientific explanation of pregnancy which recognised that the foetus was alive long before the pregnant woman could feel it moving. This provided a shift that allowed the separation of the foetus from the woman in discourse if not in biology. The concept of 'viability' then became important in the licensing of increased state regulation of pregnancy (Science and Technology Subgroup 1991).

The concept of viability has become central to the judicial discussion of abortion, particularly in the United States where it was central to the Supreme Court judgment in the case of *Roe v. Wade*. In 1973, the US Supreme Court ruled that State laws that outlawed abortion violated the right to privacy and so were unconstitutional. The court argued that the state has a different interest in a pregnancy at different gestational stages. During the first trimester of pregnancy, the right of privacy in the doctor–patient relationship is paramount, and no legislature should try to intervene in the doctor's professional judgment. During the second trimester, the physical risks of abortion for the pregnant woman are much greater than in the previous few months; in addition the foetus is approaching the stage of development at which it could live independently (viability). Therefore, States might set criteria for terminations of these more advanced pregnancies. It is only during the final trimester, when the foetus has a good chance of survival if born alive, that the State has an interest in the preservation of its life that would permit it to overrule the right to privacy and thus prohibit abortion.

As women in the United States have discovered, Roe did not establish a woman's right to abortion. The ruling did not formally address the rights of women to either privacy or decision making; it is the doctor–patient relationship that is protected. The judgment makes this very clear, '[t]he abortion decision in all its aspects is inherently, and primarily, a medical decision, and basic responsibility for it must rest with the physician' (*Roe v. Wade*, 410 US 113 (1973)). The trimester argument was based on medical 'best practice' at the time and on the assumption that only doctors would be performing abortions. First trimester abortions were safer than childbirth for pregnant women, later abortions were more dangerous. At the time when the case was argued, few foetuses born at 28-weeks gestation survived, so the 'viability' test provided a margin for misjudgment about the length of gestation. In the Webster case in 1989, the US Supreme Court foreshadowed the possibility of reviewing the trimester doctrine, but the changing politics of the court and country has delayed that review. Neo-natal intensive care has become more successful at saving very small newborns, thus raising questions about the meaning of viability. Indeed, in the United Kingdom parliamentarians have relied on this and other technological changes to restrict the availability of mid-trimester abortion (Science and Technology Subgroup 1991).

The second approach to the question of the meaning of abortion laws is to start outside the abortion laws and try to understand where the legal prohibition of abortion fits with broader social changes. Petchesky (1985) provides a thorough account of abortion politics in the United States in the context of the social relations of reproduction. She argues that women have made reproductive choices within the constraints of class and race as well as gender divisions within specific societies. Available choices change over time as do the meanings of the various courses of action. Such an approach requires wide-ranging reading and the synthesis of research about reproduction from many disciplines including history, anthropology, law, sociology, health studies and public policy.

When considering the contradictory place of abortion laws in the lives of women it is important to seek out information about the meaning of fertility for women. This is always a complex task because the meanings are social and cultural, and so change according to circumstances even during the life of an individual woman. Is childbearing the only indicator of adult femininity for a particular group of women, or must a woman provide sons for her husband's family before she is finally accepted by them? What are the accepted circumstances for childbearing? Must a woman be married before she gives birth in order to have social and financial support for mothering? Are cultural norms of 'good mothering' applied across class and race boundaries with devastating results for women and their children? How do public figures speak about women and reproduction? This approach leads to an analysis that acknowledges women's experiences as they exist parallel with the public posturing of professional experts in the abortion debates. Chapter 6 includes a discussion of some of the broader meanings of fertility and motherhood in the lives of Australian women.

Abortion laws and contemporary liberal democracies

The state is a central focus for an analysis of the contemporary struggles about abortion for many reasons: not only is it the site of legislative and electoral politics discussed here, but it is also the site of the several apparatuses of law enforcement—police, judiciary, prisons; it is a respected and legitimate source of information about society; it is an acknowledged provider of welfare and health services. While it is important to acknowledge that the state is only a fictive unity, with many contradictory policies, abortion activists, whatever their politics, continue to work for some level of state recognition. They attempt to influence the direction of state intervention in the struggles by encouraging policy making and implementation, if not on their side, at least against the side of the most reviled opponent (usually there are more than two sides). In fact much of the public policy literature about abortion in the United States has turned on the question of what policy initiatives would help resolve the political conflict, casting the state as an agent of national unity (Davis 1993a, 1993b; Tribe 1992; Tatalovich and Danes 1981).

In Australia there have been campaigns about legislation and law reform, about specific arrests or the lack of law enforcement, about public funding of medically induced abortion, about the relationship between State ministers and pregnant State wards, about the availability of medical services, about the quality and quantity of the medical services available. Allen called for detailed work in discrete areas of state activity as a contribution to understanding the complexity of fertility control (Allen 1990a). However, the investigation of concepts that provide insights into the linkages and contradictions revealed by the detailed studies is also needed. In the regulation of reproduction, policy makers do not wait for social historians to fully investigate the past; activists always have to make interventions on the basis of partial information. On the other hand, since similar language and arguments are repeated in each new round of the abortion debate, it is important to try to understand the political processes and public fears that seem to give impetus to the controversy in order to better intervene in and change the terms of the public debate.

Law makers in English-speaking countries have taken up abortion during the past two hundred years or so, but the moral concerns that are so much a part of the contemporary debates have gained prominence since the beginning of the twentieth century (Brookes 1988). This is the period that coincides with other struggles in and against the state for an expansion of bourgeois rights of citizenship to all, for state intervention against the worst excesses of capitalism, and for the extension of the role of the state from the maintenance of social order to the provision of social amenity. The various state interventions in abortion politics and service delivery were not necessarily directly related to these other struggles—neither were they completely separate (cf. Shaver 1992). In any case they took the form of established state activity—legislation, law enforcement, public inquiry and the bureaucratic administration of services.

Often these interventions have been at odds with each other. For example, in Australia the Medicare rebate, which has been important for the provision of abortion services, was instituted as one among many items in the original Medibank tables in 1975. The feminist desire for abortion to be treated like an ordinary medical procedure was established by bureaucratic fiat. By 1979, this was the cause of considerable moral indignation by anti-abortion members of the national parliament who wanted to remove the item number and thus put abortion in the category of medically provided services that users had to pay for with no rebate, justifying the removal in terms of the moral sensibilities of taxpayers. Law enforcement in the realm of abortion has been a site of police corruption and sensationalism in response to moral panics (Wainer 1972). Health services for women are not always administered according to the principles of equity enshrined in democratic notions of health care provision. Parliaments, of course, remain the 'bully pulpit' for the playing out of the current state of the debate, regardless of the measured tones of government reports. In public debate, the call for quality health care for women seems to be a pale opponent to the robust symbolic appeal of motherhood, nation and duties to the innocent which are recurrent themes in the anti-abortion speeches. However, an 'item number' for vacuum aspiration of a gravid uterus (the main method of early abortion) remains on the medical benefits schedule, though it is still open to challenge. In spite of the continuing controversy, abortion seems to have become 'normalised' in Australia. While anti-abortion activists have borrowed language and tactics from the United States, they have not been able to create an ongoing sense of moral panic about abortion; governments of all persuasions have refused to engage in the kind of grandstanding played out in the United States, and legislative attempts by private members to limit the availability of abortion have suffered clear defeats. However, when newly elected governments face an upper house without a clear majority, as happened in New South Wales in 1988 and in the Commonwealth in 1996, they may permit an upsurge of anti-abortion initiatives. In addition, legislatures may be forced to act by other government agencies. In 1998 the WA parliament debated abortion bills after charges were laid against two Perth doctors for performing an unlawful abortion. The Australian Medical Association threatened to withdraw all abortion services unless the parliament acted to clarify the law (Lamont 1998; O'Brien 1998). In the face of demands from this prestigious professional body as well as from nurses and the abortion rights activists the government presented a bill that offered members of the lower house a range of choices about the conditions under which abortion could be lawful. A member of the upper house proposed that the sections of the Criminal Code be repealed in a private member's bill (Le Grand and O'Brien 1998: 4). The final result combined these two bills by repealing the contentious sections of the Criminal Code and inserting specific conditions for the termination of pregnancy in the Health Act. Women can no longer be charged under the Criminal Code (Le Grand, 1998). Charges against the doctors were then withdrawn.

Rosalind Petchesky, in a comprehensive account of abortion politics in the United States, pointed out that the state has several interests that support its intervention in fertility control. She argued that the state has three distinct purposes when it intervenes in fertility. The interventions are as complex and contradictory in Australia as in the United States. The first is the interest in population—its size, composition, health. The second is to regulate sexual behaviour and establish sexual norms, particularly for women. These two interests often are in conflict since the dominant norms of sexual practice may contribute to a population that is larger or less healthy than desired, or that has an unacceptable racial balance. She goes on to argue that the state has to mediate the conflict between these two interests and, at the same time, it has an interest in maintaining its own legitimacy (Petchesky 1985). As it tries to balance these tasks it sometimes has to accommodate popular demands that seem in contradiction both with each other and with some declared state goals. The sources of the contradictions are clearer if the analyses of public policy that highlight the politics between different state agencies are kept in mind (cf. Davis et al. 1993).

Petchesky's argument directly addresses one of the main gaps in the non-feminist scholarly literature on abortion. A central, but usually unspoken, stake in the public abortion debate is the control of female sexuality. In Australia this has historically taken the form of a concern for population size and the 'moral fibre' of the nation; women who seek to limit their pregnancies are portrayed as both unpatriotic and selfish (Hicks 1978; Allen 1990b; Coleman 1991). They are failures both as citizens and as mothers (self-sacrifice being an important characteristic of

113

'good' mothers). At the same time, abortion is a necessary adjunct to the expression of male heterosexuality. It is likely that the charge that good women do not abort serves only to silence women, not to stop them aborting; certainly enough women have sought and found abortions to produce a series of moral panics and demands for government action in English-speaking countries since the mid-nineteenth century. Silent, non-pregnant, but sexually available women did not challenge that definition of good womanhood. The articulation of a female heterosexuality with open access to safe abortion in a form that seemed to threaten patriarchal authority had to wait until the contemporary feminist movement challenged that authority in the name of Women's Liberation. The early twentieth century radical sex reformers in Britain did not produce the same effect; perhaps they were too marginal, or perhaps their willingness to campaign for contraception as separate from and preventative of abortion was shocking enough. Today concern for the integrity of 'the family', a code for concerns with the challenges to patriarchal gender and generational relations, has been added to those historic concerns for nation and morality. Sometimes they are all combined in assertions that the breakdown of the 'family' will lead (has led) to social disorder and the call to restore national 'greatness' by a return to 'traditional family values'. In Australia, the specific threats to the family have indicated a concern with the loss of male authority—access to IVF by single women or increased availability of abortion or contraception.

Abortion debates and Australian parliaments

In Australia, abortion has become available without being decriminalised in the sense of being removed from Crimes Acts or Criminal Codes. That is, the statute law remains as it was in 1969 before Mr Justice Menhennitt specified the definition of 'unlawfully' in a ruling in the case *R. v. Davidson* and Mr Justice Levine further expanded it in his ruling in *R. v. Wald et al.* in 1971. South Australia, Western Australia, the Northern Territory and the Australian Capital Territory have amended the law to permit and regulate the practice of abortion. In laws based on the English *Offences Against the Person Act* of 1861, a variety of actions to procure a miscarriage are declared unlawful whether carried out by a pregnant woman or by another person. Likewise the supply of instruments or drugs in the knowledge they will be used for an illegal abortion is penalised (Finlay and Sihombing 1978; Graycar and Morgan 1990). This English law and similar ones in the United States were enacted as a part of the struggle by the 'scientific' medical profession against irregular practitioners (Brookes 1988; Mohr 1978). The process of legislation had two aspects: to redefine pregnancy and abortion using medical 'knowledge' rather than women's experience; and to allow medical practitioners a monopoly over legal abortion, now redefined as 'therapeutic' (medically required).

In Australia, as in many countries, the late 1960s was a time of campaigns to reform a variety of laws regulating sexual practice—homosexuality, divorce, prostitution and censorship of pornography as well as abortion (Wilson 1971). These reforms were seen as necessary for an advance in civil liberties and a recognition of the secular nature of the modern state in a pluralist society. The various state Abortion Law Reform Associations (ALRA) were offshoots of the Humanist Society and worked in cooperation with Councils for Civil Liberties (McMichael 1972; Blewett 1975). This meant that the main pressure for change came from people with backgrounds and approaches to politics similar to those of the parliamentarians to whom they addressed their concerns. While some doctors were involved in the various ALRAs, the Australian Medical Association (AMA) itself did not support abortion law reform until the campaigns around the Lusher Motion in 1979, when medical benefits were under attack (Coleman 1991). In contrast, the American Medical Association was involved in the campaigns leading to the reforms of the late 1960s (Luker 1984).

Abortion has been the topic of formal debate in various Australian parliaments since 1966 when WA member of the Legislative Council, the Hon. Dr Gordon Hislop, introduced a private member's bill similar to the abortion reform bill then being debated in the United Kingdom (later enacted as the Abortion Act 1967). It and subsequent bills failed and after 1972 no more reform bills were introduced in Western Australia (Anderson 1986). The first successful attempt to reform abortion laws in Australia took place in South Australia at the end of 1969 with the act going into effect in early 1970 (Blewett 1975). The legislatures of the Northern Territory and the Australian Capital Territory have also regulated the provision of legal abortion. Trials of doctors charged under the abortion sections of the criminal law led to a reinterpretation of the meaning of the term 'unlawfully' in regard to abortion and hence to a

115

significant increase in the availability of abortion, first in Victoria (1969) and then in New South Wales (1971). The failure of a federal bill to reform the abortion law in the Australian Capital Territory in 1973 led to the establishment of the Royal Commission on Human Relationships (Siedlecky and Wyndham 1990).

Abortion became an ordinary rebatable item under the Whitlam Labor government's original Medibank, triggering a new focus for abortion questions in parliament and finally the motion by Stephen Lusher, a member of the House of Representatives, in 1979 to remove it from the medical benefits schedule. After two days of impassioned debate the motion was defeated by a vote for an amendment that reversed its original meaning, thus endorsing the status quo. The motion itself and much of the debate turned on conflicting notions of what can be represented as 'the duty of the state' both to citizens and within a federal system (Australia, House of Representatives 1979). The findings of the 1977 *Final Report* of the Royal Commission on Human Relationships were a frequent point of reference as were the annual reports on abortion in South Australia and consideration of legal interpretations of the two judicial decisions. In a sense the various branches of the state provided the information for one another. The press coverage also debated similar issues, but drew more directly on the language and insights of activists in the social movements.

The focus of the public debate began to shift over the next couple of years, however. In 1980, the Australian Senate debated and defeated an amendment to the Human Rights Commission Bill that would have recognised the moment of conception as the beginning of human life and hence the point at which human rights could be claimed (*SMH* 7.3.80; *SMH* 15.5.80). The intention of the amendment sponsors seemed to be the possibility of flooding the new commission with complaints about the denial of human rights to aborted foetuses. During the same months the Queensland government debated and defeated a draconian anti-abortion bill (Petroechevsky 1994). At one point the Cabinet was reported as considering a way to stop women going to New South Wales for abortions (*Australian* 17.4.80). By 1983, a newspaper headline referred to an unwanted foetus as an 'unborn child' in the case of a man who wanted to prevent an abortion (he failed) (*Daily Telegraph* 24.3.83: 1). The high point of reporting the women's movement rhetoric about abortion as a woman's right seemed to have passed. Abortion was not a major issue in legislatures during the mid-1980s.

In March 1988 the NSW election gave the Liberal–National Party coalition a majority in the Legislative Assembly and thus in government, but resulted in a Legislative Council in which the balance of power was held by small political groupings. The most notable were the Australian Democrats and the Call to Australia Party (CTA), a conservative Christian group headed by a clergyman, the Reverend Fred Nile. One early rumour suggested that the government had made a deal with Nile to allow the debate and a vote on abortion matters. The Australian Labor Party (ALP) government had used parliamentary procedure to prevent a Right to Life motion sponsored by Mrs Marie Bignold (CTA) from coming to a vote. In June 1988, soon after the new parliament began sitting, the Bignold Motion, which did not have the force of law, was debated and MLCs voted according to their consciences on a motion that affirmed the 'sanctity of life' as applying 'with equal force and validity to the unborn child'; that condemned the practice and funding of 'abortion on demand' in New South Wales; that called upon 'law enforcement agencies to fully and properly enforce the existing law contained in 82–85 of the Crimes Act 1900'; and that called upon the 'Government to examine the adequacy of the existing law to protect the unborn child' and to remedy any deficiency.

The vote ended in a 20–20 tie with the president of the Legislative Council John Johnson (ALP) using his casting vote in favour of the motion. Johnson had long thought that abortion was murder and after a heart attack had decided that he would devote considerable energy towards curbing its availability in New South Wales (*SMH* 14.9.88). Throughout much of 1988 abortion was again a part of public discourse in New South Wales, though with some changes from the previous decade (Albury 1989). In 1991 an anti-abortion initiative in the NSW Legislative Council was decisively defeated.

The widespread influence of feminist ideas and the introduction of a wider range of reproductive technologies marked the two most important changes in the social context of the abortion debate since the successful law reforms of the late 1960s and early 1970s. The latter was more important during the time between the debates on the Lusher and Bignold motions, with IVF and ultrasound imaging of foetuses changing the representation of pregnancy and the relationship between the pregnant woman and the foetus (see chapter 6). In Australia, in addition to the abortion debates in various parliaments, State and national governments have been active in developing and implementing public policy in many areas of feminist concern (rape, domestic violence, unequal opportunities in education and work, women's health care) (Watson 1990; Sawer 1990; Broom 1991). They have also responded to the challenges of the new reproductive technologies, but have been unwilling to combine the two policy areas in a way that challenges the presumed central value of foetal life or acknowledges the autonomy of women regarding childbearing. These government initiatives have not gone unchallenged: a morally conservative political movement has developed to contest these changes in the name of traditional family values based on an amalgam of religious belief, appeals to 'nature' and nostalgia for a previous 'golden age' of simplicity and moral order.

Abortion in a welfare state

The development of the welfare state has provided the context for this changing emphasis in abortion politics. It has provided the apparatus for collecting information about and regulating the population. In a sense the ability to count abortions, or birth rates, has made the contribution of each woman to the size of the population an issue. Numerous publications by the NSW government statistician, Timothy Coghlan, paved the way for the 1903–04 NSW Royal Commission into the Decline of the Birth-Rate, following the depression of the 1890s when both emigration and the falling birth rate contributed to a decline in population (Hicks 1978; Allen 1982; Allen 1990b). In Australia, as elsewhere, the health and welfare institutions have been agents for spreading norms of personal behaviour—in addition to serving the needs of disadvantaged people—through infant welfare, juvenile courts, family planning and domestic science education (Donzelot 1979; Reiger 1985, Finch 1993). Likewise, post-World War II reconstruction in Australia was thought to require the alteration of the economic conditions in which women lived to enable them to have more children on the assumption that childbearing was limited only by women's sense of financial insecurity (Cass 1988).

More recently, the collection of statistics made possible by legalised abortion combined with the payment of medical benefits has meant that the number of women terminating pregnancies is public knowledge. Opponents of access to abortion have used the official statistics in a number of interesting ways. The Royal Commission on Human Relationships estimate of 60 000 abortions a year was frequently cited in the Lusher debate, and the more up-to-date (1986–87) figure of 80 000, with half in New South Wales, was cited in the Bignold debate. These were usually used to demonstrate the wilful destruction of 'human life'; to call attention to the moral dangers of such a casual attitude towards human life, and to highlight the 'unwomanly' behaviour consequent on 'permissiveness'. The cost to the taxpayer of these operations was also cited. Jane Macquarie cites the figure 75 000–80 000 without a reference to indicate the accessibility of 'safe, legal abortion' in the early 1990s (1994: 114). In the media discussion of the politics surrounding the publication of the NHMRC Expert Panel on Services for the Termination of Pregnancy in Australia in 1997, the figure of 80 000 was again quoted (Horin 1997). However, the discussion paper reports 89 521 abortions in the financial year 1993/94 including both Medicare and hospital data (Australia 1997a: 5). Opponents of abortion claim that the numbers are the result of the legalisation of abortion, but Paul Wilson reported estimates of abortion in Australia to be between 60 000 and 120 000 a year with 'an average opinion . . . at about 75 000' in 1970 (1971: 17). These earlier unofficial estimates are not cited as comparisons; it is as if during the illegal years, before uncomplicated abortions were a part of the official statistics, there was a 'hazy golden age' when 'women cheerfully had all the babies God sent them, and did not complain' (Simms 1981: 168). Yet it is clear from the sources Wilson used, the reports of any population inquiries, careful reading of health statistics and many oral history accounts, that abortion has been a part of the reproductive and sexual experience of large numbers of Australian women for over a century (Hicks 1978; Allen 1982; Baird 1990; Siedlecky and Wyndham 1990; Coleman 1991, Ryan et al. 1994; Australia 1997a).

Since the funding question was based on the notion that medical benefits should be payable for 'medically necessary' abortions, opponents of 'abortion on demand' pointed to the abuses possible under the contemporary legal interpretations. The SA statistics were cited, deploring the use of the 'mental health' indication for abortion in 96 per cent of abortions in 1977, with only 1.36 per cent for specified medical disorders (Australia, House of Representatives 1979: 966). Supporters of public funding spoke in parliamentary debates of the possibility of a return to unsafe abortions from backyard providers. Many of the reviled 'backyard' operators were doctors or nurses practising outside the law but with great skill and care. Pay-offs to police were an important part of the costs of relatively safe, but hidden, abortion through the middle of the twentieth century in Australia (Berman and Childs 1972; Wainer 1972; Allen 1990b). The early medical dominance of illegal abortion may be limited to New South Wales and Victoria, with safe non-medical providers in South Australia and perhaps other States (Baird 1990; Baird 1996). This history is discussed only by parliamentary supporters of medically safe abortion; opponents seem to be unwilling to engage with the weight of evidence against their assertions that a return to illegality would result in more births and greater 'moral' conduct by women.

At the same time as data collection has opened more domestic practices to public scrutiny, the family support provisions of the welfare state have made it possible for women and children to evade the supervision of particular men. Although some feminists have pointed to the patriarchal values embedded in the administration of welfare (Baldock and Cass 1988; Bryson 1993), those are abstract demands that may offer more scope for personal choices than the concrete demands of individual men. The state does not care what time an evening meal is served, only that a cohabitee is not there to eat it, nor does it care what is on the plate as long as the children remain healthy. Once it accepted responsibility for women and children, the state then had to confront the use of abortion as an alternative to infanticide or the burden of unwanted infants. Safe abortions may be less expensive than the alternatives of health care for septic abortions, maternity and supporting mother's benefits for single mothers, or maternity homes and adoption services. Whether it pays for child support or for abortions, moralists can argue that the state is spending taxpayers' money to support 'immorality and irresponsibility' on the part of women and men. Most of the arguments refuse to acknowledge that married as well as single women used abortion to avoid unwanted births before widespread use of the contraceptive pill. The various concerns of state agencies are in conflict when it comes to individual women seeking abortions.

The Women's Liberation Movement was just getting started as the major Australian changes in abortion law were occurring. This meant that feminists participated in those campaigns and extended arguments about abortion reform beyond the intentions of the civil-liberties-based reformers. A few non-profit abortion clinics and feminist referral services were established during the mid-1970s. The developing feminist analysis of health care meant that the 'reform' of the abortion laws as envisioned by the 1960s activists was quickly regarded as insufficient. The reforms left abortion decision making in the hands of doctors and the responsibility for continuing availability of services in the hands of legislators, police and judges. Women's Liberation abortion politics challenged medical dominance and infused subsequent campaigns with a passion for justice and women's freedom.

Free abortion on demand!

The demand to repeal the abortion laws challenged definitions of the relationship between law and morality in a secular state. The reforms of the 1960s were a part of a wider expansion of civil liberties regarding sexual expression. Feminists who argued for repeal and not reform sought to extend the liberal ideals of autonomy and free choice to women. The demand that abortion be provided free to any women who asked was a challenge to the health care delivery system as well as to notions of the special vulnerabilities of women because of their role in procreation. Reproductive health care provision became the background for the abortion debates of the 1980s and 1990s in the way that civil liberties had been in previous decades, with service provision and popular perceptions of the legal standing of abortion being strongly related (Ryan et al. 1994). Medical professionals have been willing to set up abortion services and assert the more 'permissive' interpretations of the abortion sections of the criminal law established by the two lower court judgments.

Case law, built up State by State, has reinforced the early rulings. In the District Court of New South Wales in 1971 in *R. v. Wald*, Justice Levine ruled that the jury could decide 'whether there existed in the case of each woman any economic, social or medical ground or any reason which in their view could constitute reasonable grounds upon which an accused could honestly and reasonably believe there would result a serious danger to her physical or mental health', thus extending Justice Menhennitt's clarification of 'lawful' in the Victorian Criminal Code (Finlay and Sihombing 1978: 64–7). This ruling has never been tested in an appeal: to do so would mean that a government would have to be willing to arrest a doctor for performing an abortion and then, if she or he was found 'not guilty' using this ruling as a precedent, appeal the case to a higher court. In 1971 the NSW government was not willing to appeal; nor have other

State governments tested lower court rulings. Following the legal decisions in Victoria and New South Wales, doctors established private clinics in both States, and in some cases previously 'illegal' clinics became public knowledge. A few non-profit and feminist clinics were also established. The Family Planning Association, community health centres, many general practitioners and some community services provide abortion information and referrals to specialist clinics. In Western Australia, feminist abortion activists began a referral service in 1974. They sought an opinion from the attorney-general about the legality of abortion in the State. After one brief inquiry by the police the service continued providing counselling and referrals to private practitioners in Perth (Anderson 1986; ALRAWA 1977: 9). However, in 1998, long after the apparent extension of the Menhennitt and Levine interpretations to Western Australia, the director of Public Prosecution charged two doctors under the literal terms of the Criminal Code. No compromise is final.

The unwillingness of the governments to use the criminal law to regulate abortion did not extend to Queensland until the 1980s, however. In May 1985 the Queensland police raided abortion clinics in Brisbane and Townsville, collecting medical files and summonsing doctors from the clinics. The doctors were charged with 'conspiring with persons unknown to use force with intent to procure miscarriages to women' (Loane 1985). In June, the search warrants were found to have been invalid and the files were returned to both clinics. The charges against the Townsville doctor were dropped in July when no woman would testify against him. The State attorney-general found a complainant against Dr Bayliss in Brisbane. He and an anaesthetist were tried before Justice McGuire of the Queensland District Court. Justice McGuire found that the Brisbane doctors 'had acted in good faith as medical practitioners to save the life of the mother' and therefore confirmed that abortion was not a criminal offence in certain circumstances in Queensland. The doctors were acquitted of the charges (Ryan et al. 1994: 56). Even so, some women who found their way to one of the clinics were surprised to find that they could reclaim a part of the cost through Medicare (Ryan et al. 1994: 21–4).

In Tasmania, unlike Western Australia, successive State governments have been unwilling to openly accept the applicability of the Menhennitt or subsequent rulings. In addition the medical profession was very self-protective, with the result 'in medical, legal and popular belief that abortion is illegal except in certain extreme circumstances' (Ryan et al. 1994: 25). The consequences for Tasmanian women were judgmental treatment by professionals or a trip to Melbourne for an abortion in a private day clinic. The trip to Melbourne from Tasmania is possible, though beyond the easy reach of many household budgets. It seems to me that for many years the spectre of the trip to the east from Western Australia made quasi-legality easier for politicians to accept. If abortion laws had been enforced, women would have had to travel across South Australia, which has a residence requirement, to Melbourne or Sydney in order to terminate a pregnancy.

The placing of abortion within the context of standard medical practice is, of course, contradictory. Decision making would be still in the hands of doctors or hospital boards, not pregnant women. Hospitals can limit the number of abortions performed in areas without free-standing clinics. This severely reduces the accessibility of abortion and may significantly increase the cost as women are forced to travel to obtain a fee-for-service abortion that should have been available free in their local public hospital. In Victoria during 1986–87 only 21 per cent of abortions were performed in public hospitals (Health Issues Centre 1989), while in New South Wales during the same period the figure was only 10 per cent, virtually all for women with health problems or following diagnosis of a defective foetus (according to the Abortion Providers Federation). In South Australia the requirement that abortions occur in registered hospitals meant that a significant number of women had to travel to Melbourne, Victoria to obtain an abortion in the private sector. In 1992, a specialist clinic attached to a public hospital was opened in Adelaide, thus providing in the public sector the same kind of service women in other States found in the private sector. By the financial year 1993/94 only 14 per cent of all abortions in Australia were performed in public hospitals for public patients—all of the others were in the private sector (Australia 1997a: 5).

However, the medical definition of the act of abortion has allowed it to appear on the medical benefits schedule since the first version of national health insurance was set up by the Whitlam Labor government in 1975, thus establishing a standard price and providing rebates as a matter of entitlement to health care services. The existence of rebates and the possibility for practitioners to 'bulk-bill' certain categories of people within the private health care sector have made it possible for a few of the clinics in the private sector to challenge the standard model of medical practice. These are operated by feminist collectives or by non-profit companies, and some small private practice clinics have also accepted their more woman-centred model.

This all sounds fairly positive for supporters of funded accessible abortion services within the health care system. Certainly the governments in power whether Liberal or Labor have resisted changes to laws or funding arrangements with arguments that resonate with the older civil liberties case for abortion rights. However these parliamentary responses are occurring in a climate in which linkages between abortion and infertility services are being made. Discussions about embryo experimentation frequently rely on an analogy between the disposal of early *in vitro* embryos and established pregnancies ended by abortion.

An article called, 'Embryo "massacre" mars test-tube party', juxtaposed the eighteenth birthday of the first person conceived by IVF and a requirement of the regulations governing the practice of IVF.

> A week after Louise [Brown, the first IVF birth], a Bristol teenager training to be a children's nurse, officially comes of age, the technology that gave her life will end in a kind of mass death . . .

> The 'pre-natal massacre', which the Vatican calls it, is seen by some as the inevitable outcome of a technology that fiddles with human reproduction. The Catholic Church and anti-abortion groups believe the embryos should be preserved and offered for adoption but under a British law that says unwanted or unclaimed embryos can only be kept for five years, they are to be removed from their liquid nitrogen freezers early on August 1 and destroyed. (Ellingsen 1996: 1)

Reports of political massacres and of the shortage of babies for adoption are combined unproblematically. In addition, the disposal of the embryos is linked with abortion and child neglect, but not with the possibility that many embryos would not be transferable after being thawed, or with the low success rate of embryo transfer. Embryos are usually frozen at the stage when they are four to eight undifferentiated cells. If they had been fertilised following sexual intercourse instead of during the process of IVF, they would not yet have implanted in the woman's uterus. If such an embryo failed to implant, the woman would have a menstrual period, not a miscarriage. Embryo freezing and experiments raise ethical questions, but not the problems that the article implies with its linkages to massacres, abortion and child abuse (cf. Singer et al. 1990). By early 1998, spokesmen for both the

Anglican and Catholic churches in Australia said that the disposal of unclaimed frozen embryos was preferable to keeping them indefinitely. Instead of using the analogies of massacres, Father Anthony Fisher drew parallels with the care of people at the end of their lives when artificial means are no longer justified for keeping them alive (Hawes 1998). This seems to be an approach to the issue that allows the debate to proceed in terms more appropriate to the medical processes involved in the storage and possible disposal of embryos.

Moral sex: contraception not abortion

Secular forms of moral language have been deployed about fertility and procreation and have led to interesting transformations of that tension between individual freedom and social control. Abortion in certain cases is acceptable, not because definitions of human life have changed, but because the utilitarian morality of cost and benefit has been extended to fertility. The appropriate and morally responsible method of fertility control is now efficient use of contraception, often meaning medically delivered high-technology methods. Just as today there are fears that availability of abortion will lead to irresponsibility and promiscuity with a resultant devaluation of marriage, birth control was subject to similar arguments until early in the twentieth century, being applied to all women, with the fear of uncontrolled single women lasting until very recently. Even earlier, in Britain, it was argued that adoption of illegitimate children should remain illegal to prevent promiscuity among single women (Howe et al. 1992).

Although efficient contraception has indeed offered many women freedom from unwanted pregnancy, it has also been the means of an altered form of surveillance and self-discipline of women. Women must go to clinics or doctors' surgeries to get contraception and so open their private lives to the scrutiny of medical professionals who may be moralising about the woman's choices. Women themselves have to take the pill daily or monitor their bodies in order for many methods to be used safely and effectively. Unlike barrier methods, the use of the pill, IUD and fertility awareness methods requires self-discipline even when the woman is not likely to have a sexual encounter. At the same time, the rhetoric of reliable contraception and rationally chosen fertility means that many women want an abortion when they experience an unwanted pregnancy; women who the population controllers and conservative social reformers had not expected to seek abortion. Women have applied the utilitarian morality to abortion in a way that enhances individual freedom and challenges social control over female fertility and sexuality, thus challenging the boundaries that the reforms of the late 1960s and early 1970s assumed would be maintained.

By the 1960s socially responsible couples in Western countries practised birth control, with discourses suggesting that the well-being of individual women or society as a whole might be threatened by unwanted fertility (Reed 1978). The precise content of the 'strategic unities' in the sexuality discourses of the nineteenth century that Foucault (1979) identified had changed, but the mechanisms of power–knowledge are recognisable: medical practices that gave control over effective contraceptives to doctors; economic and political discourses on population suggesting too many rather than too few people were a danger to social order ('a socialization of procreative behaviour'); a feminine body saturated with sexuality integrated into medical practices; and the linkage of the family and the social through the body and practices of the Mother ('a hysterization of women's bodies'). These mechanisms together become a part of what Jeffrey Weeks characterised as the 'family-procreation-sexuality nexus' in the web of power–knowledge relations (1981: 264).

Discourses about birth control have been a major focus in the restructuring of the linkages between family and sexuality. 'Family planning' has become an acceptable justification for the use of birth control since the early part of this century, and since the late 1960s the prevention of premarital pregnancies has replaced the prevention of premarital sex for all except conservative religious believers. During the debate on the Bignold Motion in New South Wales, as in the Lusher Motion debate, speakers emphasised the inappropriateness of abortion as a method of birth control. Many seem to share the concern of Mr J. L. Armitage, that 'abortion on demand' means the substitution of abortion for other birth control methods (Australia, House of Representatives 1979: 1074). Three NSW MLCs quoted a statement issued by the Australian Federation of Family Planning Associations in June 1979 which asserted:

1. that contraception is preferable to abortion;
2. that reliance on abortion is not a reasonable method of planned parenthood;

3. that early abortion is preferable to late abortion;
4. that skilled, legal abortion is preferable to unskilled, illegal abortion;
5. that abortion laws and practices should be legalized in order to facilitate access to medically skilled abortion; and
6. that all support services should be freely available for those women seeking abortion, or wishing to continue their pregnancy. (NSW, Legislative Council 1988: 1286–87, 1292, 1305)

They portray abortion as a necessary backup, more necessary when sex education and contraceptive services are not widely available. Note that this statement relies on both medical expertise and a morality based on 'reasonable' behaviour, not on an analysis of the complexity of heterosexual relationships in which contraceptives must be used.

The physical and emotional benefits of contraceptive use for women have been central to the birth control movement during the twentieth century. Knowledge of the risks to women's health and life of illegal abortion was a strong motivation of activists like Margaret Sanger in the United States and Marie Stopes in Britain (Fryer 1965). Concerns about health unified the English birth controllers during the 1920s and led to an increasing integration of birth control into the official machinery of the British welfare state by the late 1930s; the consolidation of the social planning emphasis is indicated by the change of the name of the National Birth Control Association to the Family Planning Association in 1939 (Weeks 1981: 195). Early during the same period in the United States, the medical profession first sought to distance itself from the voluntary birth control movement, in part for moral reasons, but also because early birth control activists were political radicals. Later, they began to support birth control in order to keep provision in medical hands and away from any hint of 'socialisation' or programs that linked birth control for poor people with more general social reforms (Reed 1978). In Australia the first 'family planning' service in New South Wales during the 1920s was called initially, the Race Improvement Society, then the Racial Hygiene Society, showing the eugenic concerns for maintaining the health and strength of the immigrant population, though the birth control ideas of Marie Stopes were also regarded as a threat to the Empire, and her books were banned for a time in Australia (Siedlecky and Wyndham 1990: 160–1). At this time diaphragms, like D. H. Lawrence novels, were obscene imports and had to be smuggled in. While importation remained a problem, the Racial Hygiene Society was able to manufacture a diaphragm called the 'Racia Cap' in Australia, patenting it in 1934. Condoms were also manufactured in Australia. The birth rate continued to fall and the reported deaths from abortion to rise (Allen 1982), so abortions must have been available for many women.

In a relatively brief but suggestive analysis of the 1960s in England, Weeks argues that a combination of commercial factors and the more general availability of birth control contributed to a shift in the balance of the arguments from one of social control of female sexuality to one that allowed for more individual freedom for women, though he admits that the new female sexuality was still largely male defined (1981: 256–260). In Australia the development of the national network of Family Planning Associations was a part of the political demands for abortion law reform in the late 1960s and early 1970s. Abortion law reformers successfully argued that the abortion rate would be reduced with the introduction of widespread availability of birth control methods and sex education (Siedlecky and Wyndham 1990). These changes, which challenged the previous norm of sexuality that suggested chastity for women before and a willingness to continue any pregnancy after marriage, were a part of the shifting economic and ideological position of women in post-World War II Australia (Matthews 1984).

The challenges to previous social norms about sexuality did not go so far as challenging the norm of procreative heterosexuality as 'the sex act'. A couple of MPs allude to the male-centredness of heterosexuality in their speeches against the Lusher Motion. John Brown caught the social relations in his remark, 'Women endure abortion, men cause the need' (Australia, House of Representatives 1979: 1110). Clyde Cameron was the most graphic: 'There is not one of us who has not released his passion upon the body of some woman'. He went on to assert that many members had 'committed adultery', more 'fornication' and some had been party to an abortion. 'No woman can get pregnant without the help of a man and most of the honourable members in this House tonight have been responsible for helping some woman get pregnant' (Australia, House of Representatives 1979: 988). Cameron's speech stands out for his willingness to discuss the sexual politics of sexuality and fertility as well as the social inequities of removing abortion from the medical benefits schedule.

Abortion debates have changed over the past thirty years. In the late 1960s, abortion seemed to civil libertarians to be a policy matter that was open to standard political resolution processes. As the consequences of changing practice, abortion made a public appearance in official statistics and women made demands on the health services. Opponents mounted new arguments. In the parliamentary debates I have studied, opponents of abortion frequently equate concern for all foetuses with respect for all human life. This is one location where the combination of new medical technology and the new visual technologies has altered the moral arguments in the public abortion debates. The elevation of each foetus to a representative of life itself is problematic for women. Among other things, it draws attention away from the social context of women's lives by making each woman individually morally responsible for honouring human life. Women have and rear children in many social and economic circumstances, but human life is nurtured by an idealised Mother. In the next chapter I will examine the ways that these representations of foetuses and mothers serve to reduce the visibility of women.

6   Motherhood and Technologies of Gender

The title of this chapter calls attention to the implications of using the image of the foetus as a symbol for human life. It highlights the contradiction of opposing demands for rights for women with calls for human rights for foetuses. Such imagery represents the everyday life of a pregnant woman as if it was not very important to the big picture, but abstracts any specific foetus from its place inside a pregnant woman to represent all of human life. In this chapter I will be examining one of the most important shapers of women's everyday lives—motherhood. Mothers have both a daily life and an idealised one. While feminist analyses have called attention to the difficulties of meeting expectations of Perfect Motherhood, some popular assumptions about mothers help to shape the feminist analysis of assisted reproductive technologies. The cultural equation of Woman with Mother and the overlap between the lists of feminine emotional characteristics and the sentimentalised characteristics of mothers mean that the lives of childless women are also shaped by motherhood as a social institution if not as a personal practice.

I will discuss some of the feminist arguments about motherhood in order to show the importance of an understanding of childbearing and childrearing for the development of the politics of reproduction. The development of new technologies with the ability to assist conception, to diagnose foetal abnormalities and to sustain the lives of very small newborns has changed the experience of motherhood for all women. What once seemed 'natural' may no longer be sufficient. As governments have addressed the challenges of the new technologies they have reiterated some cultural assumptions about motherhood and contradicted others. The new technologies have contributed to the possibility of changing representations of life by apparently separating the foetus or embryo from the body and social life of the pregnant women. They have made visible what was previously known only through the reports of the woman and opened the way for more of the medical interventions described in chapter 2.

Motherhood in the lives of women

Motherhood is the mark of adult womanhood for many people, though not all women become mothers. Pregnancy and birth have been regarded as the cure for many 'female troubles' from period pain to serious mental illness. Motherhood is spoken about as if it were a natural experience of femininity yet it is a significant point for medical and social intervention in the lives and bodies of women. There has been a lot of ink spilled over the past few centuries to tell women how to follow their supposedly 'natural maternal instincts'. The work of mothering has been central to the changing definition of 'good' womanhood for at least two centuries, with childbearing and childrearing deployed in the service of such diverse causes as nationalism, industrial reform, pacifism and the development of the disciplines of social work and home economics. In spite of the heavy emphasis on motherhood in the culture, the mother and child dyad was problematic outside a marriage relationship. This was mirrored by the suspicion that childless couples were 'selfish'. Earlier this century, adoption was regarded as a resolution to both problems: babies could be transferred from unmarried mothers to married women. In addition the supposed naturalness of nurturing behaviour has been the justification for poor pay and conditions for child care workers and nurses. Family responsibilities have been used to explain similar conditions in other female-dominated industries and the potential to bear children used to deny women workers opportunities for further training and promotion. Motherhood shapes women's lives whether they have young children or not.

What do mothers do? And more importantly for a social analysis of motherhood, what are the meanings of what they do;

what are past and present representations of motherhood and who benefits from the cultural currency of particular representations? Motherhood has long figured in feminist campaigns: nineteenth century campaigns for maternal custody and 'voluntary motherhood' were challenges to oppressive male behaviour both in law and in the home. Early twentieth century campaigns for equal pay (so single mothers could afford to keep their children), birth control and a variety of struggles to maintain a woman's voice in childbirth practices have marked concerns for the daily lives of mothers. Feminists during the 1960s through to the 1990s campaigned for what has come to be called 'reproductive freedom': abortion rights, contraception, an end to sterilisation abuse, woman-centred birth practices that are affordable and culturally appropriate, child care services, custody for lesbians and other women suffering what can be called a 'middle class deficit' (women who do not meet certain classed maternal stereotypes). Most recently these campaigns have also addressed the development of the new reproductive technologies, beginning with criticism of IVF and continuing with calls for the regulation or prohibition of embryo experimentation and surrogate motherhood.

At one level everyone knows what mothers do—they care for children. They care, not in the somewhat distanced way that a child care worker does, but in an intimate and highly personalised way: mothering does not include a 35-hour work week. In a sense that caring begins before the child is born. The woman enacts the culturally appropriate behaviour of a pregnant woman: eating and drinking the right things, avoiding the wrong things, seeking helpers, preparing her body for the rigours of birthing. In addition, she makes a social space for the coming baby: tells family and friends, discusses names, imagines a life, remembers past family births (or not, as culturally appropriate). When the baby is born it fills the constructed space: it is a son or daughter, a grandchild, a niece or nephew. At the same time, the pregnant woman begins to think of herself (and be thought of by others) as a mother.

But women are not automatically mothers; in spite of terms like 'maternal instinct', mothering is not a biological response to the stimulus of the infant or small child. Rather, motherhood is socially constituted, a developed form of subjectivity achieved by the woman through a range of social and psychic practices. In a sense, we can say that a social position of 'mother' exists and is structured according to particular cultural, economic and social relations. In a number of ways growing up helps prepare girls to become women and to take up the position 'mother' in ways similar to those in which boys are prepared to become men and take up the social position of 'worker'. The mere physiological presence of a foetus growing in a woman's uterus does not make her a mother, as we can see in this classic joke included in a study of the experiences of single pregnant women in the early 1970s:

> Doctor: 'I've got good news for you, Mrs. Brown.'
> Woman: 'It's Miss Brown, actually.'
> Doctor: 'I've got bad news for you, Miss Brown.' (Macintyre 1976: 160)

During the early 1970s, Macintyre reports that while women had a range of reactions to pregnancy, their doctors were of a single view: pregnancy and childbearing were normal and desirable only for married women. In a summary of the doctors' views it is clear that the woman's civil status colours every aspect of fertility and the social relations of procreation (Macintyre 1976: 159–60). Unmarried women who wanted to keep their children were considered to be unrealistic and selfish but any married woman who wanted to give up a child was by definition 'aberrant'. There were also assumptions that married and unmarried women would react very differently to late miscarriage, stillbirth or neo-natal death of their babies. Social workers and nurses working with pregnant women shared many of the same views as the doctors.

That we recognise and perhaps share some of these early 1970s views is symptomatic of what Teresa de Lauretis (1987) called the 'technology of gender'. She argued that gender, as both representation and self-representation, is a product of various social practices, institutional discourses, knowledge systems, critical practices like feminism and of course, the practices of daily life. Indeed, in spite of new technologies, changing government policies such as the supporting parent's benefit and many other social changes, these views have considerable currency in the late 1990s in urban Australia. A number of feminist researchers and writers, like Macintyre, have emphasised the difference between the institutional discourses of socially authorised experts and the experiences of women. As with most other areas of human life, motherhood is not experienced as purely a gendered experience, but is also constituted by other sets of interlocking social relations including class, ethnic background, religious belief and geographic location. Nevertheless, feminists began with a gendered analysis as they challenged the taken-for-granted notions of the naturalness of mothering as social behaviour founded on a physiological process (see Richardson 1993).

Many feminists have given birth and lovingly raised children, and feminists have also argued that childless women are neither deficient nor necessarily missing one of life's important experiences. Yet, there are repeated misreadings of the relationship between feminism and motherhood. Non-feminists often portray feminists as anti-child and contemptuous of motherhood; this is particularly true of those non-feminists who oppose access to abortion and child care. There are deep ambivalences in feminist discussions of motherhood, with some women arguing that feminist writing and politics have ignored motherhood and have refused to acknowledge the power of the experience in shaping women's lives. Others have argued that feminists have gone 'too far' in criticising motherhood and thus denigrating the family by focusing on women as autonomous individuals. Motherhood as a new experience is overwhelming; as a continuing experience it is constantly changing. New mothers, feminist or not, frequently comment that 'no one told me' about the feelings evoked by life as a mother. It is more likely that those women did not pay attention to the deeper meanings of mothers' conversations until a child arrived. Each welcomed first birth initiates another woman into what one feminist mother described as 'this humbling, extraordinary secret world: this milky furious love' (Dell'oso 1996).

I became a mother and a feminist in the late 1960s in a community of feminist mothers. Since that time my practices as a mother and as an activist have informed each other in ways that are difficult to explain. I read all feminist critiques of motherhood except *The Feminine Mystique* (Friedan 1963) as a practising mother: a subjective, not scholarly, reading. Ann Snitow has argued that feminists have been a part of the misreadings of the writing on motherhood. She reviewed at least 190 articles and books about motherhood by feminists published between 1963 and 1990. Snitow concluded there were three stages in the US feminist engagement with the institution of motherhood: the early 'demon texts' (1963–1974); the time of serious attempts to theorise the mixed experiences of motherhood (1975–1979); and a period of more defensive writing which reflects the strong backlash against feminism in US political life (1979–1990) (1992: 34). The timeline she provides for the United States is different elsewhere, of course, but the texts published in the United States have influenced feminist writing and popular views about feminism in other English-speaking countries. Australia is no exception. In the account of the engagement of feminism with motherhood that follows, some of the major US texts are discussed, but so are the accounts of the specifically Australian experiences of motherhood.

The 'demon texts' include some trenchant criticism of the limited horizons of women at home with small children during the 1960s and early 1970s. It is true that some writers who suggested paid work as a way to broaden those horizons underestimated the tensions in the lives of working mothers. In part this was because there were fewer working mothers in the early 1970s, few of them were speaking about their experiences and many of the feminist writers had not yet tried to combine motherhood and full-time paid work. The less privileged women who have always worked in either the taxed or black economy (cf. Matthews 1984) were not particularly visible to the white intellectuals who wrote those early books. The radical questioning of the expectation that motherhood would be the source of both identity and fulfilment of women has been read as a rejection of children and an attack on housewives. The rhetoric of Friedan (1963), Firestone (1971) and Greer (1971) may seem dated today, but many of the questions they raised have yet to be fully explored.

The mid-1970s was a period marking the first attempts at feminist scholarly accounts of women's lives since early in the century. Throughout *Damned Whores and God's Police* (1975/1994; the later edition is used in the following citations) Summers used the insights of Women's Liberation to interrogate the received versions of Australian history and to challenge the assumptions about women and the social order that informed the orthodox versions. As the title suggests, she challenged the binary definitions of women as whores or madonnas. Summers refused the personalising explanations of individual women's inability to live up to the 'God's Police' stereotype, replacing them with an account of the social structure in which state agencies played an important role. The account of women in the family is thus complex, drawing in political struggles and demands on the state for services, attempts by state workers such as baby health nurses to regulate the lives of women as well as the efforts by women to maintain a reasonable standard of living for themselves, their children and husband.

Summers argued that a major achievement of the earlier feminist movement in Australia was respect for the work of housewives. The existence of a separate sphere of women's work allowed women to feel and be recognised for their competence, particularly during the years between the first and second world wars.

> An impressive repertoire of skills and accomplishments was necessary to be able to be an Australian Mum. She had to be an implacable creature, the mainstay of the home, the human bulwark against any forces (such as unemployment, death and family scandals) which might undermine family harmony and happiness. She had to clean houses . . . and to satisfy family appetites with a sparse available menu of acceptable foods . . . At the same time she had to demonstrate thrift by sewing children's clothes and soft furnishings, by preserving fruits and making jams and chutneys. She had to be tireless . . .
>
> She had to be mother and lover, enduring in silence the ceaseless worry of an unplanned pregnancy—because contraception was never perfect and abortions were hard to procure—for Such Things were not discussed between husband and wife. All this as well as keeping up a lively interest in what the children were learning in school, how husband was getting on at work, corresponding with relatives interstate, organizing visits of reluctant children to aging grandparents. (Summers 1994: 489)

Summers went on to describe the changes of the post-World War II decades in which the life of a mother in the home became increasingly impossible for many Australian women. The changes in the economy were not reflected in family life where women were still doing the majority of the physical and emotional upkeep, however. Indeed, at the time *Damned Whores and God's Police* was published, there is evidence that many couples raising small children expected a pattern of childrearing based on their own childhoods and were ambivalent about the changes. Mothers with full-time paid employment were regarded by many people interviewed in two studies for the Royal Commission on Human Relationships as 'ambitious, selfish, arrogant, or simply hassled', women with little time or concern for their children. Part-time work seemed to pose fewer tensions between the interviewees' notion of good mothering and workforce participation (Harper and Richards 1979).

By the mid-1970s feminists were well engaged in the task of analysing the sources of the popular notions of good mothering and the effects of those notions on the lives of women. In *Of Woman Born*, American poet Adrienne Rich (1976, the tenth anniversary edition (1986) is cited below) examined the experience of motherhood as embedded in its social context—the political institution of motherhood under conditions of patriarchy. She drew on historical, literary and mythological accounts, personal experience and contemporary social research to provide a feminist (now understood as radical feminist) account of motherhood. Rich argued that the institution of motherhood was structured patriarchally, governed by the law of the father in both actual and symbolic ways. Children and women were inserted into a cultural nexus determined neither by them nor by their needs. Rich described a summer holiday spent in a friend's weekender while her husband was abroad. She and her primary-school-aged sons lived according to their own pattern: informal meals, no set timetable and still enough reading and writing time for the mother. She reflects, 'We were conspirators, outlaws from the institution of motherhood; I felt enormously in charge of my life' (Rich 1986: 194–5). One of the most powerful aspects of the book is this evocation of the tensions in the daily life of mothers, the love for children and the pleasures of seeing them grow set against the need to live always in the 'rhythms of other lives' (1986: 33), rhythms determined not only by human needs but also by the demands of the market economy and social expectation.

From the perspective of twenty years, this powerfully written account of the development of scientific 'experts' of childbearing and childrearing, the male take-over of obstetrics, mother–daughter and mother–son relationships and the potential for violence at the heart of maternal responsibility, is also flawed. Rich pointed out that guilt is so often a part of a mother's experience because of the changing demands of mothering and the inability to tell if one is doing 'enough' or in the right way, but she was less revealing about the complicity of women in the enforcement of the institution. It was a book of its time, as Rich comments in the introduction to the tenth anniversary edition. She was insensitive to the differences of race and class, turning similarities into universals, attempting to collapse the contradictions of being brought up by a black nurse/housekeeper into the category of mother–daughter relations (Rich 1986). Even so, the book remains one of the few that both affirms the complexity of mothering in the lives of women and criticises the conditions that shape those experiences.

Australian writers have taken up the complicity of women in the enforcement of the institution of motherhood. Jill Julius

Matthews (1984) and Kerreen Reiger (1985) built on the insights of 1970s feminist scholarship and activism to analyse the social shaping of femininity in twentieth century Australia. Matthews regarded mothering as one of three arenas of life in which the impossible demands of femininity are lived out. In a sense the practice of mothers has been shaped by a concern for the quality of the population in a vast and unpopulated country. Following Foucault (1979), she argued that in Australia women's bodies were the focus of a population ideology with specific concerns about the size and standard of living of the population. Campaigns to meet these concerns were aimed at the mothering practice of women by public health officials, infant and child welfare proponents and activists for social purity. By following the precepts of a variety of experts and activists, women were to have more and healthier children through cleanliness, good nutrition and sexual purity (Matthews 1984). Later authors have pointed to the differential effects of these demands on working class women who were being asked to change more and for whom the failure to meet the higher standards might mean the loss of their children to the welfare system (Finch 1993; van Krieken 1991).

In spite of the growing trends towards scientific childrearing there was no change in the assumption that women would do the work involved. Why do *women*, not humans, mother? Some commentators answer this by claiming that motherhood is 'natural' for women. Biological determinist arguments suggest that women care for small children because they have breasts or because they gave birth. A somewhat more social, but still biologically determinist, account says that it is hard to hunt wild animals with a baby so women have to stay 'home' to care for children. Of course, gathering women did not stay at 'home' either; they caught and brought home fish and small animals along with plant foods. Anyway, social and technological changes over a long passage of human history have resulted in urbanised or settled agricultural populations and safe baby-feeding technology. Those who promote natural motherhood have turned to the notion of 'maternal instinct', today sometimes reduced to 'hormones' (cf. Vines 1993).

The question remains: given the many problems with childrearing under patriarchal conditions why do women mother? Feminists have been unwilling to accept an explanation that suggested that women were simply victims of patriarchy or unthinking products of their socialisation. It is also clear that possession of power and wealth alters other conditions of parenthood. Wives have freed most men, and servants relieve wealthy women from the provision of daily care for small children (Polatnick 1983; see also: Dally 1982; Badinter 1981). It's not a surprise that feminists challenged the functionalist interpretation of family life; the needs of small children seemed to serve as an all-purpose barrier to opportunities for women in the workforce, civil society or political life. Yet, of course, the children of feminists are children with the needs and desires of children; they are born with neither a political understanding of the evils of nuclear families nor a good critique of sex roles. Feminists with children do the work of mothering in the same conflicted ways as other women (Dowrick and Grundberg 1980; Wearing 1984; Adelaide 1996). Politics or sophisticated theory does not get up to provide a night feed!

In trying to understand how girls become culturally appropriate women and why women mother, some feminist theorists turned to the insights of psychoanalysis. This involved (and still does) a rereading of the originating texts and strong theoretical development in the area of femininity. Whereas the authors of some of the 'demon texts' of early feminism rejected all of psychoanalysis because many practitioners were a part of the social control of women from the early twentieth century, Juliet Mitchell began the rereadings. She ended *Women's Estate* (1971) with a statement about the importance of psychoanalysis for understanding the ideology of the family. In *Psychoanalysis and Feminism* (1975) she demonstrated how Freudian theory offered an important way of understanding 'the devil you [we] have got'; that is, a patriarchal capitalist culture.

Traditional psychoanalysis regards mothers as a part of an individual's past experience. The good or at least 'good enough' mother thus was a woman who raised children without neuroses. What happens to adult women who mother? It was as though the question could not even be asked. Yet, if psychoanalysis is useful to sociology and cultural studies because it helps to explain how culture is reproduced without relying on the insulting assumption that women are 'cultural dopes' and regularly act against their own interests, then the questions about the reproduction of the social practices of mothering had to be asked.

What do mothers do?

It isn't good enough just to meet the basic physical needs of the baby—to keep it clean and dry, to feed it regularly—babies need reliable emotional relationships in order to take their places as functioning adults in society. One group of writers has used psychoanalytic concepts to explain how women learn to care for babies by being cared for themselves. Nancy Chodorow used object relations theory to argue that men are prepared for their lives in the less affective public realm and women are prepared for mothering. According to Chodorow the sexual and familial division of labour thus produces a psychic division which in turn reproduces the sexual and familial division of labour (1978).

There have been numerous criticisms of her work, in part because it universalises the middle class white experience (a criticism of most psychoanalytic theory); it ignores lesbianism and male homosexuality as adult outcomes of the psychic processes; and it seems to tread dangerously close to a form of feminine essentialism, though Chodorow does not claim that nurturance is a solely feminine capacity. Rather, she suggests that men should consciously tap their latent capacities and share childrearing as a way out of the social reproduction of gendered child care. While I do not want to discourage shared child care, I wonder if this solution underestimates the power of the combined technologies of gender by suggesting that a particular individual behavioural change could be a solution for a problem that is so pervasive.

Also I wonder if it overestimates the explanatory power of a particular psychoanalytic story. That is, while the story she retells may help explain the social relations of mothering among a specific social group this century, it may not explain social relations in general. In spite of her intentions to reshape gender relations, the story Chodorow tells can also be an argument for the necessity of mothering for women; an explanation for why women should put up with the rigours of infertility programs in their search for motherhood; an excuse for paying them less; and a foundation for a re-sentimentalising of the mother–child bond.

Chodorow herself was not particularly guilty on any of these counts. She warned about the dangers for feminism of reproducing 'The Fantasy of the Perfect Mother'. She and a co-author examined psychoanalytic themes in feminist writing about motherhood during the late 1970s and early 1980s. 'These themes include[d] a sense that mothers are totally responsible for the outcomes of their mothering, even if their behaviour is in turn shaped by male-dominant society' (Chodorow and Contratto 1982: 55). They were concerned that these accounts of motherhood had an unprocessed quality (in a sense, they were written from the unconscious) and shared much with general cultural understandings of motherhood, particularly anti-feminist ones.

The undercurrent of mother blaming and mother idealisation has some practical consequences, as well as the theoretical ones Chodorow and Contratto point out. To blame a past flesh-and-blood mother for something she could do nothing about—the fact that a child grew up or that she was an 'ordinary' woman—is also to blame contemporary adults for being 'bad' mothers to their own children or to suggest that they refrain from childbirth because of supposed imperfections. This keeps motherhood special and separated from everyday life which is otherwise full of conflicts and failures as well as successes. It contributes to a refusal to examine the ways individuals constitute themselves as women or mothers. It also accepts in an unquestioning way a set of womanly or perfect motherly personality traits (self-sacrificing, nurturing, loving, altruistic, organised and so on)—yet no living woman can meet these ideals.

Writing at the same time, philosopher Sara Ruddick focused her analysis on the intellectual work of mothering, which she called 'maternal thought'. 'The discipline of maternal thought consists in establishing criteria for determining failure and success, in setting priorities, and in identifying the virtues and liabilities the criteria presume' (Ruddick 1982: 77). Ruddick does not presume that women achieve all that is set out in the criteria, but rather thinks that they develop an understanding of achievement that may be different from the dominant public definitions of what mothers do. She argued that all thought arises out of social practice; in their practice, people respond to what seem like demands; maternal responses are shaped by interests in preserving, reproducing, directing and understanding individual and group life (Ruddick 1982: 77).

So maternal thought can be seen to arise from the demands of the child and the demands of the mother's social group. Children 'demand' that their lives be preserved and their growth fostered, and the social group 'demands' that the growth be shaped in socially acceptable ways. The woman's maternal practice then is governed by at least three interests in satisfying the demands for preservation, growth and acceptability. These begin, typically, when a woman knows that she is pregnant and that she will continue the pregnancy and raise the child. Like all interests, these maternal interests in preservation, growth and acceptability come into conflict. Consider the mother who sees her child push another aside to climb a tree. She worries about physical danger but knows the child must develop confidence and skill. She is concerned that the social values of moral restraint embodied in turn-taking might inhibit the development of the social value of competitiveness if she stepped in to make the child wait (Ruddick 1982: 79). Similar temptations and errors exist for the other interests.

Ruddick argues that the characteristics of maternal thought are undervalued in our society, largely because they are seen as virtues of subordinates. She says practitioners of maternal thought develop the capacity of attention, a watchfulness of the needs of children which, with the virtue of love, invigorates preservation and enables growth. Together, attention and love help to undermine the temptation to inauthentic obedience in the shaping of a child that is socially acceptable. This 'attentive love' is what mothers do. It is an intellectual discipline that accompanies the physical labour; a discipline that shapes mothering practice (Ruddick 1982). As one critic points out, these are not specifically 'maternal' patterns and could be found among any group of 'care-giving' workers (Morell 1994).

Christine Everingham (1994) recognised that in much social theory the everyday work of mothers is relegated to the background or just appears as a given, not in need of explanation. While she found Ruddick's ideas useful as a starting point, Everingham was interested in emphasising maternal practice as socially constructed and constrained rather than as the intellectual discipline of an individual. Instead of asking, why do women mother or where do women go wrong? Everingham asked, how do women mother? In changing the question, she changed the focus from the motivations of individual women to the activities of communities of women in the process of interpreting and responding to the needs of their children.

Everingham reported that mothers accepted personal responsibility for the care of their infants, frequently believing that the baby's needs would be self-evident. This is seldom the case and new mothers became preoccupied with trying to understand the baby's needs. The child care literature based on the notion that mothers have an intuitive ability to meet the baby's needs contributes to this preoccupation as does the apparent assumption by others that the mother knows the child best. These ideas meant that mothers felt responsible for the social behaviour of their children, though the children continued to act in disapproved ways, frequently embarrassing their mothers (Everingham 1994).

The mothers attended to the personal needs and social

behaviour of the children according to the ethos of their particular social group and the differences among the children. The mothers demonstrated a variety of ways of balancing the desire to be a good mother with their own self-interests to have some free time and a relatively predictable daily schedule. For example some mothers interpreted 'demand feeding' to mean that the baby should be offered a breast whenever it fussed, but other women used an alternative interpretation that included feeding when the baby was likely to be hungry and offering other comforts like 'jiggling' or a dummy. Different babies within the same family also elicited redefinitions of needs and comforts (Everingham 1994: 90). Everingham fills in some of the gaps in social theory by her detailed account of the ways that women work with their children and their friends to create personal identity for both mothers and children.

Taken together these writers provide many of the elements of a nuanced account of what is sometimes called 'socialisation' as if the concept explained the process. The work that mothers do with children is central to the transformation of babies into acceptable human adults. Many feminists have pointed to the costs of this process for women. The analysis of the costs is too frequently regarded as the only feminist engagement with motherhood, to the extent that some people assume that supporting feminism means rejecting motherhood. Yet, most people realise that those who criticise capitalism and the social relations of the workplace are in paid work. The challenging insight that motherhood is itself a social institution, not a natural 'fact', keeps getting lost. Since the 'demon texts' of the early years of Women's Liberation, feminists have been urging changes in the institution of motherhood.

But woman does not equal mother

The institution of motherhood not only shapes the lives of women who bear children, but also assigns a lesser value to those who do not. When motherhood is assumed to be the role and identity of adult women, childless women occupy an ambiguous position. Feminists from at least the nineteenth century forward have valued childless women. Single, childless women were prominent in the struggles for the vote and to open higher education and the professions to women; Rose Scott is but one Australian example (Allen 1994). They supported each other and their sisters and fellow activists with children. For some childlessness was a choice; until contraception was fairly reliable, women who wanted a public life often had to choose to be single as well as childless. Others formed close emotional and perhaps physical relationships with other women; many lesbians have pointed to such women as precursors to contemporary lesbian partnerships and communities (Faderman 1981).

Some women remained single because they put their duties towards their families before their personal lives, caring for invalid or elderly parents or sickly siblings into middle age. In addition, wars and colonial expansion reduced the number of available men in Europe during the second half of the nineteenth and the first quarter of the twentieth centuries. Economic depressions further delayed marriage and childbearing for some women. Familiar as they were with this range of reasons for remaining single and childless in a culture that sentimentalised married motherhood, it is no wonder that some nineteenth century feminists promoted celibate spinsterhood as a good life for women (Jeffreys 1985). Since existing factory and domestic work was viewed as inappropriate for women of their class, the opening of careers for single middle class women was important because jobs with reasonable pay would allow spinsters to be independent. Women entered nursing, teaching and office work in significant numbers during the late nineteenth century. In addition to making demands to enter professions such as law and medicine, women were in the forefront of the new human services such as social work and infant welfare.

During the first quarter of the twentieth century, with the popularisation of psychoanalysis and sex reform as sexology, a number of writers discussed the dangers of lesbianism between close female friends. Jeffreys describes contemporary accounts that suggest that single women might suffer poor health or inadequate moral character in the absence of an emotional and physical relationship with a man (1985: 102–27). Indeed, the employment of virginal single women in the teaching profession was regarded by some as a danger to the children as early as 1914—they might make the girls critical of men (Jeffreys 1985: 180). In earlier times, a single working life was an alternative to marriage for some women when religious values such as chastity regulated women's conduct. But with the decline of religion and the rise of science, even in such a diluted form as sexology, marriage and motherhood became the only acceptable adult life for women, though celibate single women and lesbians did not disappear. This denigration of the single or childless life existed at the same time as the enhanced respect for the 'Australian Mum' discussed by Summers (1994: 489). It also led society to forget about the lives and communities of single women until the 1960s and the early historical research of the Women's Liberation Movement, when new studies were written and old books reprinted.

Married women, too, have been childless. Cultural expectations have meant that childless married women have been viewed with suspicion unless they were known to be infertile. The expectation that family life will follow marriage is so strong that voluntarily childless couples are assumed to be selfish, inadequate or immature in some way (Morell 1994). Casual acquaintances and even strangers seem willing to ask why an established couple have remained childless. At the same time, childless couples reported that friends' relationships had been damaged by children, though as Marshall (1993) suggests, it is difficult to separate the fact of the children from the ways that the parents tried to meet social expectations of parenthood. Lesbian couples are expected to be childless, often having to fight for custody of children from previous heterosexual relationships or being excluded from infertility services such as donor insemination programs on the basis of their sexual orientation. This suggests that Rich's analysis of motherhood needs to be extended to include the place of not-mothers within the institution of motherhood. In important ways the discriminatory treatment of lesbians is a warning to women who might stray outside the institution by refusing to marry, or remaining childless: not-mothers are flawed women. That allegation of flawedness is a part of the stigma that those who are involuntarily childless suffer even though they want to be mothers (Pfeffer 1987). Married women are culturally expected to be mothers regardless of their inclinations or circumstances just as single heterosexual women and lesbians are expected to be not-mothers. Other life courses may be regarded as 'unwomanly conduct' and as a challenge to good social order.

Adoption and motherhood

Married women have been childless by circumstances as well as by choice. It is difficult to know the rates or causes of infertility in the past (Napier 1987). Today adoption is suggested as one way of providing babies for childless couples, but prior to the twentieth century in Britain, adoption was not a socially approved solution to illegitimacy. It gave the 'lewd' woman an easy way out of her problem and later there was a concern about 'bad blood' being passed on to the child and polluting a 'good' home (Howe et al. 1992). However, by the early twentieth century, with the rise of the welfare state, illegitimate children and their mothers posed a problem of social order as well as personal morality. The collection of social statistics and the growing dominance of the medical definition of women's bodies as inherently unstable meant that middle class people could no longer claim that infanticide, abortion and contraception were practised only by poor people (Smart 1992). Unmarried mothers became subject to regulation beyond the previous concerns to prevent economic burdens on the parish. Attempts were made to lessen the public fears about adoption. During the 1920s the practice of a form of closed or secret adoption was legislated in many English-speaking countries as a response to the infants of unmarried women, with increasing secrecy developing in the 1950s and 1960s. Certainly parliamentarians in the State of Victoria claimed to be protecting the adopted child from the 'slur of illegitimacy' as well as protecting the adoptive parents from the insecurity of unregulated adoption practice when they legislated in 1928 (Swain and Howe 1995: 136–7). The woman who bore the child was pushed to the background and treated as a moral risk to her child.

Adoption practice has changed over the past twenty years to better acknowledge the ongoing emotional and psychological impact both of relinquishing a child or being adopted. The reassertion of feminism during the 1970s made it possible for women to speak openly about their experiences of being pregnant and unmarried during the previous two decades. In addition, changing popular attitudes towards ex-nuptial children in Australia were consolidated by the extension of social benefits to unmarried single mothers (Swain and Howe 1995). Despite these changes, two notions deeply embedded in common-sense constructions of gender through ideologies of motherhood and family life reappear in the debates about adoption in Australia and New Zealand (Shawyer 1979; Winkler and van Keppel 1984; Inglis 1984; Harkness 1991; Swain and Swain 1992). The first is the continuing shame of many women who relinquished their babies and the second is the fear of adoptive parents that any detailed knowledge about the personality and circumstances of their child's birth mother will destroy their family life. The adoption literature stresses the importance of the silences left by the practice of closed adoption: women who have given birth but cannot claim the name of 'mother'; adoptees who cannot find answers to certain questions about their origins. The accounts are moving, and it is clear that the assurances by adoption workers seriously underestimated the difficulty of establishing personal relationships based on a pretence. Closed adoption did not guarantee 'normal family life' for parents and adoptees, nor did it ease the experience of 'putting the pregnancy and birth behind her' for the relinquishing mother.

Unmarried women who demonstrated their 'unruly' sexual behaviour by giving birth were reintegrated into the social order by the practice of closed adoption, but at considerable personal cost. The explanations of the costs draw on aspects of contemporary constructions of femininity. One is the continuing social distinction between 'good' and 'bad' women based on sexual behaviour; pregnancy outside of marriage was, and for many still is, a clear marker of inappropriate or irresponsible sexual activity on the part of women, the same marker used in the abortion debate. An unmarried woman could become a good woman again only by the act of self-sacrifice involved in relinquishing the baby. Yet, relinquishing mothers report varying degrees of distress using the language of bereavement, experiencing unresolved grief at the loss of their babies. During the period of closed adoption, relinquishing mothers were denied access to their babies after birth on the grounds that if a women did not see or touch the baby, she would not 'bond' with it and would not feel its loss. Today, those women are asserting the imaginative and physical processes of pregnancy that were previously denied. Some are claiming that the mother–child bond has a biological beginning in pregnancy and hence that their distress is 'natural' for a mother who has lost a child. They argue that the disruption of that 'natural' bond has ongoing social effects for both mother and child. In a sense, they remain 'unruly' by claiming the 'good' title of 'mother' without the respectable title of 'wife'. Furthermore, if motherhood was to be the reward of married womanhood, childless marriage was also a problem for social order. The practice of closed adoption addressed this problem by supplying babies with altered birth certificates to married couples.

While closed adoption provided solutions to the social problems of unruly, inappropriate fertility (both too much and too little), it created a significant gap in the lives of all parties. All of the parties speak of personal difficulties that they trace to the perceived need for a sense of genetic relatedness as a basis for the formation of personal identity and 'normal' family life. The adoptive parents had neither the experience of pregnancy, nor an extended family with whom their child shared physical characteristics. The birth mother lost an intimate physical relationship with a small infant and had no knowledge of how the child grew to adulthood. The adoptee had no reliable account of the circumstances leading to her or his birth and no extended family as a point of reference for personal peculiarities. The desire to know (or fear of the disruption that knowledge might bring) may have become stronger in recent decades with the popularity of family history research using public records like marriage and birth certificates, the tracing of 'roots' by those who know their parents and grandparents. The invisibility of relinquishing mothers and adopted people in much of this work that celebrates the respectability of married childbearing is not a surprise. In addition, the adoptive parents are frequently reminded that, though they appear to be a 'normal family', they were unable to enact biological reproductivity within their respectable marriage; yet their visible family life renders any continuing pain of infertility invisible.

Technologies and motherhood

Medical technologies, with their potential to promote conception, to diagnose foetal abnormality, or to sustain the life of very small newborns, seem to present a resolution to some of the tensions of adoption by providing genetically related babies to a few more married couples. The technologies also offer new choices to specific women while changing the experience of motherhood for all women; what seems 'natural' may not be good enough. The technologies that offer assistance with conception, however, are only the most obvious of the technologies that shape motherhood. A range of other practices may also be regarded as cultural 'technologies'—child care services, images of motherhood in popular media, maternity leave provisions, patterns of housing and transport, for example. Among these are social practices that encourage or discourage motherhood in particular groups of women ranging from media beat-up of the ticking 'biological clock' through to the use of adoption to remove babies from inappropriate (i.e. young, black, drug-using) mothers. The practice of mid-trimester abortion of foetuses with certain abnormalities has also raised questions about the valuation of the lives of people with disabilities and the social policies needed to improve their participation in the wider society.

It would be a mistake to think that these recent events represent a significant break with the past. Just as the medical technologies are a part of several centuries of medical and social practice, the cultural technologies of motherhood also have a history. Handbooks for mothers began in early modern times drawing together many of the ideas about infant care, feeding, home management, and child development, and were being widely promoted by the late nineteenth century (Ehrenreich and English 1979; Badinter 1981; Dally 1982). During the late nineteenth and early twentieth centuries some of these ideas became the basis for expert knowledge in the fields of public health and social welfare. A range of social activists and new professionals promoted programs of social reform and contributed to both the development of the welfare state and the reconstruction of the experience of motherhood.

Many of the activists and the new professionals were women, some of the very women Summers argued were responsible for raising the status of motherhood. In a discussion of the rise of professional service provision in the 1950s and 1960s, Matthews noted the lack of a clear-cut distinction between women service providers and recipients:

> The nurse needed childcare in order to work, so too did the migrant factory worker. The social worker needed contraceptive advice, as did the Aboriginal teenager. The right of married women to work and to obtain maternity leave was not specific to class. (1984: 106)

The efforts of professionals and activists led to a redefinition of the apparent naturalness of motherhood (Reiger 1985). The social changes described as rationalisation by sociologist Max Weber in the late nineteenth century were applied to several domestic concerns in the early twentieth century. By the 1930s there was a strong movement promoting mothercraft training and 'the application of rational, scientific knowledge to the process of childbearing' (Reiger 1985: 139). Feeding by the clock was promoted even for very young breastfed babies and mothers were reprimanded for playing with their babies, offering dummies or carrying and cuddling fretful infants. Some, perhaps many, mothers ignored the reprimands and took care of babies without the interference of professionals (Reiger 1985: 148–9). The daily

149

lives of mothers were shaped not only by the needs of their children, but also by advice from women working as baby health nurses, kindergarten teachers, child welfare workers and others. The new women experts of course also faced the tensions between the individuality of particular babies and the generality of the rules; like other mothers faced with an overtired baby they sometimes 'broke the rules and gave a little nurse and held his hand' (Reiger 1985: 150).

Three-quarters of a century of 'expert' constructions of good womanhood has meant that ideas supporting motherhood as central to female identity are widespread and readily available to medical practitioners, journalists and other writers about assisted reproductive technologies (Van Dyck 1995). The practices of reproductive technologies rest on and are constructed by discursive technologies of gender, including representations of motherhood as the main or only form of subjectivity for adult women. There seems to be a return to a nostalgic, sentimental stance towards motherhood and family in film and advertising, with debates about surrogacy frequently turning on the biological nature of dominant mother–child relations (Kaplan 1992). Women seeking surrogates to grow babies for them are constructed in terms that are common in popular accounts of career women—cold, unfeeling and selfish—whereas surrogates are warm, nurturant and altruistic, perhaps so much so that they are prey to manipulation by men and cold women. Women in IVF programs are sometimes constructed (by feminists) as manipulated by husbands or patriarchal values (cf. Arditti et al. 1984; Spallone and Steinberg 1987; Scutt 1988) or (by anti-feminists) as previously manipulated by the ideology of permissiveness, so in a sense paying for past mistakes with infertility (Sandelowski 1990). Some religious opponents of the technologies try, not to attribute blame, but to limit the experience of pregnancy and birth to those who can become pregnant via sexual intercourse within a marital relationship (cf. Nichols and Hogan 1984; Daniel 1982). These accounts want to close the IVF programs and limit, for different reasons, the subject position 'mother' to women who can get pregnant using the traditional method.

Reproductive technologies have posed several problems for feminist writers and activists. The demand for access to safe contraception and abortion was shared by feminists, regardless of their perspective on the causes of women's subordination or their political priorities. A shared position about the technologies that assist conception has been less obvious. The claims and practices of the medical providers of IVF and related technologies were regarded with suspicion. To many activists they sounded like extensions of the professional attitudes and practices that feminists had criticised about doctors and reproductive health more generally (see chapter 2). The new treatments for infertility were experimental, of unproven worth and potentially dangerous to women's health (Klein 1989a). Nevertheless, they were offered to women as a 'choice' that would allow an opportunity for motherhood to a few more women. Though the success rates of the technologies were and still are not high (less than 20 per cent, except for donor insemination), the treatments have been regularly justified in terms of the anguish or desperateness of infertile people, especially women (Franklin 1990; Pfeffer 1987; Albury 1987). That 'desperateness' is frequently described as a failure to fulfil social norms that project a life story in which parenthood follows marriage. Indeed, childless women use the word themselves to explain why they began invasive and uncomfortable medical procedures and continued several courses of treatment. Yet, those women are describing a particular emotional state that changes over time, not the version of self-identity that seems to shape the popular press accounts of the new technologies.

The emphasis on feelings of desperateness raises another concern for feminist writers: assisted reproductive technologies reinforce the equation of womanhood with motherhood. There is a tension in the writing by feminists who oppose the technologies. While recognising the desire for children, they want 'women to say "no" to reproductive technology' as a result of knowledge of the dangers and limitations of the medical techniques (Klein 1989b: 49). Yet, the differences between the stories Klein reports and those reported by supporters of the technologies are matters of interpretation. The two IVF stories in chapter 1 report on similar treatment regimes, one successful for the couple and one not. Having 'the family we wanted' as a result of a variety of medical interventions over seven IVF cycles for two full-term pregnancies seemed acceptable to one woman, though she and her husband had decided to quit if the last cycle had been unsuccessful (Wood and Riley 1992: 42). However, three cycles that 'didn't work' led another to think the next one, with already-frozen embryos, would be her last (Stuart 1989: 82). Anne Stuart discussed the ambivalences involved in being on the IVF program: changed expectations in her marriage, continuing hope for a child, the frustration of life being at a standstill, shame about her inability to have a child, fears about the drugs, the tension of being able neither to 'drift along' in life nor to control the treatment process. For her, the apparently simple choice of staying on the program or leaving and accepting her infertility was more complex (Stuart 1989: 88–9).

A political campaign based on asking women with fertility problems to say 'no' to reproductive technologies does not address those complexities. This approach feels to many women like victim blaming because it asks for individual action in the face of a contradictory social problem. It argues that exploitation at the hands of doctors is the fate of 'desperate' women. The tension between the need to quit the program in order to continue in a life 'at a standstill' and the desire 'to be able to say well we did everything we possibly could' (Wood and Riley 1992: 49) may be a reflection of the pervasiveness of the assumption that women who are voluntarily not-mothers are morally flawed (Morell 1994). It is as if 'doing everything' is a demonstration of being a good woman, in the way that using highly effective contraception is a demonstration of good womanhood for a woman who is fertile. Feminists may be able to contribute to public debate in ways that begin to acknowledge the diversity of individual resolutions of infertility (Pfeffer 1987). The social meanings of the mother and the not-mother will have to be addressed in more sophisticated ways in order for the interventions to have the impact of 'a woman's right to choose'. This is not the place for a new slogan; it is already difficult enough to separate the idealised mother from the experiences of everyday women struggling with childbearing and childrearing. I will discuss some aspects of new contributions to the debates in the final chapter.

The public foetus and human rights

This chapter began with the assertion that the image of the foetus has come to represent human life. A number of visual technologies, beginning with photography, have made it possible for the foetus to have a public presence. In 1965, *Life* magazine published a series of now famous photographs of the 'beginning of life' by Lennart Nilsson. Those photos that showed a little figure in a bubble were of beautifully lit specimen foetuses that had been removed from dead women or, that were the result of a tubal pregnancy. In 1965 the optical fibre technology that makes fetoscopy possible was still in its early stages; only a small section of the foetus could be made visible on any one picture (Duden 1993: 14). The photographs of early foetuses have become commonplace; for example, such an image was on the cover of an issue of *The Australian Magazine* with a story debating the ethics of pre-natal diagnosis (Eccleston 1996). Also in 1996, *Life* Magazine featured similar photographs of foetuses from several species, including human, by Nilsson as a part of a story on scientific theories about the relatedness of mammals (Miller 1996). The frequent analogy used with these photos is of the foetus as an astronaut, protected by 'his' ship in space. Such a reading is only possible by treating the woman as absent or peripheral to the life of the foetus or as a threat to its existence (Petchesky 1987).

Ultrasound provides a much fuzzier picture of the foetus, but one that many pregnant women who can afford high-technology ante-natal care see. Obstetricians found ultrasound and other monitoring technology exciting because it removed their dependence on the woman for information about the foetus, which then became a second patient (Arney 1982). The 1960s were the experimental years of ultrasound, with doctors measuring various parts of the foetus in order to learn how to interpret the images (Oakley 1984; Petchesky 1987). They learned fast, and by 1982 a doctor could write about ultrasound 'stripping the veil of mystery from the dark inner sanctum, and letting the light of scientific observation fall on the shy and secretive fetus' (quoted in Hubbard 1984: 148). This kind of language makes it sound as if the woman is deliberately hiding the foetus instead of nurturing it and preparing its social existence. Or perhaps women have nothing to do with pregnancy and small foetuses are engaged in a secret frolic of their own.

If this representation of foetuses as second patients was the only effect of ultrasound, it would still be worth consideration because of the way it changes the experience of pregnancy for women. But there have been a couple of more worrying effects as well. The anti-abortion movement has used the images to lend the weight of science to their belief that human personhood begins at conception. The repeated use of the photographic images and the production of the video *The Silent Scream*, which purports to show an abortion in 'real time' ultrasound, have contributed to popular recognition of foetal images as babies (Petchesky 1987; Condit 1995). The popularisation of technical discourses serves to make the woman invisible by optical fibre and ultrasound imaging of the foetus. If, as a viewer, one identifies with the foetus as a subject, then the real, material, complex woman disappears and the imaginary mother takes her place. The human woman then may be measured against some version of the impossible 'perfect' mother or demonised as heartlessly seeking abortion (Petchesky 1987; Condit 1995), if not endangering the foetus through 'drug abuse' (Young 1995). The 'shy and secretive foetus' has become a political symbol, a public foetus. In the United States the public foetus also has gone to court against its traditional ally and necessary companion, its mother. Doctors and child protection officers have applied for and sometimes gained injunctions to require medical treatment against a pregnant women's will or to charge drug-taking pregnant women with 'child' neglect (Condit 1995; Daniels 1993). The construction of the public foetus has, in the striking phrase of Barbara Duden (1993), disembodied women.

The representation of the human foetus as life itself is a step beyond the argument for human rights for foetuses, which at least seems to leave open the possibility that women also have human rights. Unfortunately the usual interpretation of the claim also implies that women's rights are opposed to human rights. The current thinking about international human rights law by some feminists explains this strange conclusion by calling attention to the way in which the public/private distinction is present in the definitions of civil and political rights (Peters and Wolper 1995; Bahar 1996).

Human rights are there to protect men from public actions. That is, the 'right to life' in Article 6 of the *International Covenant on Civil and Political Rights* 'is concerned with the arbitrary deprivation of life or liberty through public action'. Just being a woman is risky in some societies, with threats to life from infanticide, cultural pressure to have sons or to feed sons more than daughters, poor access to health care, and both public and domestic violence. 'Yet the right to life is not regarded as extending these threats to women's lives' (Charlesworth 1995: 107). Feminists working for reproductive rights and the development of women's reproductive health services have produced many examples of violence against women by doctors and others in the public sphere related to reproduction; however, it has been hard to have these included as examples of human rights abuses (Hartmann 1987; Heise 1995; Cook 1995). The public foetus seems to have arrived in time to enjoy public rights. Women still struggle against being reduced to the background of human life rather than being full participants (cf. Bunch and Fried 1996).

The everyday experiences of motherhood continue to be elided into the institution of motherhood that Rich described in 1976. It is possible to analyse the processes that contributed to the building of the institutional relationships by state welfare provisions during the past century. But those relationships are constantly reconstituted by the cultural equation of Woman with Mother. The ease with which the public foetus has displaced the diverse experiences of everyday women is sobering for activists in reproductive politics. In the next chapter I will explore some of the ways that feminists themselves have contributed to cultural reconstructions of women, with contradictory results.

7 Acknowledging the Complexity of Fertility

I return to the device of storytelling I introduced in the first chapter because stories are a familiar way of making sense of disparate events. Eyewitness and first-person accounts are compelling reading, listening or viewing, but each story is only one person's observation or experience. Often when a number of stories are put side by side differences emerge making further interpretation necessary. Feminists have made it possible to speak of the differences, but have also tried to fit a single interpretation over the conflicting accounts on the grounds that all the experiences happened to women. Repeatedly some theorists and activists have reminded each other that the differences are profound and should be a part of any account of the lives of women. Just as frequently, the simple explanations creep back.

What follows are stories about how feminists have represented themselves and others while engaged in a variety of political struggles, which I have already discussed. There are feminist challenges to some of these representations, yet those critical analyses contribute to the reconstructions of gender. 'If the deconstruction of gender inevitably effects its (re)construction, . . . in which terms and in whose interest is the de-re-construction being effected?', de Lauretis asked (1987: 24). I will try to answer her question by examining the contradictory effects of the traces of the ongoing abortion campaigns in the constitution of assisted reproductive technologies as a public issue from 1980 to the present. I want to explore the possibility of thinking about a politics of human fertility and reproduction from outside the conventional heterosexual social contract without seeming to require the end of woman–man sexual contact and childrearing by different-sex couples. Such a politics would happen, to use a term from film making, 'elsewhere', off the main screen in that surrounding area that we must imagine in order to make sense of what we see on the screen (de Lauretis 1987: 25–6). It would mean developing a politics that would seriously challenge the institutions of heterosexuality and motherhood, without denying the complexity of the experiences of heterosex and motherhood for diverse women. This strikes me as difficult, but filled with possibility because it suggests that on the level of theory, at least, we can work towards a construction of subjectivity that is at once embodied and engendered in terms of race and class as well as sex (and all at the same time), and furthermore does not keep sliding into that equation Woman = Mother. The interactions of feminist and non-feminist women's demands with public policy making and professional practice have been caught in the con-tradictions of such a politics. The stories that follow demonstrate both the possibilities of changing the 'elsewhere' of reproductive politics and the constant pull of the institutional conventions of marriage, motherhood and family life.

A story about medicalised childbirth

When feminists address issues of reproduction, they respond to available representations of women, especially women as mothers or at least potentially reproductive beings. A number of stories can be told about the political processes whereby pregnancy and birth have been transformed from women's business into a medical event. Changing representations of birthing have been one part of this process, with labour and birth shifting from natural though not without danger to inherently pathological (Leavitt 1986). This shift has taken place during the codifications of knowledge that produced 'science' as a privileged form based on abstract theorising, differentiated from empirical practices or crafts. Privileged knowledge was certified by universities while trades were learned through a system of apprenticeship.

During the nineteenth century these processes came together as university-educated 'scientific' medical practitioners were strug-gling to gain ascendency over their 'craft-like' competitors, the empirical healers, among whom were midwives (cf. Friedson 1970; Arney 1982). Midwives and other healers learned their skills from older practitioners by watching and practising under close supervision. Women knew and trusted village or neighbourhood midwives who also often provided other kinds of health care beyond the skills of family members. As a part of the campaign to replace midwives as the authorised birth attendants, the university-educated male doctors faced serious problems of representation, both of themselves and of the reliability of midwives. Not surprisingly they attacked the problem on several fronts. While there is a large literature on aspects of this topic, the following short account is drawn from Donnison (1988), Barker-Benfield (1976) and Leavitt (1986).

In Britain, doctors claimed a monopoly on the use of obstetric instruments, building on the convention of the previous century in which male midwives had been called in to use forceps, the lever or posthumous caesarean section in order to remove a foetus alive or dead from the body of the woman, also alive or dead. This sexual division of obstetrical labour meant that the male midwives only rarely saw ordinary labour that resulted in a live birth. In addition, for most women, the presence of a male practitioner in the birthing room meant likely injury or death for herself, her foetus or both. To overcome this suspicion, doctors claimed that female midwives were responsible for high numbers of maternal and early infant deaths, especially for deaths from childbed fever. Poverty, ignorance, dirt and femaleness were posed against education, middle class sensibility and maleness in order to entice middle class women to use male doctors as birth attendants. University educations and middle class lifestyles were no substitute for careful hand-washing in the prevention of septicaemia, however.

In the United States, some nineteenth century medical educators claimed it was unnecessary for trainee doctors to view female genitals in order to learn about birth. Many young doctors thus had no practical knowledge when called upon to assist women in childbirth. Nevertheless, they felt they had to intervene in the process to demonstrate their superiority to traditional midwives. Leavitt (1986) reports some horrific obstetrical injuries as a result of the ignorant use of instruments. Neither side of that great struggle gives much credit for saving the lives of women and babies to the public health measures that produced fresher food, clean water and better sanitation for city and town dwellers.

Medical professionals took their campaign for a monopoly

over health service delivery to the legislators. Again, these campaigns took several forms and were played out differently in the particular circumstances of various countries. English midwives were placed under the supervision of doctors, losing their right to independent practice somewhat earlier than Australians. The shortage of doctors in country Australia meant that without midwives, some women might have no skilled help available during labour and birth (Donnison 1988; Willis 1983). In England and the United States during the nineteenth century, medical practitioners also campaigned for strict anti-abortion sections in the criminal law (Brookes 1988; Mohr 1978). The argument was based on a representation of the male medical practitioner as possessed of both scientific knowledge and an ethical stance based on principle. The doctor 'knew' what shameless women refused to recognise: the foetus was alive and growing before 'quickening'. The doctor could be relied upon to judge correctly the circumstances in which an abortion might be therapeutic, whereas a midwife might help a woman terminate a pregnancy out of sympathy and female solidarity. Here again, maleness was associated with rationality and femaleness with ignorance and unprincipled behaviour on the part of both the pregnant woman and the midwife. Legislation was passed from the beginning of the nineteenth century that ultimately served to authorise the medical definition of pregnancy and to establish a medical monopoly over legal abortion. University medical degrees also became the prerequisite for a medical licence.

Throughout the nineteenth and twentieth centuries the self-representation of doctors as a social category has used the entwined themes of scientific knowledge, development of new technology and techniques, and a heroic commitment to humankind. It would be easy to fill many pages with outrageous quotations from medical books, popular journals and speeches to medical associations. As only one example, the inventor of the speculum, from the south in the United States, assumed the persona of an explorer by asserting that his 1845 invention allowed him to see what no man had seen before: 'I felt like an explorer in medicine who views a new and important territory' (Sims cited in Barker-Benfield 1976: 95). With a different consciousness he might have made the more modest claim that he had invented a device to better allow a visual inspection of an area of the female body that had been culturally forbidden to the medical male gaze. Perhaps other males and females had seen, but were forbidden by modesty or convention from publishing an account of their experience, or perhaps they had seen in non-medical settings and so outside the range of the medical gaze entirely. Nevertheless, this invention and the heroic surgery Sims developed working on the bodies of young slave women, and later, poor urban women before trying it on middle class women produced fame and fortune, though perhaps not as much as his heart desired (Barker-Benfield 1976).

The promoters of ultrasound used similar language. So too do today's reproductive technologists. It is hard to imagine a pregnancy initiated using a new technique being announced with a modest speech about the social and historical conjuncture that has made possible the development and use of particular drugs and pieces of equipment. This is partly a result of the current competition for funding, partly of the shared language of sport, but also of the history of representation of medical science as work on the frontiers of knowledge. An early 1980s account of IVF justified the interference in 'the natural system of conception' with an appeal to the goals of medicine: 'Medicine has always had the objective of trying to overcome nature's defects . . . To deny man the objective of trying to overcome nature's errors is to obliterate a substantial portion of current medical practice' (Wood and Westmore 1983: 97).

Stories about reproductive women

The representation and self-representation of medical men as knowing subjects must be juxtaposed with the representation of women, in this case reproductive women, as objects of knowledge. Again, the infuriating quotations can be piled up from many sources over the past 150 years (at least). While one can cite the medical representations of women as little more than bodies around uteruses or bodies governed by hormones, or those of female pathologies that can be cured by motherhood, these representations have changed over time and were often developed in response to claims by women or changes in knowledge from outside the profession of medicine (Scully and Bart 1972; Koutroulis 1990; Leavitt 1986; Arney 1982).

As some women challenged dominant images of women through political campaigns and publication, some medical professionals drew on and developed previous representations to oppose the demands. In addition, medical discourses and social sciences were used to recommend legislative regulation in response to a variety of moral panics about motherhood, especially among the urban poor during this same period. Smart (1992) argues that English legal regulations of female sexuality and motherhood in the second half of the nineteenth century both constructed women's bodies as 'unruly', dangerous to the social order, and proposed married motherhood as the appropriate social protection.

The conflicting themes of women as irresponsible about reproduction or fertility and women as victims of 'biology' are not limited to the medical literature and debate about public policy on reproduction in the nineteenth century. Both of these representations of women were deployed by parliamentarians in the UK debate on the Abortion Act 1967 (Sheldon 1993). Opponents of the act held out the image of a feckless single young woman, a 'girl' who would turn to abortion in response to unwanted pregnancy as easily as she might see a dentist about a rotten tooth—might have an abortion because the pregnancy interfered with a planned holiday. Supporters, on the other hand, represented women seeking abortion as victims of drunken husbands, of poverty, of too many children too close together and of depression as a result of these social problems. Many parliamentarians thought that doctors were both able to distinguish the deserving from the undeserving and in some situations able to offer the sort of advice that would change a woman's mind about the need for an abortion. Thus, doctors were placed as both medical professionals and as agents of the welfare state, providing a remedy for those few women the social order had failed. These representations were soon proved wrong as all kinds of women applied for legal abortions once the act became practice. The National Health Service was unable to meet the demand, at least in part because of the mistaken representations in the public debate (Greenwood and Young 1976). It is also likely that the bill was passed because of the power of the representations of women as victims or minors in need of ethical and medical care by male doctors. Neither of the positions about abortion law reform challenged the notions of women as mothers or doctors as responsible professionals.

Similar representations have been deployed in Australian parliamentary abortion debates, but with changes. Women were portrayed as either irresponsibly rejecting 'the central essence of womanhood' (NSW, Legislative Council 1988: 1334) by adopting an unfeminine and selfish attitude of individualism or as potential victims of their own refusal of motherhood. Concern has been

161

expressed by both opponents and supporters of legal publicly funded abortion that women might turn to abortion rather than use reliable birth control to prevent unwanted pregnancy. Doctors have been presented in a more contradictory way than in the 1967 debate in the United Kingdom. While many parliamentarians did not question the ability of doctors to make ethical judgments, opponents of abortion recognised that doctors could not be relied upon to share the most conservative ethical position; hence there was also a concern with the doctor who would abuse the system (Albury 1994). Here the representation of doctors was not that of the detached ethical professional, but rather was that of the greedy unprincipled businessman.

No abortion debate I have read has seriously challenged the notion that women are mothers. Indeed, parliamentary and some extra-parliamentary supporters of access to abortion seem to cast the termination of particular pregnancies in terms that reinforce the motherly responsibility of women. Some women can be good mothers by refusing to give birth to babies they cannot afford for financial or emotional reasons or if the needs of that particular foetus when grown to babyhood would compromise the care of existing children or others who depend on the woman. De Lauretis (1987) suggests that the representation of Woman as Mother destabilises the attempt to question the 'natural' motherliness of women. Claiming that some aborting women display the characteristics of maternal sacrifice and responsibility undermines the feminist attempt to represent women as able to refuse motherhood. This is the tactic identified by de Lauretis as 'one of the most deeply rooted effects of the ideology of gender', the reduction of the complexity of women's lives to 'a simple equation: women = Woman = Mother' (1987: 20).

The feminist critiques of representations of women as sexually passive and desiring only motherhood have served as points of resistance to the hegemonic discourses of masculine heterosexuality (cf. de Lauretis 1987: 18). Feminists have promoted an independent female sexuality ranging across lesbian separatism, non-penetrative heterosexual practices, positively valued celibacy, more egalitarian heterosexuality and woman-defined procreation. Yet, only the feminist language of choice was incorporated into the more popular discourses, not the more radical aspects of the challenges to the notion of passive maternity. The rhetoric of contraceptive choice seems to have effected a reconstruction of women as heterosexually active, responsible contraceptors who have one or two planned children. This reconstruction preserves a range of benefits: to heterosexual men who can expect freedom from concerns about unintended pregnancy; to medical professionals who have a monopoly on the delivery of the most highly recommended contraceptives; and of course to the drug companies; as well as to women who do benefit from possibilities for greater sexual freedom and increased decision making about childbearing. I am arguing not that activists should not have engaged in the political and intellectual work that has made that 'de-re-construction' possible, but that the task is not finished.

Launched in 1993, the Family Planning Choices Charter demonstrated the need for continuing the task of critically analysing dominant representations of women. The charter sought to intervene in the polarised abortion debate and to reduce the number of abortions by promoting social and medical research, the inclusion of 'comprehensive sexuality education' in personal development programs in schools, the wider diffusion of contraceptive information and education of men about their responsibility in sexual relationships (Larriera 1993; FFPA 1993). Many of the charter's recommendations were laudable in themselves, but there were several problems with its presentation. It accepted without question the conservative assertion that current abortion rates are unacceptably high by citing US President Ronald Reagan's surgeon-general, Dr. C. Everett Koop, without discussing the comparability of data about abortion in the United States and Australia. It was silent about the political investments that compelled Koop, a man 'well known for his anti-abortion views', to recommend a program for reducing abortions in the face of the continuing 'high' rates of unintended and unwanted pregnancies despite information about the safety of abortion.

The 'most important aim' of the charter, 'to ensure that easy-to-understand information on the need for effective contraceptive use is available to reduce the number of unplanned pregnancies', is problematic in terms of the common-sense understandings of gender. An 'educative, preventive approach to the issue of abortion' reinforces popular expectations that fertility can always be controlled and that morally responsible women become pregnant as a rational choice, with abortion a necessity for a minority of women in exceptional circumstances. That approach contradicts the experience of women for whom contraception fails and requires that those women feel ashamed that they have 'failed' to be 'good' women (cf. Ripper 1993; Horin 1993: 20). With no counter to common-sense notions of masculinity and femininity in the charter, the recommendations are likely to promote information, public discussion and medical practice that recognise heterosexually active women as 'good' or 'responsible' only when they avoid abortion (see chapter 4). The Choices Charter was an approach to abortion in which the varied and contradictory meanings of women's experiences of sexuality and reproduction were ignored and a range of experts were called upon to 'reduce the need for abortion' and thus reduce the heat of the abortion debate. It demonstrates that the attempts to secure services for women are open to destabilisation when they rely on discourses that seek to define and confine women as both heterosexual and reproductive.

The rush to report Naomi Wolf's 1995 'discovery' of the ambivalence that many women feel about abortion was more problematic than attempts to reduce the heat in the abortion debate by calling for better access to birth control. Wolf's views were authorised by her status as an international icon. Her desire to cast the abortion debate in terms of 'sin and redemption' in an article reprinted in the *Weekend Australian* (1995) was deeply disturbing for many feminists. During the 1970s abortion had a clear symbolic meaning for feminists—freedom and choice. The abortion of an unwanted pregnancy represented for women a way out of a closed domestic role, an opportunity to have some greater measure of control over their lives, freedom from the stigma of continuing the pregnancy and from the pain of relinquishing the child. The feminist slogan 'Abortion Is a Woman's Right to Choose' came into widespread popular use. It was also used by anti-feminists as a marker of unwomanly behaviour, a condensation of all the evils of feminism. Womanly women, it seemed, were always ready to put aside their personal concerns for the needs of others even if the other was an unexpectedly conceived foetus.

Now in the 1990s the symbolism is more mixed. Freedom is sometimes read as irresponsibility; choice is too frequently read as simple consumerism. The relationship between politics and personal life has been reversed from the heady days of the assertion that 'the personal is political'. Instead of there being an analysis that perceives personal experience as a consequence of social power relations, personal experience is being used to generalise from the particular to the universal. Unbelievably this can mean that a public feminist like Naomi Wolf can argue that because she thinks of her welcome four-month foetus as her 'baby', it and all foetuses *are* babies and that all pregnant women should value their foetuses as she does. Further she reinforces that powerful guilt-inducing argument of right-to-lifers when discussing a mid-trimester foetus, 'looks like a baby, therefore is a baby', even while asserting her continued support for legal abortion.

In chapter 6 I discussed some of the effects of ultrasound and fibre optics which allow the visualisation of a foetus as separate from those of a pregnant woman. If a foetus can be represented as separate, then it is easier to think of it as separable rather than as completely dependent. In addition, it is now possible to use visual technologies to diagnose certain foetal abnormalities before birth. The foetus then ceases to be in some sense unknown and turns into another patient with needs separate from those of the pregnant woman. Using the same technology, anti-abortionists urge women to see their foetuses as separate and already the babies they could become.

When she re-stated this rhetorical move, Wolf put the spotlight on pregnant women and their behaviour, not on the wider cultural context or even the social relations in which the pregnancy occurred. She supported her assertion that feminists should think about abortion in more religious terms with anecdotes about a couple of middle class high school girls who took sexual risks (Wolf 1995: 27). This individualisation of social issues poses difficulties for feminist politics in a time of family values versus feminism rhetoric. Naomi Wolf may continue to think that many abortions are morally justified by the circumstances of the pregnant women, but those who oppose access to abortion services do not agree. Wolf seemed to agree with critics of open access to abortion that some women are not as deserving of abortions. Less deserving women are those who do not articulate 'reasons' for terminating the pregnancy that she supports: poverty or failed contraception. In an analysis of the longer version of Wolf's article that appeared in the United States, Leslie Cannold (1998: 25-7) points to the reiterated fear that 'trivial, selfish women' might have abortions for 'trivial, selfish reasons'.

In *Fire With Fire* (1993), Wolf argued that accepting responsibility is a necessary component of the demand for rights. In the same section, she reported that her own history of careful contraception was the result of fear of being 'at the mercy of [her] reproductive system' and an intuitive feeling that she would feel guilty about having an abortion. She collapsed the political concept of rights for groups (women) with the individual use of those rights and the moral responsibilities that may accompany them. She also projected her own fears about loss of control onto other women who might find that an abortion is a way to reassert control. Furthermore, there is no obvious reason to rule out having an abortion as a responsible action for a woman faced with an unplanned and unwanted pregnancy. Women who have described their decisions about pregnancies emphasise the importance of the complex web of responsibilities in their lives (Gilligan 1982; Ryan et al. 1994; Cannold 1998).

Feminists, like most people, may deplore the circumstances of some women's lives that make taking sexual risks likely, but I think it is dangerous to suggest that risk-taking is 'wicked'. I say this because opponents of abortion argue that all abortion is 'wicked' and no reason is 'good enough'. While Wolf does not suggest that risk-taking women should be denied abortions, plenty of opponents of abortion would deny abortions to most women in order to 'teach' the lesson of moral responsibility. Yet, Wolf's argument rests on the assumption that because some or even many women feel 'bad' after an abortion that means that the abortion itself was morally wrong. Women feel bad about many decisions or events in their lives that do not call for analyses within the framework of 'sin and redemption' (Cannold 1998: 25–6).

Two years later, Wolf continued to be promoted as a feminist who 'had second thoughts about abortion' and as a woman who broke some kind of feminist taboo about recognising ambivalent feelings about abortion (Abraham 1997: 57, 60). This representation and self-representation is both a denial of the diversity of the feminist politics and scholarship about abortion and a recuperation of a standard media representation of most feminists as out of touch with the feelings and lives of 'ordinary' women. The assertion that many or some women have only silly, trivial reasons for abortions has been repeated again and again by opponents of access to abortion, including members of the WA parliament during the law reform debates in 1998.

Leslie Cannold's work on how women think about the abortion decision slips into the reduction of the complexity of women's lives to the equation of Woman = Mother when she argues that the 'abortion debate' could be renamed the 'motherhood debate' (1998: 110–11). The pro- and anti-choice women that she interviewed discussed the morality of abortion first in terms of the familiar conflicting rights of the woman and the foetus, then in terms of the responsibilities of motherhood. Both groups of women thought that pregnant women had certain moral responsibilities to any foetus, and they shared aspects of a definition of a 'good mother' which included a willingness to make sacrifices for a child. While the anti-abortion women thought this responsibility entailed continuing an unplanned and unwanted pregnancy and finding a way to rearrange their lives to enable them to keep and raise the resulting child, pro-choice women disagreed. The pro-choice women thought that abortion was a morally justifiable form of 'care' for specific foetuses within their understandings of the meanings of mothering children. Since both groups of women thought that the bonds with the foetus established during pregnancy made the alternative of adoption unacceptable for themselves, continuing a pregnancy was, in a sense, an expression of their willingness to mother a child. They differed on the level of sacrifice implied by the equation Good Mother = Good Woman (Cannold 1998: 58–117).

The women made judgments within what Cannold calls a 'moral circle'; that is, they thought that some abortions were morally justified and that others were not. Even anti-choice women expressed ambivalence about requiring a young woman who was raped or the victim of incest to continue a pregnancy to term; some were willing to consider abortion for themselves if the pregnancy was the result of rape. Even pro-choice women expressed ambivalence or disapproval towards a hypothetical situation posed by Cannold, in which a woman who might use pregnancy as a means to better athletic performance, aborting after the meet (Cannold 1998: 127–9). The extreme cases served to demonstrate that most women are willing to draw moral lines that include and exclude specific pregnancies. This is a good way to talk about what individual women do when making fertility decisions. They think about specific situations, their own immediate contexts and social relationships. This is only partly about motherhood, however, so to reframe the moral debate about abortion as a moral debate about motherhood serves to hide the other things it is about.

Cannold mentions some of those other things: male control over women, the moral meanings of human foetuses, trust in women as ethical decision makers, the role of powerful social institutions in the constitution of femininity and masculinity. She points to the danger of institutionalising the moral circle in panels of people who would test women's decisions, but finds it difficult to place her insights about women's moral decision making into the political debate. She is not alone: this is one of the most difficult problems in reproductive politics.

There is an apparent impasse in wanting to defend access to

abortion services while taking seriously the moral aspects of terminating a pregnancy. One way out is to resist taking the either/or stance towards moral reasoning and political action suggested by the assertion that the demand for political rights implies a rejection of moral reasoning. Activists need to analyse the uses of moral reasoning within the political discourses. Morality, especially the morality that defines 'good mothers', is a technology of gender and is totally implicated in the power relations in which women live their lives. Having a political right does not always mean that each citizen exercises that right in the most responsible manner. Reproductive rights activists may have to find the words to publicly acknowledge their own ambivalences about some abortion decisions. At the same time they will have to resist, as Cannold does, any calls to 'police' decision making or to establish a 'best practice' abortion decision-making process that assumes economic security, high-level verbal skills, consistent contraceptive use and a familiarity with approved patterns of rational decision making. In the face of media demands for talk in short 'grabs', and in view of the cultural status of motherhood and the widespread desire for certainty and simple explanations, expressions of ambivalence and ambiguity are very difficult. They are unlikely to be any easier regarding abortion than they have been about assisted reproductive technologies.

Stories about new technologies

Many of the interventions in the debates about IVF and related reproductive technologies have questioned the equation Woman = Mother. The media images of women with fertility problems as 'desperate' and willing to endure anything in hope of a baby, of family life as the only source of fulfilment for women, or of doctors as only interested in benefiting patients, have all been challenged. There is a danger that these challenges will be incorporated into a reconstruction of womanhood that is not necessarily of any more benefit to women than the one it replaced. In addition to the particular feminist accounts I discuss here, there are accounts of analyses of notable examples of abuses of the new reproductive technologies from other perspectives. Many feminists have included discussions of some aspects of the social issues raised by the technologies as cases of particular theoretical problems; for example, Pateman (1988: 209–18) considered 'surrogate mother' contracts as a part of her exploration of women

and the concept of contract in liberal p
(1994) used a variety of ethical proble
interventions in human reproduction to p
weakness of ethical theory to take acc‹
sexual difference. New reproductive te‹
an explosion of publishing, with schol‹
addressing the challenges raised by the

The policy debates about the prac
tion have been informed by the mo1
interventions. Health activists have raised quesuu... ..
term effects of drugs and other medical interventions on women
and their children. Welfare activists have provided a language
and speaking positions that have challenged the smug assumptions
about adoption practice. Few today assume that once the baby
was handed over the birth mother 'got on with her life' or that
the new 'family' that was formed by the adopting couple and
the baby would be exactly like nuclear families formed as a result
of procreation by a husband and wife. These interventions have
developed as a part of the broader feminist project of resistance
to dominant discourses of heterosexuality that represent women
in terms of their reproductive relationships to men as virgin
daughters or fecund wives. They have tried to break down the
claims that the resolution of the social problems of childlessness
is properly the domain of medical practice following a diagnosis
of 'infertility'. In doing so, however, some activists have engaged
in rhetorical practices that create a sharp distinction between male
medical scientists and female infertility service clients. In doing
so they rely on versions of the gendered assumptions they were
attempting to challenge: the power of masculine rationality and
'natural' biological victimisation of women.

In the attempt to call into question the language and practices
of doctors working in reproductive technologies, some feminist
arguments introduce a rhetorical demonisation of the doctors,
calling them 'pharmacrats', 'technodocs' (Corea 1985) or 'tech-
nopatriarchs' (Rowland 1987), who 'mine women's bodies'
(Spallone 1989) and/or turn women into 'mother machines'
(Corea 1985), 'baby machines' (Scutt 1988) or 'living laboratories' (Rowland 1992) while speaking 'reprospeak' (Rowland
1992). It is easy to demonstrate that doctors do not necessarily
work to benefit women. Indeed, the doctors themselves have
provided the material for this representation by their inappropriate
reassurances that greater success is only a matter of time
(Trounson and Wood 1981) and that reproductive technology

efficient or produce 'better' babies than procreation
from heterosexual intercourse; by the use of a technical
that reduces women to body parts and chemicals (Leung
1983), sometimes using agricultural metaphors (e.g. egg
resting); and by their willingness to subject women to medical
intervention as a treatment for male infertility (Matson et al.
1986). Women who seek medical assistance in their attempt to
become pregnant have complained that they were not treated
with dignity (Klein 1989a). Doctors themselves focused on
research success rather than client satisfaction, changing some of
the process only in response to a high 'drop out' rate that made
it hard to discover how many attempts it would take to achieve
a pregnancy (Mao and Wood 1984; Kovacs 1986). But demonisation is little more than the obverse of the medical self-representation as ethical scientists who work selflessly to meet human
needs. The critical analysis of that particular representation needs
to be done in a way that moves away from the good and evil
dichotomy, the characterisation of science and technology as the
domain of men, or the popularisation of the notion that doctors
somehow give women babies.

The problem with demonisation is that it does not challenge
the power claimed by the profession but argues that it is power
with evil effects; the benign, rational and scientific helper of
women is replaced with a dehumanised and malignant figure, the
'technodoc'. More modest representations of doctors might assert
that doctors are part of interlocking social processes as their
clients are. Medical scientists practise certain experimental and
sometimes dangerous techniques that allow a few more women
to grow their own babies rather than acting as a vanguard for
an attempt to destroy women (Rowland 1984). Given the robust-
ness of the strategies of the profession, its critics have to work
particularly hard to promote changes in the current self-representation, rather than assist in its reassertion.

In an account of the deployment and transformation of power
in the profession of obstetrics, William Arney identified four
strategies that have been used by the profession since its struggle
with midwives:

> appeals to ethics and other aspects of 'professionalism,' manip-
> ulation of the public's views of birth by exploitation of meta-
> phors developed earlier, the touting of 'advances' which would
> have been impossible but for the ideological changes and fragile
> structural reforms effected earlier, and the ability to rebuff or
> ignore critics of their practices. (1982: 49–50)

Medical practitioners involved in reproductive technologies use each of these strategies. Experiments with egg freezing have been justified as providing an ethical alternative to embryo freezing (*Age* 7.3.85), though embryo freezing itself was earlier described as an 'ethical obligation' (Trounson et al. 1982). The public view that fertility, pregnancy and birth are controllable by safe, modern medical practices is manipulated to gain support for experimental interventions in cases of infertility (Leeton et al. 1984). Technological advances used in obstetrics and gynaecology during the 1980s were claimed to be the result of IVF research (Trounson 1987). The 'ability to rebuff or ignore critics' has been reinforced by the recruitment of supporters in the fields of law and ethics (Singer and Wells 1984), and by appeals to the social acceptance of women's agency in reproductive decision making as a justification of reproductive technologies as a part of the increased 'choices' for women who cannot become pregnant (Jansen 1988). This process has contributed to public perceptions of IVF and related technologies shifting from potentially dangerous experimental procedures to mainstream medical treatment, in other countries as well as Australia (Van Dyck 1995).

Confrontation with these strategies is more likely to happen in campaigns that challenge the patterns of medical and health service decision making rather than in those that issue calls to outlaw particular practices related to reproduction alone. Reproduction-related critiques have been the site for the recuperation of cultural constructions of woman as mother by anti-feminist opponents of the technologies as well as by feminists interested in stopping the exploitation of women. In addition, during the nineteenth century, the opposed figures of the medical practitioner and the reproductive woman were deployed in campaigns that led to the criminalisation of abortion, midwife deregistration and medical monopoly. It is important to develop a critical stance that avoids essentialising conclusions like 'women's bodies must have the same freedom from intervention, intrusion, and invasion as men's' (Raymond 1987: 65). Men with prostate disease or polyps in their colon experience a distressing amount of 'intervention, intrusion and invasion'. The widespread assumption that medical technology can or ought to 'cure' any physical problem in the human body is the context of the enthusiasm for reproductive technology, not the limit of its application. The focus on specific medical practices or the apparent contrast between the treatment of women and men draws attention away from the institutional and cultural structures and processes that reproduce the individual instances of exploitation.

Family stories

The abuses of a past attempt to regulate female reproductive capacities in the name of the family have been the basis of a powerful intervention in the policy debate about reproductive technologies, with the development of an analogy between adoption and surrogacy or gamete donation. A strong feminist intervention in the debates has relied on discussions of the importance of the mother–child bond and the role of knowledge of genetic parentage in the construction of personal identity (Dietrich 1990). The adoption experience is used as an analogy both for surrogacy—in which a woman grows a baby and after birth hands it over to a couple to raise—and for sperm, egg or embryo donation—in which gametes or embryos are made available to a woman so she can become pregnant and grow the baby she and her partner will raise. None of these alternatives to conventional baby-making by sexual intercourse and childrearing by biological parents is without problems. However, it is unclear whether the problems are best set out in a simple analogy with the past closed adoption practice of the 1950s through to the 1970s. Indeed, in many arguments it is not clear what the 'lessons' of adoption are in the particular technology being considered.

What are the problems with adoption? The literature suggests that the silences that surrounded all participants are at the centre of the problems. Since that silence was a part of a lie, there is also distrust and anger at adults who make decisions without considering the consequences for future offspring. It is not a denial of the pain and confusion felt by the parties to adoption to suggest that there are other secrets in families, other sources of feelings of difference, and other sources of distrust and anger. The much publicised examples of the surrogacy arrangements between the Kirkman sisters in Victoria (Kirkman and Kirkman 1988; Docherty 1993) and Vickie Hillary and her sister Susan Ferry in Western Australia (Pritchard 1993) suggest silence can be avoided, that children can understand the circumstances of their births and good family relations be maintained. Yet, other sisters have not found the relationship easy; in response to American Lori-Jean Jasso's ambivalence about giving up the child to her sister, the sister moved away and continued to refuse contact with her. Jasso believed that the child was unaware of its origins in an informal and do-it-yourself surrogacy arrangement (Lewis 1993). The coercion of women to give up their children and to maintain silence about their experience under the adoption regime might also be difficult in families, though a different kind of coercion might be deployed to prove love through having a baby for a sister, daughter or other close relation as seems to have occurred in Jasso's family (Meggitt 1991).

The greatest number of known surrogacy arrangements is not between sisters or close friends, however, but between strangers. In commercial arrangements, the pregnancy is frequently achieved by insemination of the surrogate with the sperm of the man in the couple who will raise the hoped-for child. The resulting child is therefore the biological child of the birth mother and the 'commissioning' man. While there has been judicial recognition of contract to bear and give up children in the United States, such contracts are deemed unenforceable in all Australian jurisdictions. In addition, all children are considered to be the child of the woman who gives birth and her legally recognised partner (not a sperm donor).

The distress that some commercial surrogates feel after giving up the child is represented in part as a result of the broken mother–child bond. As the pregnancy progresses women who previously thought that they were having the sperm donor's child begin to feel that it is, indeed, their own baby. Even without the analogy of adoption, this is no surprise. There are problems with using the notion of a biologically based mother–child bond to explain the distress, however. In the immediate post-World War II period the notion of maternal bonding was used to encourage women to stay at home and provide full-time care for children. Social problems were explained as the result of the failure of women to bond with their babies; thus urging 'us to look inward to our biology for solutions to major social ills' (Arney 1982: 173). To extend the explanation backwards to include pregnancy is to reinforce the individualising of the problems that have arisen from adoption and may arise from surrogacy arrangements.

In much of the public discussion of surrogacy, there is a collapsing of what seems to be an easily defined physical experience of pregnancy and birth with the more varied social meanings attributed to those experiences at any given time. Opponents of surrogacy point to the strong maternal feelings that develop for many women during pregnancies which will continue into mother–child relationships. These feelings develop well before birth as women who experience grief following miscarriage can attest (Borg and Lasker 1981; Oakley et al. 1984). It seems to me that one source of the ongoing pain of relinquishment is the denial of mixed feelings in most social explanations of the act of giving up the baby. There is an attempt to fix the meaning of a complex and contradictory act, to make what was once an adequate justification or meaning last forever. Women who gave up babies for adoption thought their reasoned 'consent' should preclude feelings of loss, and women who act as surrogates think the selflessness of their 'gift' of a child will preclude other feelings (Meggitt 1991). These women report both their own surprise and a lack of support when they express feelings of loss, betrayal, anger or a desire to see or to care for the child. Women who suffer serious depression following the birth of a wanted child also experience the contradiction between the simple story of joyful motherhood and their more complex reaction. Few women are completely unambivalent about motherhood, even when they are content with their reproductive experiences and positive about relationships with their children or their nieces and nephews. This could hardly be otherwise in a culture that collapses complex experiences of womanhood into simplistic images of motherhood.

Women who regret acting as surrogates and relinquishing their babies describe themselves as having acted out of a self-representation of generous womanhood. A part of their sense of self was tied to self-sacrifice and a desire to please. They also felt sorry for women without children and found it hard to imagine themselves without the identity of mother. When they look back on the pregnancy they remember feeling cared for and valued, perhaps more so than ever before. Either late in the pregnancy or after the birth of the baby, the identity as mother to this particular child began to contradict the generosity and desire to help an unfortunate woman. As one regretful woman reported, '[T]he baby I promised was theoretical. The baby I wanted to keep was real' (Meggitt 1991). She and others found that they felt used, were unable to mediate the experience to their other children and sometimes became estranged from family members. They became doubly 'bad' mothers, unable to live up to either side of the tension: no longer cheerfully self-sacrificing, nor able to keep the loved baby. Women who have broken their agreement and kept their baby have sometimes lost their husbands who were unable to live with another man's child (Rowland 1992: 156–94). These women, like those who regret giving up a baby, have found the tensions of their previous notions of 'good' womanhood impossible to reconcile with their feelings.

The difficulties faced by individual women are reflected in the feminist literature on surrogacy. Shanley (1993) has claimed that feminist arguments cluster around two positions: women as free individuals with rights to make choices about their bodies including their reproductive activities; and women as people with strong commitments to the recognition and preservation of non-contractual relationships. The experiences of the women who found their surrogacy arrangements too difficult suggest the situation is even more complicated. Surrogacy may require a woman to preserve one set of relationships (with the commissioning parties or her partner) rather than another (with the child she gestated), even if the contract is not legally binding. Feminist political philosophers have pointed to the inability of liberal democratic notions of autonomy and rights to adequately account for the dilemmas facing pregnant citizens. The focus on pregnant citizens serves as a telling reminder that no citizen, male or female, is completely free from ties with other citizens and therefore that no contract is in practice made between two abstract and freely choosing individuals. Likewise, the existence of conflicting non-contractual relationships may point to the limits of the alternative offered by the ethic of care (Gilligan 1982; Tronto 1993). The shift in focus to responsibilities in relationships does not guarantee that several compelling personal responsibilities will not be in conflict in a way similar to the frequently discussed conflict among rights. Shanley concludes that the experiences of women will contribute to a better political theoretical understanding of the 'individual-in-relationship' (1993: 636). In addition, I would suggest that contributions towards this theory will need to be careful to avoid reducing the diversity of women's experience into a single understanding of motherhood as a defining relationship and identity, thus reconstituting the familiar gendered representations of liberal democratic citizens.

As popular knowledge of genetics has increased there have been appeals to the importance of genetic 'heritage' as the basis of identity in discussions of surrogacy and some aspects of IVF. Reproductive scientists have suggested that gametes and embryos are the same as kidneys or blood and can be donated in the same way. A powerful challenge to this argument relies on another part of the analogy with adoption: the confusion that some adopted people feel about their identity (Dietrich 1991; van Keppel 1991; Ley 1992; Lewis 1993). People who were conceived by donor insemination have also raised similar questions about the need to know their genetic heritage as a part of knowing themselves (Robinson 1997). Like the notion of bonding, the concept of a genetic basis of personal identity serves to individualise a social issue, to reduce it to a concern of specific individuals. Yet, the claim made by medical practitioners that the pregnant woman can avoid the contradictions of surrogacy through IVF and the use of an embryo created from the gametes of the commissioning couple needs serious criticism. A foetus is not 'carried' around as if hidden in the boot of a car for nine months; a woman is pregnant. She feels the growing foetus and conducts her life among people who expect pregnant women to become mothers. While supporters of IVF-assisted surrogacy also use a genetic argument as an individual solution to a complex social issue, it may be politically more effective for feminists to challenge directly the notion that a woman can emotionally ignore her pregnant embodiment while acting as a surrogate. The argument that centres on the genetic basis to personal identity for the resulting child does not address the reduction of the complexity of the experience of pregnancy for all women implied in the suggestion that it is easy for a woman to separate her physical, social and emotional responses. A few women have said it was important for them to have gestated an embryo made from their sister's egg, but these few got pregnant quickly with embryo transfer. No one talks about the number who have not, or about the added potential for physical and emotional complications for the two women involved.

While considerable energy is devoted to various analyses of 'woman' and 'mother', representations of 'man' and 'father' are relatively unquestioned in feminist as well as popular literature about ART. Men's desire for a child is trivialised or seen as a form of exploitation of women or reduced to the aspects of fatherhood that are subject to claims in legal proceedings: biological paternity and legal inheritance. Reproductive scientists, on the other hand, offer micro-injection of sperm in the context of an IVF program as a way to provide a biologically related child for the infertile or sub-fertile husband of a fertile woman. The relatively successful process of donor insemination is replaced by the frequently unsuccessful process of IVF. In addition, the man's desire to have his 'own' child within marriage in spite of the inability of his sperm to fertilise eggs is accepted as a reason for a woman to undergo a series of medical and surgical interventions. There are relatively few attempts to challenge the representation of fatherhood as necessarily implying a biological rather than a social connection, though the husbands of surrogates sometimes are represented as 'fathers' by virtue of closeness with their wives during pregnancy. The previously discussed notions of genetic heritage as a part of identity provide further support for the biological definitions of fatherhood.

Robyn Rowland (1992) includes a section titled 'The Commissioning Party' in the surrogacy chapter of *Living Laboratories*, a strong radical feminist attack on reproductive technologies. She discusses couples who have a child by adoption or in which one partner has a child by a previous relationship. In her account she argued that in the publicity about these cases '[T]he emphasis is on the genetic relationship for *men*' (Rowland 1992: 181, original italics); indeed the main focus of the section was men. It seems to me that these are not 'bad' men, just as the relinquishing mothers were not 'bad' women, but rather men caught in a representation of manhood that included having their 'own' child. Rowland relied on second-hand accounts about the cases to discuss the meaning of infertility and surrogacy for the partners of these men. Yet the media accounts of particular surrogacy relationships are written in the social context in which many more couples seek to complete their self-representation as a committed couple by having their 'own' child. Even (or especially) G-rated comedies represent the problems of raising children who are hers, his and 'ours'. The cultural representation marriage = parenthood is as powerful as any representation of gender.

The notion that every life partnership (marriage) should be marked by biological offspring in spite of previous sterilisation or even age of the partners has received little attention by critics of reproductive technologies. It only seems to become problematic when the woman is unable to become pregnant by sexual intercourse. Then, the question of using limited medical resources is raised, especially when childless couples are on waiting lists with those who have children from previous relationships. For some women and men, a chosen sterilisation for contraception in one partnership may become the pain of infertility in the next. For couples, the inability to achieve pregnancy may be a bigger issue when one partner has children from a previous relationship and the other is childless. In late 1993, there was media coverage of the use of donor eggs and IVF by reproductive medicine practitioners to enable an older post-menopausal woman to have a baby with (for) her younger, though middle-aged, partner; the effects of her age on the growing child were the focus of criticism (Van Dyck 1995). I doubt if the same storm of condemnation would have arisen had she been a woman in her mid-thirties who had experienced a 'premature menopause'. The assumptions behind the equation of parenthood with marriage deserve greater attention from feminists since the birth of a child is a powerful symbol of commitment to adulthood and to a relationship for so many women and men.

Feminists had criticised the ideal of self-sacrificing womanhood before any of the women currently describing their experiences became surrogates. That critique was marginal to the hegemonic discourses of religion, family obligation and selfless generosity that played an important role in the constitution of many women. Yet, in the critical accounts of feminine sacrifice there seems to be a willingness to accept motherly care as an unproblematic feminine value (Dietrich 1991; Meggitt 1991). Just as the shame of being caught with an unwanted or unsanctioned pregnancy silenced women who gave up children for adoption or sought abortions, the shame of inappropriate 'unmotherly' feelings may silence other women. Certainly the popular notion that giving birth means having the ability to take physical and emotional responsibility for the baby means too many women cannot get assistance until they injure or kill their children. Therefore, representations of women in campaigns against the promotion of the use of so-called surrogate mothers as simply another treatment modality may also contribute to the portrayal of reproductivity in ways that do not benefit women.

Obviously, the representation of pregnancy as merely instrumental and the growing and giving of a baby as being like babysitting needs to be challenged, since these representations are not congruent with either the dominant cultural representations of pregnancy or the self-representation of both contented and regretful surrogate/birth mothers. While arguments that rely on appeals to maternal feelings and mother–child bonds as 'natural' or 'what every mother knows' have a powerful political and emotional appeal, they also effect the constitution of women as 'natural' mothers, one of the representations of women the promoters of surrogacy, and reproductive technologies more generally, also use.

Challenges for the next decade

To argue either that all women need children or that no woman can give up a child after birth is to reinforce the equation

178

Woman = Mother. It is an argument that does not necessarily benefit the diversity of women living everyday lives rather than abstracted ahistorical existences. This is all the more important in the late 1990s with the rhetoric of 'family values' being used to justify all manner of defunding of community services. Woman the nurturer, Woman the self-sacrificing Mother, seems to be a shadowy figure just out of sight, expected to fill the gaps. It may seem like too big a leap to suggest that the reconstruction of motherhood in the reproductive technology debates helps conservative governments cut benefits. I do not want to suggest a simple cause and effect relationship; rather I wish to issue a reminder that the stories circulating in a culture are not respecters of analytic boundaries. Indeed, a variety of news stories are indicators of attempts to reinstate the traditional 'heterosexual social contract' of marriage, women's paid work taking second place, child care at home by mothers, expressions of suspicion of all single mothers and increased discomfort at the separation of sexual expression from procreation.

Times have changed since the 1950s when some of the Liberal–National Party coalition leaders were young. More women are spending more of their adult lives in the paid workforce, more men are experiencing unemployment or other forms of job insecurity. Women and men expect to make and act on decisions about how many children they will have. Marriage is not the only publicly acknowledged pattern of adult life: more people are single for longer, more are divorced, homosexuality is discussed openly and more gay men and lesbians are 'out' at work and with their parents. Public policy has addressed these changes in a variety of ways, both contributing to them and responding to the demands of citizens. The stories of less privileged lives are also circulating, a reminder that change has not removed social problems. Given the insecurity of high unemployment, the awkwardness of intercultural relations at home and abroad, and the structural changes of globalisation, the past seems to have a rosy glow of security. Feminists have argued that the rosy glow is based on a discredited representation of the 1950s woman; similar analyses should be applied to attempts to reconstruct her for the new millennium.

Are other stories possible? They already exist: people are living complex and contradictory lives. The story of love, marriage, household formation and childrearing within what I have called the conventional heterosexual social contract is very strong. It tells people what to expect at various stages of their lives and provides a common language for the complexities of social relationships. The common language relies on simplifications and symbols, the slogans of daily life, to reduce the sense of contradiction and confusion that people often feel. Telling the stories without simplistic reduction of the contradictions to familiar representations of gender and power relations will be more difficult. Yet, versions of the other stories will resonate with experience because they address the gaps in the conventional and simplified accounts. Women have never been only daughters, wives or mothers, just as men have not been only workers.

In this chapter I have argued that many campaigns that engage in policy intervention in the polarised areas of abortion and reproductive technologies have relied on language and symbolism that are unable to challenge the equation of Woman with Mother. As the repeal of abortion laws from all State criminal laws becomes politically imaginable, it will be important to understand the interaction of other forms of regulation of fertility. In this book I have canvassed some of those forms of regulation, ranging from the constitution of reproduction as an area of medical rather than popular expertise, and the cultural construction and reconstruction of notions of the good mother, to the shifts in the institution of heterosexuality as sexual expression has been separated from procreation. These forms of regulation are a part of the politics of reproduction; that is; they express aspects of the social power relations in which fertility and procreation are expressed. The challenge for the next decade is to intervene in the debates without slipping into simple reductions of complex experiences. There needs to be more acknowledgment that the 'elsewhere' outside the frame of the shared language and symbols of social institutions, policy documents and media stories is contradictory and diverse. I do not think that repeal of the criminal sanctions on abortion will make debates about abortion go away any more than the Victorian legislation regulating infertility services has made the debate about reproductive technology go away. The terms of the debates will change, the demands for public policy will change, but the politics of reproduction will continue.

Bibliography

Abortion Law Repeal Association of Western Australia (ALRAWA) 1977, *Report on Legal, Medical, Social and Political Aspects of Abortion Relevant to Western Australia*, ALRAWA, Claremont, WA

Abraham, Y. 1997, 'The Devine Ms. W.', *HQ Magazine*, May/June, p. 56ff

Adelaide, D. ed. 1996, *Mother Love: Stories about Births, Babies and Beyond*, Random House Australia, Sydney

Albury, R.M. 1987, '"Babies Kept on Ice": Aspects of Australian Press Coverage of IVF', *Australian Feminist Studies*, no. 4 (Autumn), pp. 43–71

——1989, 'Abortion?—But I Thought that was Settled Years Ago', *Refractory Girl* , no. 31–32 (May)

——1990, 'Sexual Politics in the 1990s: Making Sex Safer?', *Social Alternatives*, vol. 9, no.1 (April), pp. 42–6

——1994, 'Speech and Silence in Abortion Debates in Australian Parliaments', *Abortion: Legal Right, Women's Right, Human Right, Proceedings of the Abortion Rights Network of Australia 1993 National Conference,* ARNA (Queensland), Brisbane

——1998, 'Reproductive Rights and Technologies: Feminist Campaigns and Debates', *Australian Feminism: A Companion,* eds B. Caine, M. Gatens, E. Graham, J. Larbalestier, S. Watson and E. Webby, Oxford University Press, Melbourne (Forthcoming)

Allen, J. 1982, 'Octavius Beale Reconsidered: Infanticide, Babyfarming and Abortion in NSW 1880–1939', *What Rough Beast: The State and Social Order in Australian History,* ed. Sydney Labour History Group, George Allen & Unwin, Sydney

Allen, J. A. 1990a, 'Does Feminism Need a Theory of "The State"?', *Playing the State,* ed. S. Watson, Allen & Unwin, Sydney

181

——1990b, *Sex & Secrets: Crimes Involving Australian Women Since 1880*, Oxford University Press, Melbourne

——1994, *Rose Scott: Vision and Revision in Feminism*, Oxford University Press, Melbourne

Anderson, D. 1986, Abortion in Western Australia: How Legislation was Changed Without Legislating, Unpublished paper in possession of author

Ang, I. 1995, 'I'm a Feminist but . . . "Other" Women and Postnational Feminism', *Transitions: New Australian Feminisms*, eds B. Caine and R. Pringle, Allen & Unwin, Sydney

Anthias, F. and Yuval-Davis, N. 1993, 'Resisting Racism: Multi-culturalism, Equal Opportunities and the Politics of the "Community"', *Racialised Boundaries*, eds F. Anthias and N. Yuval-Davis, Routledge, London

Arditti, R., Duelli-Klein, R. and Minden, S. eds 1984, *Test-Tube Women: What Future for Motherhood?*, Pandora Press, London

Arney, W. R. 1982, *Power and the Profession of Obstetrics*, University of Chicago Press, Chicago and London

Australia 1977, *Final Report, Royal Commission on Human Relationships*, AGPS, Canberra

Australia 1985, *Creating Children: A Uniform Approach to the Law and Practice of Reproductive Technology in Australia*, Family Law Council, AGPS, Canberra

Australia 1986, *Human Embryo Experimentation in Australia*, Report of the Senate Select Committee into the Human Embryo Experimentation Bill 1985, AGPS, Canberra

Australia 1989, *National Women's Health Policy: Advancing Women's Health in Australia*, Commonwealth Department of Community Services and Health, AGPS, Canberra

Australia 1997a, *An Information Paper on the Termination of Pregnancy in Australia*, Report of an Expert Panel of the NHMRC, AGPS, Canberra

Australia 1997b, *Bringing Them Home*, Report of the National Inquiry into the Separation of Aboriginal and Torres Strait Islander Children from Their Families by the Human Rights and Equal Opportunity Commission, AGPS, Canberra

Australia 1997c, *Women's Year Book*, Office of the Status of Women, Australian Bureau of Statistics, Catalogue no. 4124.0, AGPS, Canberra

Australia, House of Representatives 1979 *Debates*, vol. 113 HR, pp. 963–1006, 1061–1126

Backhouse, C. and Flaherty, D. H. eds 1992, *Challenging Times: The Women's Movement in Canada and the United States*, McGill-Queen's University Press, Montreal and Kingston

Badinter, E. 1981, *The Myth of Motherhood: An Historical View of the Maternal Instinct*, Souvenir Press, London

Bahar, S. 1996, 'Human Rights are Women's Right: Amnesty International and the Family', *Hypatia: A Journal of Feminist Philosophy*, vol. 11, no. 1 (Winter), pp. 105–34

Baird, B. 1990, '*I Had One Too . . .*' An Oral History of Abortion in South

Australia Before 1970, Women's Studies Unit, The Flinders University of South Australia, Bedford Park, SA

——1996, '"The Incompetent, Barbarous Old Lady Round the Corner": The Image of the Backyard Abortionist in Pro-Abortion Politics', *Hecate*, vol. 22, no. 1, pp. 7–26

Baldock, C.V. 1988, 'Volunteer Work as Work; Some Theoretical Considerations', *Women Welfare and the State*, eds C.V. Baldock and B. Cass, Allen & Unwin, Sydney

Baldock, C. V. and Cass, B. eds 1988, *Women, Social Welfare and the State*, 2nd edn, Allen & Unwin, Sydney

Barbach, L. 1976, *For Yourself*, Signet, New York

Barker-Benfield, G. J. 1976, *The Horrors of the Half-Known Life: Male Attitudes Toward Women and Sexuality in Nineteenth-Century America*, Harper & Row, New York

Bartky, S. L. 1990, *Femininity and Domination: Studies in the Phenomenology of Oppression*, Routledge, New York and London

Basen, G., Eichler, M. and Lippman, A. eds 1993/1994, *Misconceptions: The Social Construction of Choice and the New Reproductive and Genetic Technologies*, vols. 1 (1993) and 2 (1994), Voyageur Publishing, Hull, Quebec

Bass, M. 1998, 'Toward Coalition: The Reproductive Health Technologies Project', *Abortion Wars: A Half Century of Struggle, 1950–2000*, ed. R. Solinger, University of California Press, Berkeley

Baxter, J. and Gibson, D. with Lynch-Blosse, M. 1990, *Double-Take: The Links Between Paid and Unpaid Work*, AGPS, Canberra

Berman, P. with Childs, K. 1972, *Why Isn't She Dead!*, Gold Star Publications, Melbourne

Berger, J. 1973, *Ways of Seeing*, Penguin Books, Harmondsworth

Billings, E. and Westmore, A. 1988, *The Billings Method: Controlling Fertility Without Drugs or Devices*, Anne O'Donovan, South Yarra

——1992, *The Billings Method: Controlling Fertility Without Drugs Or Devices*, new edn, fully revised and updated, Anne O'Donovan, South Yarra

Birke, L., Himmelweit, S. and Vines, G. 1990, *Tomorrow's Child: Reproductive Technologies in the 90s*, Virago, London

Bittman, M. 1991, *Juggling Time: How Australian Families Use Time*, Office of the Status of Women, Canberra

Bittman, M. and Pixley, J. 1997, *The Double Life of the Family: Myth, Hope and Experience*, Allen & Unwin, Sydney

Bland, L. 1995, *Banishing the Beast: English Feminism and Sexual Morality 1885–1914*, Penguin Books, London

Blewett, J. 1975, 'The Abortion Law Reform Association of South Australia 1968–73', *The Other Half*, ed. J. Mercer, Penguin Books, Ringwood

Boling, P. ed. 1995, *Expecting Trouble: Surrogacy, Fetal Abuse and New Reproductive Technologies*, Westview Press, Boulder

Bordo, S. 1993, *Unbearable Weight: Feminism, Western Culture and the Body*, University of California Press, Berkeley

Borg, S. and Lasker, J. 1981, *When Pregnancy Fails: Families Coping with Miscarriage, Stillbirth and Infant Death*, Beacon Press, Boston

Boston Women's Health Book Collective 1985, *The New Our Bodies, Ourselves*, Penguin Books, Ringwood

Brennan, D. 1994, *The Politics of Australian Child Care*, Cambridge University Press, Melbourne

Bretherton, R. and Mather, K. 1997, *Abortion: RU486—Anecdotes of Anguish and Hope*, Rod Bretherton, Daylesford

Brook, B. 1997, 'Femininity and Culture: Some Notes on the Gendering of Women in Australia', *Contemporary Australian Feminism*, ed. K.P. Hughes, Longman, South Melbourne.

Brookes, B. 1988, *Abortion in England: 1900–1967*, Croom Helm, London

Broom, D. 1991, *Damned if We Do: Contradictions in Women's Health Care*, Allen & Unwin, Sydney

Brough, J. 1996a, 'Abortion Drugs: Bid to Ban Imports', *Sydney Morning Herald*, 10 May

——1996b, 'Family planning cut in Harradine deal', *Sydney Morning Herald*, 23 August, p. 1

——1996c, 'NHMRC Split Over Abortion Report', *Sydney Morning Herald*, 21 October

Bryson, L. 1993, *Welfare and the State*, Macmillan, London

Bunch, C. and Fried, S. 1996, 'Beijing '95: Moving Women's Human Rights from Margin to Center', *Signs: Journal of Women in Culture and Society*, vol. 22, no. 1 (Autumn), pp. 200–4

Burgmann, M. 1984, 'Black Sisterhood. The Situation of Urban Aboriginal Women and their Relationship to the White Women's Movement', *Australian Women and the Political System*, ed. M. Simms, Longman Cheshire, Melbourne

Burgmann, V. 1993, *Power and Protest: Movements for Change in Australian Society*, Allen & Unwin, Sydney

Burton, C. 1991, *The Promise and the Price: The Struggle for Equal Opportunity in Women's Employment*, Allen & Unwin, Sydney

Caine, B. and Pringle, R. 1995, *Transitions: New Australian Feminisms*, Allen & Unwin, Sydney

Callahan, D. 1970, *Abortion: Law, Choice and Morality*, Macmillan, New York

Canada 1993, *Proceed with Care: Final Report of the Royal Commission on New Reproductive Techologies*, Canada Communications Group–Publishing, Ottawa

Cannold, L. 1998, *The Abortion Myth: Feminism, Morality and the Hard Choices Women Make*, Allen & Unwin, Sydney

Carrington, K. 1993, *Offending Girls: Youth, Sex and Justice*, Allen & Unwin, Sydney

Cass, B. 1988, 'Population Policies and Family Policies: State Construction of Domestic Life', *Women, Social Welfare and the State in Australia*, eds C. V. Baldock and B. Cass, Allen & Unwin, Sydney

Charlesworth, H. 1995, 'Human Rights as Men's Rights', *Women's Rights*

Human Rights: International Feminist Perspectives, eds J. Peters and A. Wolper, Routledge, New York and London

Chodorow, N. 1978, *The Reproduction of Mothering: Psychoanalysis and the Sociology of Gender*, University of California Press, Berkeley

Chodorow, N. and Contratto, S. 1982, 'The Fantasy of the Perfect Mother', *Rethinking the Family*, eds B. Thorne and M. Yalom, Longman, New York and London

Church, C. A. and Geller, J. S. 1990, *Voluntary Female Sterilisation: Number One and Growing*, Population Reports Series C, no. 10, Johns Hopkins University, Population Information Program, Baltimore

Cica, N. 1991, 'The Inadequacies of Australian Abortion Law', *Australian Journal of Family Law*, vol. 5, January, pp. 37–68

Clough, P. T. 1994 *Feminist Thought: Desire, Power, and Academic Discourse*, Blackwell, Oxford, UK and Cambridge, MA

Cockburn, C. 1985, *Machinery of Dominance*, Pluto Press, London

Coleman, K. 1988, 'The Politics of Abortion in Australia: Freedom, Church and State', *Feminist Review*, no. 29, pp. 75–97

——1991, 'Discourses on Sexuality: The Modern Abortion Debate', unpublished PhD thesis, Macquarie University, Sydney

Collins, P. H. 1991, *Black Feminist Thought: Knowledge, Consciousness and the Politics of Empowerment*, Routledge, New York and London

Condit, D. M. 1995, 'Fetal Personhood: Political Identity Under Construction', *Expecting Trouble: Surrogacy, Fetal Abuse and New Reproductive Technologies*, ed. P. Boling, Westview Press, Boulder

Connell, R. W. 1987, *Gender and Power*, Allen & Unwin, Sydney

——1995, *Masculinities*, Allen & Unwin, Sydney

Connell, R.W. and Dowsett, G. W. eds 1992, *Rethinking Sex: Social Theory and Sexuality Research*, Melbourne University Press, Melbourne

Cook, R. J. 1995, 'International Human Rights and Women's Reproductive Health', *Women's Rights Human Rights: International Feminist Perspectives*, eds J. Peters and A. Wolper, Routledge, New York and London

Corea, G. 1977, *The Hidden Malpractice*, Harcourt Brace Jovanovich, New York

——1985, *The Mother Machine: Reproductive Technologies from Artificial Insemination to Artificial Wombs*, Harper & Row, New York

Corrêa, S. with Reichmann, R. 1994, *Populations and Reproductive Rights: Feminist Perspectives from the South*, Zed Books (in association with Dawn), London and New Jersey

Coveney, L., Jackson, M., Jeffreys, S., Kaye, L. and Mahoney, P. 1984, *The Sexuality Papers: Male Sexuality and the Social Control of Women*, Hutchinson, London

Cummings, B. 1990, *Take This Child . . . From Kahlin Compound to the Retta Dixon Children's Home*, Aboriginal Studies Press, Canberra

Curthoys, A. 1992, 'Doing it for Themselves: The Women's Movement Since 1970', *Gender Relations in Australia: Domination and Negotiation*, eds K. Saunders and R. Evans, Harcourt Brace Jovanovich, Sydney

——1994, 'Australian Feminism since 1970', *Australian Women: Contemporary Feminist Thought*, eds N. Grieve and A. Burns, Oxford University Press, Melbourne

Dally, A. 1982, *Inventing Motherhood: The Consequences of an Ideal*, Burnett Books, London

Daniel, W. 1982, 'Sexual Ethics in relation to IVF and ET: The Fitting Use of Human Reproductive Power', *Test-Tube Babies*, eds W. Walters and P. Singer, Oxford University Press, Melbourne

Daniels, C. R. 1993, *At Women's Expense: State Power and the Politics of Fetal Rights*, Harvard University Press, Cambridge, MA

Davis, G., Wanna, J., Warhurst, J. and Weller, P. 1993, *Public Policy in Australia*, Allen & Unwin, Sydney

Davis, N. A. 1993a, 'The Abortion Debate: The Search for the Middle Ground, Part 1', *Ethics*, vol. 103, no. 3 (April), pp. 516–36

——1993b, 'The Abortion Debate: The Search for the Middle Ground, Part 2', *Ethics*, vol. 103, no. 4 (July), pp. 731–78

Davis, N. J. 1985, *From Crime to Choice: The Transformation of Abortion in America*, Greenwood Press, Westport, CT

de Lauretis, T. 1987, 'The Technology of Gender', *Technologies of Gender*, Indiana University Press, Bloomington and Indianapolis

Dell'oso, A. M. 1996, 'Harvest Day', *Mother Love: Stories about Births, Babies and Beyond*, ed. D. Adelaide, Random House Australia, Sydney

Devlin, P. 1965, *The Enforcement of Morals*, Oxford University Press, London

Dietrich, H. 1990, 'Dissenting View 2', *Surrogacy Report 1*, National Bioethics Consultative Committee, Commonwealth of Australia, Canberra

——1991, 'Motherhood and the Feminist Vision: The Lessons from the New Reproductive Technologies', *Surrogacy—In Whose Interest?*, Proceedings of the National Conference, Melbourne February 1991, ed. M. Meggitt, The Mission of St James and St John, Melbourne

Diprose, R. 1994, *The Bodies of Women: Ethics, Embodiment and Sexual Difference*, Routledge, New York and London

Docherty, M. 1993, 'Maggie's Little Miracle', *New Idea*, 19 June

Donnison, J. 1988, *Midwives and Medical Men: A History of the Struggle for the Control of Childbirth*, 2nd edn, Historical Publications, London

Donzelot, J. 1979, *The Policing of Families*, Pantheon Books, New York

Douglas, S. J. 1994, *Where the Girls Are: Growing Up Female with the Mass Media*, Penguin Books, Harmondsworth

Dowrick, S. and Grundberg, S. eds 1980, *Why Children?*, Penguin Books, Ringwood

Duden, B. 1993, *Disembodying Women: Perspectives on Pregnancy and the Unborn*, Harvard University Press, Cambridge, MA and London

Dunn, K. and Leeton, J. 1982, *Birth Control*, Pitman Publishing, Carlton, Vic

Eccleston, R. 1996, 'Death Before Deformity', *Australian Magazine*, 20–21 January, pp. 10–15

Ehrenreich, B. and English, D. 1979, *For Her Own Good: 150 Years of the Experts' Advice to Women*, Pluto Press, London

Eichler, M. 1993, 'Frankenstein Meets Kafka: The Royal Commission on New Reproductive Technologies', *Misconceptions*, vol. 1, eds G. Basen et al., Voyageur Publishing, Hull, Quebec

Eisenstein, H. 1991, *Gender Shock: Practicing Feminism on Two Continents*, Allen & Unwin, Sydney

——1996, *Inside Agitators: Australian Femocrats & the State*, Allen & Unwin, Sydney (also published by Temple University Press, Philadelphia)

Eisenstein, Z. R. 1981, *The Radical Future of Liberal Feminism*, Longman, New York and London

Ellingsen, P. 1996, 'Embryo "Massacre" Mars Test-tube Party', *Sydney Morning Herald*, 25 July, pp. 1 and 12

Evans, M. 1997, *Introducing Contemporary Feminist Thought*, Polity Press, Oxford

Everingham, C. 1994, *Motherhood and Modernity*, Allen & Unwin, Sydney

Faderman, L. 1981, *Surpassing the Love of Men: Romantic Love and Friendship between Women from the Renaissance to the Present*, William Morrow and Co., New York

Fernandez-Kelly, M. P. 1992, 'A Chill Wind Blows: Class, Ideology, and the Reproductive Dilemma', *Challenging Times*, eds C. Backhouse and D. H. Flaherty, McGill-Queen's University Press, Montreal and Kingston

FFPA 1993, *Family Planning Choices Charter*, Family Planning Association, Sydney

Finch, J. 1989, *Family Obligations and Social Change*, Polity Press, Oxford

Finch, J. and Groves, D. eds 1983, *A Labour of Love: Women, Work and Caring*, Routledge and Kegan Paul, London

Finch, L. 1993, *The Classing Gaze: Sexuality, Class and Surveillance*, Allen & Unwin, Sydney

Finlay, H. A. and Sihombing, J. E. 1978, *Family Planning and the Law*, Butterworths, Sydney

Firestone, S. 1971, *The Dialectics of Sex, The Case for Feminist Revolution*, Cape, London

Flick, B. 1990, 'Colonization and Decolonization: An Aboriginal Experience', *Playing the State: Australian Feminist Interventions*, ed. S. Watson, Allen & Unwin, Sydney

Foucault, M. 1975, *The Birth of the Clinic: An Archaeology of Medical Perception*, Vintage Books of Random House, New York

——1978, *Discipline and Punish: The Birth of the Prison*, Random House, New York

——1979, *The History of Sexuality, Volume 1: An Introduction*, Allen Lane, London

——1980, 'Two Lectures', *Power/Knowledge: Selected Interviews & Other Writings 1972–1977*, ed. C. Gordon, Pantheon, New York

Franke, L. B. 1978, *The Ambivalence of Abortion*, Penguin Books, Harmondsworth

Franklin, S. 1990, 'Deconstructing "Desperateness": The Social Construction of Infertility in Popular Representations of New Reproductive Technologies', *The New Reproductive Technologies*, eds M. McNeil, I. Varcoe and S. Yearley, Macmillan, London

Franklin, S., Lury, C. and Stacey, J. 1991, *Off-Centre: Feminism and Cultural Studies*, HarperCollins Academic, London

Friedan, B. 1963, *The Feminine Mystique*, Penguin Books, Harmondsworth

Friedson, E. 1970, *The Profession of Medicine*, Dodd Mead, New York

Fryer, P. 1965, *The Birth Controllers*, Stein and Day, New York

Game, A. and Pringle, R. 1983, *Gender at Work*, Allen & Unwin, Sydney

Gamman, L. and Marshment, M. eds 1988, *The Female Gaze: Women as Viewers of Popular Culture*, The Women's Press, London

Gatens, M. 1991, *Feminism and Philosophy: Perspectives on Difference and Equality*, Polity Press, Cambridge, UK

Gilding, M. 1991, *The Making and Breaking of the Australian Family*, Allen & Unwin, Sydney

Gilligan, C. 1982, *In a Different Voice: Psychological Theory and Women's Development*, Harvard University Press, Cambridge, MA

Ginsberg, F. D. 1989, *Contested Lives: The Abortion Debate in an American Community*, University of California Press, Berkeley

——1998, 'Rescuing the Nation: Operation Rescue and the Rise of Anti-Abortion Militance', *Abortion Wars*, ed. R. Solinger, University of California Press, Berkeley

Ginsberg, F. D. and Rapp, R. eds 1995, *Conceiving the New World Order: The Global Politics of Reproduction*, University of California Press, Berkeley

Gordon, L. 1976, *Woman's Body, Woman's Right: A Social History of Birth Control in America*, Penguin Books, Harmondsworth

——1982, 'Why Nineteenth Century Feminists Did Not Support Birth Control and the Twentieth Century Feminists Do: Feminism, Reproduction and Family', *Rethinking the Family: Some Feminist Questions*, eds B. Thorne and M. Yalom, Longman, New York

Graycar, R. and Morgan, J. 1990, *The Hidden Gender of Law*, Federation Press, Sydney

Greenland, H. 1997, 'Time and Tied', *HQ*, May/June

Greenwood, V. and Young, J. 1976, *Abortion in Demand*, Pluto Press, London

Greer, G. 1971, *The Female Eunuch*, Paladin, London

Grimshaw, P. and May, A. 1994, '"Inducements to the Strong to Be Cruel to the Weak": Authoritative White Colonial Male Voices and the Construction of Gender in Koori Society', *Australian Women: Contemporary Feminist Thought*, eds N. Grieve and A. Burns, Oxford University Press, Melbourne

Grimwade, J. with Fraser, I. and Farrell, E. 1995, *The Body Of Knowledge: Everything You Need To Know About The Female Cycle*, William Heinemann Australia, Port Melbourne

Grossberg, L., Nelson, C. and Treichler, P. eds 1992, *Cultural Studies*, Routledge, New York and London

Haraway, D. 1991, *Simians, Cyborgs and Women: The Reinvention of Nature*, Routledge, New York and London

——1997, *Modest_Witness@Second_Millennium.FemaleMan© _Meets_Onco Mouse™: Feminism and Technoscience*, Routledge, New York and London

Harkness, L. 1991, *Looking for Lisa*, Random House Australia, Sydney and Melbourne

Harper, J. and Richards, L. 1979, *Mothers and Working Mothers*, Penguin Books, Ringwood

Hart, H. L. A. 1963, *Law, Liberty and Morality*, Oxford University Press, Oxford

Hartmann, B. 1987, *Reproductive Rights and Wrongs: The Global Politics of Population Control and Contraceptive Choice*, Harper & Row, New York

Hawes, R. 1998, 'Churches Want Unclaimed Embryos Destroyed', *Australian*, 14 January, p. 5

Health Issues Centre 1989, 'Just When You Thought It Was Safe . . . The Crisis in Public Abortion Services; *Health Issues*, 18

Heise, L. L. 1995, 'Freedom Close to Home: The Impact of Violence Against Women on Reproductive Rights', *Women's Rights Human Rights; International Feminist Perspectives*, eds J. Peters and A. Wolper, Routledge, New York and London

Hepburn, L. 1992, *Ova-dose? Australian Women and the New Reproductive Technologies*, Allen & Unwin, Sydney

Hicks, N. 1978, *'This Sin and Scandal': Australia's Population Debate 1891–1911*, Australian National University Press, Canberra

Himmelweit, S. 1988, 'More than "A Woman's Right to Choose"?', *Feminist Review*, no. 29 (Spring)

Hindell, K. and Simms, M. 1971, *Abortion Law Reformed*, Peter Owen, London

Homans, H. ed. 1985, *The Sexual Politics of Reproduction*, Gower, Aldershot, Hants

hooks, b. 1990, *Yearning: Race, Gender, and Cultural Politics*, South End Press, Boston

Horin, A. 1993, 'New life for moral dictators', *Sydney Morning Herald*, 9 June, p. 20

——1997, 'Abortion is a Fact of Life Many Politicians Ignore', *Sydney Morning Herald*, 24 May, p. 41

Howe, D., Sawbridge, P. and Hinings, D. 1992, *Half A Million Women: Women Who Lose Their Children by Adoption*, Penguin Books, Harmondsworth

Hubbard, R. 1984, 'Personal Courage is Not Enough: Some Hazards of Childbearing in the 1980s', *Test-Tube Women*, eds R. Arditti et al., Pandora, London

Huggins, J. 1994, 'A Contemporary View of Aboriginal Women's Relationship to the White Women's Movement', *Australian Women: Contemporary*

Feminist Thought, eds N. Grieve and A. Burns, Oxford University Press, South Melbourne

Huggins, J. and Blake, T. 1992, 'Protection or Persecution? Gender Relations in the Era of Racial Segregation', *Gender Relations in Australia: Domination and Negotiation*, eds K. Saunders and E. Evans, Harcourt Brace Jovanovich, Sydney

Inglis, K. 1984, *Living Mistakes: Mothers Who Consented to Adoption*, George Allen & Unwin, Sydney

Jackson, M. 1987, '"Facts of Life" or the Eroticization of Women's Oppression? Sexology and the Social Construction of Heterosexuality', *The Cultural Construction of Sexuality*, ed. P. Caplan, Tavistock, London

Jackson, S. and Scott, S. eds 1996, *Feminism and Sexuality: A Reader*, Edinburgh University Press, Edinburgh

Jaffe, F. S., Lindheim, B. L. and Lee, P. R. 1981, *Abortion Politics: Private Morality and Public Policy*, McGraw Hill, New York

Jakubowicz, A. ed. 1994, *Racism, Ethnicity and the Media*, Allen & Unwin, Sydney

Jansen, R. 1988, 'Reproductive Technology: Where to Now?', *Healthright*, vol. 7, no. 2, pp. 9–15

Jeffreys, S. 1985, *The Spinster and Her Enemies: Feminism and Sexuality 1880–1930*, Pandora Press, London

——1990, *Anticlimax: A Feminist Perspective on the Sexual Revolution*, The Women's Press, London

Johnson, L. 1993, *The Modern Girl: Girlhood and Growing Up*, Allen & Unwin, Sydney

Johnson, T. 1972, *Professions and Power*, Macmillan, London

Jordanova, L. 1989, *Sexual Visions: Images of Gender and Science and Medicine between the Eighteenth and Twentieth Centuries*, University of Wisconsin Press, Madison, Wisconsin

Kabeer, N. 1994, *Reversed Realities: Gender Hierarchies in Development Thought*, Verso, London

Kane, P. and Porter, J. 1988, *Choice Guide to Birth Control*, Nelson and Australian Consumers Association, Melbourne

Kaplan, E. A. 1983, 'Is the Gaze Male?', *Powers of Desire*, eds A. Snitow, C. Stansell and S. Thompson, Monthly Review Press, New York

——1992, *Motherhood and Representation: The Mother in Popular Culture and Melodrama*, Routledge, London and New York

Katz, J. N. 1995, *The Invention of Heterosexuality*, Dutton, New York

Kelly, E. ed. 1994, *Australian Women's Health Handbook*, Gore and Osment Publications, Rushcutters Bay

Kelly, J. 1979, 'The Doubled Vision of Feminist Theory', *Feminist Studies*, vol. 5, no. 1, pp. 216–27

Kerby-Eaton, E. and Davies, J. eds 1986, *Women's Health in a Changing Society*, Proceedings of the Second National Conference on All Aspects of Women's Health, Adelaide, September, 1985, Festival City Conventions, Adelaide

Kilic, S. 1997, 'Who is an Australian Woman?', *Contemporary Australian Feminism 2*, ed. K. P. Hughes, Longman, Melbourne

Kirkby, D. ed. 1995, *Sex, Power and Justice: Historical Perspectives on Law in Australia*, Oxford University Press, Melbourne

Kirkman, M. and Kirkman, L. 1988, *My Sister's Child*, Penguin Books, Ringwood

Klein, R. D. ed. 1989a, *Infertility: Women Speak Out About Their Experiences of Reproductive Medicine*, Pandora Press, London

——1989b, *The Exploitation of a Desire: Women's Experiences with In Vitro Fertilisation, An Exploratory Survey*, Women's Studies Summer Institute, Deakin University, Geelong

Koedt, A. 1972, 'The Myth of the Vaginal Orgasm', *Radical Feminism*, ed. A. Koedt, Quadrangle, New York

Koutroulis, G. 1990, 'The Orifice Revisited: Women in Gynaecological Textbooks', *Community Health Issues* , vol. 14, no. 1, pp. 73–84

Kovacs, G. 1986, 'In-vitro Fertilization and Embryo Transfer: Prospects of Pregnancy by Life-table Analysis', *Medical Journal of Australia*, vol. 144, no. 13, pp. 682–3

Kovacs, G. and Westmore, A. 1986, *The Complete Guide to Contraception and Family Planning*, Hill of Content, Melbourne

Lader, L. 1973, *Abortion II: Making the Revolution*, Beacon Press, Boston

Lamont, L. 1998, 'Abortion in the Dock', *Sydney Morning Herald*, 19 February

Lanson, L. 1983, *From Woman to Woman*, revised edn, Penguin Books, Harmondsworth

Larriera, A. 1993, 'Charter Aims to Reduce Need for Abortions', *Sydney Morning Herald*, 31 March, p. 6

Leavitt, J. W. 1986, *Brought to Bed: Childbearing in America, 1750 to 1950*, Oxford University Press, New York and Oxford

Leeton, J. et al. 1984, 'Unexplained Infertility and the Possibilities of Management with In Vitro Fertilization and Embryo Transfer', *Australian and New Zealand Journal of Obstetrics and Gynaecology*, vol. 24, pp. 131–4

Le Grand, C. 1998, 'Bill Ends Women's Doubts on Abortion', *Australian*, 22 May, p. 8

Le Grand, C. and O'Brien, N. 1998, 'Historic Bill allows Abortion on Demand', *Australian*, 3 April, p. 4

Leung, P. et al. 1983, 'A Histochemical Study of Cumulous Cells for Assessing the Quality of Preovulatory Oocytes', *Fertility and Sterility*, vol. 39, no. 6, pp. 853–5

Lewis, J. 1993, 'In Search of Parenthood' and 'Bill's Story: A Search for True Identity', *Sydney Morning Herald*, 16 August

Ley, P. 1992, 'Reproductive Technology—What Can We Learn from the Adoption Experience', *To Search for Self*, eds P. Swain and S. Swain, Federation Press, Sydney

Libesman, T. and Sripathy, V. 1996, *Your Body Your Baby: Women's Legal*

Rights from Conception to Birth, Redfern Legal Centre Publishing, Sydney

Liskin, L., Benoit, E. and Blackburn, R. 1992, *Vasectomy: New Opportunities*, Population Reports, Series D, no. 5, Johns Hopkins University, Population Information Program, Baltimore

Llewellyn-Jones, D. 1986, *Everywoman: A Gynaecological Guide for Life*, Faber and Faber, London

——1996, *Everywoman: A Gynaecological Guide For Life*, 7th edn, Penguin Books, Ringwood

Lloyd, G. 1984, *The Man of Reason*, Methuen, London

Loane, S. 1985, 'Abortion Raids: A Grisly Circus for the TV Cameras', *The National Times*, 24 May, p. 11

Luker, K. 1975, *Taking Chances: Abortion and the Decision not to Contracept*, University of California, Berkeley

——1984, *Abortion and the Politics of Motherhood*, University of California Press, Berkeley

Lumby, C. 1997, *Bad Girls: The Media, Sex & Feminism in the 90s*, Allen & Unwin, Sydney

McFerren, L. 1990, 'Interpretations of the Frontline State: Australian Women's Refuges and the State', *Playing the State*, ed. S. Watson, Allen & Unwin, Sydney

McGrath, A. 1993, '"Beneath the Skin": Australian Citizenship, Rights and Aboriginal Women', *Journal of Australian Studies*, no. 37 (Women and the State), pp. 99–114

Macintyre, S. 1976, '"Who Wants Babies?" the Social Construction of "Instincts"', *Sexual Divisions in Society: Process and Change*, eds D. L. Barker and S. Allen, Tavistock Publications, London

Mackenzie, F. 1994, *The Penguin Guide to Women's Health: Puberty to Menopause and Beyond*, Viking, Penguin Books, Ringwood

MacKinnon, C. A. 1989, *Toward a Feminist Theory of the State*, Harvard University Press, Cambridge, MA

——1979, *Sexual Harassment of Working Women: A Case of Sexual Discrimination*, Yale University Press, New Haven

McLaren, A. 1990, *The History of Contraception: From Antiquity to the Present Day*, Blackwell, Oxford

McMichael, T. 1972, *Abortion: The Unenforceable Law*, Council For Civil Liberties, Sydney

McNay, L. 1992, *Foucault and Feminism*, Polity Press, Cambridge

McNeil, M. ed. 1987, *Gender and Expertise*, Free Association Press, London

McNeil, M., Varcoe, I. and Yearley, S. eds 1990, *The New Reproductive Technologies*, Macmillan, London

Macquarie, J. 1994, *Below The Belt: An Owner's Guide To Gynaecology*, Text Publishing Company, Melbourne

Mao, K. and Wood, C. 1984, 'Barriers to Treatment of Infertility by In-vitro Fertilization and Embryo Transfer', *Medical Journal of Australia*, vol. 140, no. 9, pp. 532–3

Marr, D. 1997, 'Balancing Acts', *Sydney Morning Herald*, 1 February, pp. 15, 65

Marshall, H. 1993, *Not Having Children*, Oxford University Press, Melbourne

Martin, E. 1987, *The Woman in the Body: A Cultural Analysis of Reproduction*, Beacon Press, Boston

——1991, 'The Egg and the Sperm: How Science Has Constructed a Romance Based on Stereotypical Male-Female Roles', *Signs: Journal of Women in Culture and Society*, vol. 16, no. 3, pp. 485–501

——1994, *Flexible Bodies: Tracking Immunity in American Culture—From the Days of Polio to the Age of AIDS*, Beacon Press, Boston

Martin, J. 1991, 'Multiculturalism and feminism', *Intersexions: Gender/Class/Culture/Ethnicity*, eds G. Bottomley, M. de Lepervanche and J. Martin, Allen & Unwin, Sydney

Matson, P. et al. 1986, 'Oligospermic Infertility Treated by In-Vitro Fertilization', *Australian and New Zealand Journal of Obstetrics and Gynaecology*, vol. 26, pp. 84–7

Matthews, J. J. 1984, *Good and Mad Women: The Historical Construction of Femininity in Twentieth Century Australia*, George Allen & Unwin, Sydney

——1992, 'The "Present Moment" in Sexual Politics', *Rethinking Sex: Social Theory and Sexuality Research*, eds R. Connell and G. Dowsett, Melbourne University Press, Melbourne

Meggitt, M. 1991, 'The Dismantling of Motherhood and One Woman's Story', *Surrogacy—In Whose Interest?, Proceedings of the National Conference, Melbourne February 1991*, ed. M. Meggitt, The Mission of St James and St John, Melbourne

Mercer, J., Summers, A. and Graham, C. 1975, 'WEL and the Women's Liberation Movement', *The Other Half*, ed. J. Mercer, Penguin Books, Ringwood

Mill, J. S. 1859/1956, *On Liberty*, Bobbs-Merrill, Indianapolis and New York

Miller, K. 1996, 'What Does it Mean to Be One of Us?', photographs by Lennart Nilsson, *Life* Magazine, November, pp. 38–50, 54, 56

Mitchell, J. 1971, *Women's Estate*, Penguin Books, Harmondsworth

——1975, *Psychoanalysis and Feminism: Freud, Reich, Laing and Women*, Vintage Books, New York

Mohanty, C. T. 1991, 'Introduction: Cartographies of Struggle, Third World Women and the Politics of Feminism', *Third World Women and the Politics of Feminism*, ed. C. T. Mohanty, A. Russo and L. Torres, Indiana University Press, Bloomington

Mohr, J. 1978, *Abortion in America: Origins and Evolution of National Policy*, Oxford University Press, New York

Morell, C. M. 1994, *Unwomanly Conduct: The Challenges of Intentional Childlessness*, Routledge, New York and London

Morrissey, G. 1996, *Sex in the Time of Generation X*, Macmillan, Sydney

Mulvey, L. 1975, 'Visual Pleasure and Narrative Cinema', *Screen*, no. 16, pp. 6–18

Mumford, K. 1989, *Women Working: Economics and Reality*, Allen & Unwin, Sydney

Murdolo, A. 1996, 'Warmth & Unity with All Women?', *Feminist Review*, no. 52 (Spring), pp. 69–86

Napier, L. 1987, 'Nature's Reprisals?' Some Aspects of the Development of Medical Involvement in Infertility', unpublished MSW thesis, University of Sydney, Sydney

Nelson, M. K. 1994, 'Family Day Care Providers: Dilemmas of Daily Practice', *Mothering: Ideology, Experience, and Agency*, eds E. N. Glenn, G. Chang and L. R. Forcey, Routledge, New York and London

New South Wales, Legislative Council 1988, *Parliamentary Debates*, vol. 202, by Authority, Sydney, pp. 1253–6, 1270–1336

Nichols, A. and Hogan, T. 1984, *Making Babies: Test Tube Ethics and Christian Ethics*, Acorn Press, Canberra

Nozick, R. 1974, *Anarchy, State and Utopia*, Basic Books, New York

Oakley, A. 1984, *The Captured Womb: A History of the Medical Care of Pregnant Women*, Blackwell, Oxford

Oakley, A., McPherson, A. and Roberts, H. 1984, *Miscarriage*, Fontana Paperbacks, Glasgow

O'Brien, N. 1998, 'Abortion: AMA tells politicians to act now', *Australian*, 17 February

Okin, S. M. 1979, *Women in Western Political Thought*, Princeton University Press, Princeton, NJ

——1989, *Justice, Gender and the Family*, Basic Books, New York

Oudshoorn, N. 1994, *Beyond the Natural Body: An Archeology of Sex Hormones*, Routledge, London and New York

Overduin, D. C. and Fleming, J. I. 1982, *Life in a Test-Tube: Medical and Ethical Issues Facing Society Today*, Lutheran Publishing House, Adelaide

Pateman, C. 1988, *The Sexual Contract*, Polity Press, Oxford

Petchesky, R. P. 1985, *Abortion and Woman's Choice: The State, Sexuality and Reproductive Freedom*, Northeastern University Press, Boston (also published by Verso, London, 1986)

——1987, 'Foetal Images: The Power of Visual Culture in the Politics of Reproduction', *Reproductive Technologies*, ed. M. Stanworth, Polity Press, Cambridge, UK

——1995, 'The Body as Property: A Feminist Re-Vision', *Conceiving the New World Order: The Global Politics of Reproduction*, eds F. D. Ginsberg and R. Rapp, University of California Press, Berkeley

Peters, J. and Wolper, A. eds 1995, *Women's Rights Human Rights: International Feminist Perspectives*, Routledge, New York and London

Petroechevsky, J. 1994, 'The Story of Children by Choice', *Women Working Together: Lessons From Feminist Services*, ed. W. Weeks, Longman Cheshire, London

Pettman, J. 1992, *Living in the Margins: Racism, Sexism and Feminism in Australia*, Allen & Unwin, Sydney

——1996, *Worlding Women: A Feminist International Politics*, Allen & Unwin, Sydney

Pfeffer, N. 1985, 'The Hidden Pathology of the Male Reproductive System', *The Sexual Politics of Reproduction*, ed. H. Homans, Gower, Aldershot, Hants

——1987, 'Artificial Insemination, In-vitro Fertilization and the Stigma of Infertility', *Reproductive Technologies: Gender, Motherhood and Medicine*, ed. M. Stanworth, Polity Press, Cambridge, UK

——1993, *The Stork and the Syringe: A Political History of Reproductive Medicine*, Polity Press, Cambridge, UK

Pfeffer, N. and Wollett, A. 1983, *The Experience of Infertility*, Virago, London

Phillips, A. 1993, *Democracy and Difference*, Polity Press, Cambridge, UK

Pitt, H. 1997, 'Outrage after NHMRC backs abortion pill', *Sydney Morning Herald*, 19 May, p. 2

Polatnick, M. R. 1983, 'Why Men Don't Rear Children: A Power Analysis', *Mothering: Essays in Feminist Theory*, ed. J. Trebilcot, Rowman and Allenheld, Totowa, NJ

Pollack, S. 1984, 'Refusing to Take Women Seriously: Side Effects and the Politics of Contraception', *Test-Tube Women*, eds R. Arditti et al., Pandora, London

——1985, 'Sex and the Contraceptive Act', *The Sexual Politics of Reproduction*, ed. H. Homans, Gower, Aldershot, Hants

Poole, R. 1991, *Morality and Modernity*, Routledge, New York and London

Poovey, M. 1992, 'The Abortion Question and the Death of Man', *Feminists Theorize the Political*, eds J. Butler and J. W. Scott, Routledge, New York and London

Pringle, R. 1988, *Secretaries Talk: Sexuality, Power, and Work*, Allen & Unwin, Sydney

Pritchard, C. 1993, 'Surrogate Three Turn Five', *New Idea*, 4 September

Probert, B. 1997, 'Women's Working Lives', *Contemporary Australian Feminism 2*, ed. K. P. Hughes, Longman, Melbourne

Purdy, L. 1996, *Reproducing Persons: Issues in Feminist Bioethics*, Cornell University Press, Ithaca and London

Ramazanoglu, C. 1989, *Feminism and the Contradictions of Oppression*, Routledge, New York and London

Rawls, J. 1971, *A Theory of Justice*, Harvard University Press, Cambridge, MA

Raymond, J. 1987, 'Fetalists and Feminists: They are Not the Same', *Made to Order: The Myth of Reproductive and Genetic Progress*, eds P. Spallone and D. L. Steinberg, Pergamon Press, Oxford

Read, P. 1983, *The Lost Generations*, NSW Department of Aboriginal Affairs, Occasional Paper no. 1, Sydney

Reade, K. 1994, '"Struggling to be Heard": Tensions Between Different Voices in the Australian Women's Liberation Movement of the 1970s and 1980s', *Contemporary Australian Feminism*, ed. K. P. Hughes, Longman Cheshire, Melbourne

Reed, J. 1978, *From Private Vice to Public Purpose: The Birth Control Movement and American Society Since 1830*, Basic Books, New York

Reiger, K. M. 1985, *The Disenchantment of the Home: Modernizing the Australian Family 1880–1940*, Oxford University Press, Melbourne

Rich, A. 1976/1986, *Of Woman Born: Motherhood as Experience and Institution* (10th anniversary edn), Norton, New York

——1980, 'Compulsory Heterosexuality and Lesbian Existence', *Signs: Journal of Women in Culture and Society*, vol. 5, no. 4, pp. 631–60

Richards, L. 1978, *Having Families: Marriage, Parenthood and Social Pressure in Australia*, Penguin Books, Ringwood

Richardson, D. 1993, *Women, Motherhood and Childrearing*, Macmillan, London

Ripper, M. 1993, 'The Experience of Abortion in Queensland, South Australia and Tasmania', unpublished paper at Annual Biological Sciences Symposium of the Family Planning Federation of Australia, 28–30 May, Surfers Paradise

Robinson, N. 1997, 'I Don't Know Who I Am', *Sun-Herald*, 13 April, p. 41

Rothman, B. K. 1982, *In Labour: Women and Power in the Birthplace*, Junction Books, London

Rowland, R. 1984, 'Reproductive Technologies: The Final Solution to the Woman Question?', *Test-Tube Women: What Future for Motherhood?* eds R. Arditti et al., Pandora Press, London

——1987, 'Of Woman Born, But for How Long? The Relationship of Women to the New Reproductive Technologies and the Issues of Choice', *Made to Order: The Myth of Reproductive and Genetic Progress*, eds P. Spallone and D. L. Steinberg, Pergamon Press, Oxford

——1992, *Living Laboratories: Women and Reproductive Technologies*, Sun, Sydney

Rubin, G. 1984, 'Thinking Sex: Notes for a Radical Theory of the Politics of Sexuality', *Pleasure and Danger*, ed. C. S. Vance, Routledge and Kegan Paul, New York and London

Ruddick, S. 1982, 'Maternal Thinking', *Rethinking the Family: Some Feminist Questions*, eds B. Thorne and M. Yalom, Longman, New York and London

Ryan, E. and Conlon, A. 1989, *Gentle Invaders: Australian Women at Work 1788–1974*, Penguin Books, Ringwood

Ryan, L., and Ripper, M. 1993, 'Women, Abortion and the State', *Journal of Australian Studies*, no. 37 (Women and the State), pp. 72–87

Ryan, L., Ripper, M. and Buttfield, B. 1994, *We Women Decide: Women's Experience of Seeking Abortions in Queensland, South Australia and Tasmania 1985–1992*, Women's Studies Unit, Faculty of Social Sciences, Flinders University, Adelaide

Sandelowski, M. J. 1990, 'Failures of Volition: Female Agency and Infertility in Historical Perspective', *Ties that Bind: Essays on Mothering and Patriarchy*, eds J. F. Barr, D. Pope and M. Wyer, University of Chicago Press, Chicago

Sawer, M. 1990, *Sisters in Suits*, Allen & Unwin, Sydney

Sawer, M. and Groves, A. 1994, *Working from Inside: Twenty Years of the Office of the Status of Women*, Department of the Prime Minister and Cabinet, AGPS, Canberra

Sawicki, J. 1991, *Disciplining Foucault: Feminism, Power, and the Body*, Routledge, New York and London

Science and Technology Subgroup 1991, 'In the Wake of the Alton Bill: Science, Technology and Reproductive Politics', *Off-Centre*, eds S. Franklin, C. Lury and J. Stacey, HarperCollins Academic, London

Scott, J. W. 1992, '"Experience"', *Feminists Theorize the Political*, eds J. Butler and J. W. Scott, Routledge, New York and London

Scully, D. and Bart, P. 1972, 'A Funny Thing Happened on the Way to the Orifice: Women in Gynecology Textbooks', *American Journal of Sociology*, vol. 78, no. 4, pp. 283–8

Scutt, J. A. ed. 1988, *The Baby Machine: Commercialisation of Motherhood*, McCulloch Publishing, Melbourne

Sexton, M. 1998, 'Disability Rights and Selective Abortion', *Abortion Wars: A Half Century of Struggle, 1950–2000*, ed. R. Solinger, University of California Press, Berkeley

Shanley, M. L. 1993, '"Surrogate Mothering" and Women's Freedom: A Critique of Contracts for Human Reproduction', *Signs: Journal of Women in Culture and Society*, vol. 18., no. 3, pp. 618–39

Shaver, S. 1992, *Body Rights, Social Rights and the Liberal Welfare State*, Discussion Paper no. 38, SPRC, University of New South Wales, Sydney

Shawyer, J. 1979, *Death by Adoption*, Cicada, Auckland

Sheldon, S. 1993, 'Who is the Mother to Make the Judgement?: The Constructions of Woman in English Abortion Law', *Feminist Legal Studies*, vol. 1, no. 1, pp. 3–22

Shorter, E. 1984, *A History of Women's Bodies*, Penguin Books, Harmondsworth

Siedlecky, S. and Wyndham, D. 1990, *Populate and Perish: Australian Women's Fight for Birth Control*, Allen & Unwin, Sydney

Simms, M. 1981, 'Abortion: The Myth of the Golden Age', *Controlling Women: The Normal and the Deviant*, eds B. Hutter and G. Williams, Croom Helm, London

Singer, P. , Kuhse, H., Buckle, S., Dawson, K. and Kasimba, P. 1990, *Embryo Experimentation: Ethical, Legal and Social Issues*, Cambridge University Press, Melbourne

Singer, P. and Wells, D. 1984, *The Reproductive Revolution: New Ways of Making Babies*, Oxford University Press, New York and Melbourne

Smart, C. 1989, *Feminism and the Power of Law*, Routledge, New York and London

——1992, 'Disruptive Bodies and Unruly Sex: The Regulation of Reproduction and Sexuality in the Nineteenth Century', *Regulating Womanhood: Historical Essays on Marriage, Motherhood and Sexuality*, ed. C. Smart, Routledge, London

Smith, D. E. 1987, *The Everyday World as Problematic: A Feminist Sociology*, Open University Press, Milton Keynes

Snitow, A. 1992, 'Feminism and Motherhood: An American Reading', *Feminist Review*, no. 40 (Spring), pp. 32–51

Solinger, R. 1992, *Wake Up Little Susie: Single Pregnancy and Race Before Roe V. Wade*, Routledge, New York and London

Spallone, P. 1989, *Beyond Conception: The New Politics of Conception*, Macmillan, London

Spallone, P. and Steinberg, D. L. 1987, *Made to Order: The Myth of Reproductive and Genetic Progress*, Pergamon, Oxford

Stanworth, M. ed. 1987, *Reproductive Technologies: Gender, Motherhood and Medicine*, Polity Press, Oxford

Stevens, J. 1995, *Healing Women: A History of Leichhardt Women's Community Health Centre*, First Ten Years History Project, Sydney

Stone, D. A. 1988, *Policy Paradox and Political Reason*, Scott Foresman/Little Brown, Glenview, Illinois

Strathern, M. 1992, *Reproducing the Future: Anthropology, Kinship and the New Reproductive Technologies*, Routledge, New York

Stuart, A. 1989, 'Is it Worth It? I Just Don't Know', *Infertility: Women Speak Out about their Experiences of Reproductive Medicine*, ed. R. D. Klein, Pandora Press, London

Sullivan, L. 1989, 'Social Legislation for the Reproductive Technologies', *Australian Journal of Social Issues,* vol. 24, no. 2 (February), pp. 33–43

Summers, A. 1975/1994, *Damned Whores and God's Police*, Penguin Books, Ringwood

Swain, P. and Swain, S. eds 1992, *To Search for Self*, Federation Press, Sydney

Swain, S. with Howe, R. 1995, *Single Mothers and Their Children: Disposal, Punishment and Survival in Australia*, Cambridge University Press, Melbourne

Sykes, B. 1975, 'Black Women in Australia: A History', *The Other Half*, ed. J. Mercer, Penguin Books, Ringwood

Tatalovich, R. and Danes, B. W. 1981, *The Politics of Abortion: A Study of Community Conflict in Public Policy Making*, Praeger Publishers, New York

Thomas, H. 1985, 'The Medical Construction of the Contraceptive Career', *The Sexual Politics of Reproduction*, ed. H. Homans, Gower, Aldershot, Hants

Tingle, L. 1996, 'Senators Deal Women Out', *Australian*, 7 June, p. 13

Tong, R. 1989, *Feminist Thought: A Comprehensive Introduction*, Westview Press, Boulder

Tribe, L. 1992, *Abortion: The Clash of Absolutes*, Norton, New York

Trinh, T. M. 1989, *Woman, Native, Other: Writing, Postcoloniality and Feminism*, Indiana University Press, Bloomington

Tronto, J. C. 1993, *Moral Boundaries: A Political Argument for an Ethic of Care*, Routledge, New York and London

Trounson, A. 1987, 'In-vitro Fertilization', *Medical Journal of Australia*, no. 146 (April), pp. 338–40

Trounson, A. and Wood, C. 1981, 'Extracorporeal Fertilization and Embryo Transfer', *Clinics in Obstetrics and Gynaecology*, vol. 8, no. 3, pp. 681–713

Trounson, A., Wood, C. and Leeton, J. 1982, 'Freezing of Embryos: An Ethical Obligation', *Medical Journal of Australia*, vol. 2, no. 7, pp. 332–3

Turner, B. S. 1987, *Medical Power and Social Knowledge*, Sage, London

Turney, L. 1993, 'Risk and Contraception: What Women Are not Told about Tubal Ligation', *Women's Studies International Forum*, vol. 16, no. 5 (September/October), pp. 471–86

Van Dyck, J. 1995, *Manufacturing Babies and Public Consent: Debating the New Reproductive Technologies*, Macmillan, Hampshire and London

van Keppel, M. 1991, 'The Children are the Losers', *Surrogacy—In Whose Interest?, Proceedings of the National Conference, Melbourne February 1991*, ed. M. Meggitt, The Mission of St James and St John, Melbourne

van Krieken, R. 1991, *Children and the State: Social Control and the Formation of Australian Child Welfare*, Allen & Unwin, Sydney

Vance, C. S. ed 1984, *Pleasure and Danger: Exploring Female Sexuality*, Routledge and Kegan Paul, New York

Victoria 1984, *Report on the Disposition of Embryos Produced by In Vitro Fertilization*, Victorian Government Printer, Melbourne

Vines, G. 1993, *Raging Hormones: Do They Rule Our Lives?*, Virago, London

Wainer, B. 1972, *It Isn't Nice*, Alpha Books, Sydney

Wajcman, J. 1991, *Feminism Confronts Technology*, Allen & Unwin, Sydney

Walby, S. 1989, *Theorising Patriarchy*, Blackwell, Oxford

Waldby, C. 1996, *AIDS and the Body Politic: Biomedicine and Sexual Difference*, Routledge, New York and London

Waring, M. 1988, *Counting for Nothing: What Men Value and What Women Are Worth*, Allen & Unwin New Zealand, Wellington

Watson, S. ed. 1990, *Playing the State*, Allen & Unwin, Sydney

Wearing, B. 1984, *The Ideology of Motherhood*, George Allen & Unwin Australia, Sydney

Weedon, C. 1987, *Feminist Practice and Poststructuralist Theory*, Blackwell, Oxford and New York

Weeks, J. 1981, *Sex, Politics and Society: The Regulation of Sexuality Since 1800*, Longman, London

——1985, *Sexuality and Its Discontents: Meanings, Myths and Modern Sexualities*, Routledge and Kegan Paul, London

——1986, *Sexuality*, Ellis Horwood and Tavistock, Chichester and London

Weeks, W. ed. 1994, *Women Working Together: Lessons from Feminist Women's Services*, Longman Cheshire, Melbourne

Williams, G. 1957, *The Sanctity of Life and the Criminal Law*, Knopf, New York

Willis, E. 1983, *Medical Dominance: The Division of Labour in Australian Health Care*, George Allen & Unwin, Sydney

Wilson, E. 1977, *Women and the Welfare State*, Tavistock, London

Wilson, P. 1971, *The Sexual Dilemma: Abortion, Homosexuality, Prostitution and the Criminal Threshold*, University of Queensland Press, St Lucia

Winkler, R. and van Keppel, M. 1984, *Relinquishing Mothers in Adoption: Their Long-Term Adjustment*, Institute of Family Studies Monograph 3, Institute of Family Studies, Melbourne

Wolf, N. 1990, *The Beauty Myth*, Vintage, London

——1993, *Fire With Fire*, Chatto and Windus, London

——1995, 'The "Evil" in Abortion', *Weekend Australian*, 7–8 October, p. 27

Wood, C. and Riley, R. 1992, *I.V.F. In Vitro Fertilisation*, Hill of Content, Melbourne

Wood, C. and Westmore, A. 1983, *Test-Tube Conception*, Hill of Content, Melbourne

Yeatman, A. 1994, *Postmodern Revisionings of the Political*, Routledge, New York and London

Young, I. M. 1990, *Justice and the Politics of Difference*, Princeton University Press, Princeton, NJ

——1995, 'Punishment, Treatment, Empowerment: Three Approaches to Policy for Pregnant Addicts', *Expecting Trouble*, ed. P. Boling, Westview Press, Boulder

Index